Mother Earth and Uncle Sam

# Mother Earth and Uncle Sam

## How Pollution and Hollow Government Hurt Our Kids

RENA I. STEINZOR

University of Texas Press  *Austin*

# 129952363

First edition, 2008

Requests for permission to reproduce material from this work should be sent to:
Permissions
University of Texas Press
P.O. Box 7819
Austin, TX 78713-7819
www.utexas.edu/utpress/about/bpermission.html

⊗ The paper used in this book meets the minimum requirements of ANSI/NISO
Z39.48-1992 (R1997) (Permanence of Paper).

**Library of Congress Cataloging-in-Publication Data**

Steinzor, Rena.
Mother Earth and Uncle Sam : how pollution and hollow government hurt our
kids / Rena I. Steinzor. — 1st ed.
        p.      cm.
Includes bibliographical references and index.
ISBN 978-0-292-71689-6 (cloth : alk. paper)
ISBN 978-0-292-71690-2 (pbk. : alk. paper)
1. Environmentally induced diseases in children—United States.    2. Pollution—
Government policy—United States.    3. Pollution—Law and legislation—United
States.    4. Pollution—Health aspects—United States.    5. Environmental policy—
United States.    6. Children and the environment—United States.    I. Title.
[DNLM:    1. Child Welfare—United States.    2. Environmental Pollution—adverse
effects—United States.    3. Environment—United States.    4. Environmental
Exposure—adverse effects—United States.    5. Politics—United States.
6. Prenatal Exposure Delayed Effects—United States.    7. United States
Government Agencies—United States.      WA 671 S823m 2007]
RJ383.S74    2007
618.92′98—dc22
2007019522

# Contents

Acknowledgments   vii

Prologue   1

PART I. **Diagnoses**   5

Introduction to Part I   7

1.   Predicates   9

2.   The Rise of Special-Interest Conservatism   26

3.   Battered-Agency Syndrome   45

4.   Corporations and the Commons   75

PART II. **Symptoms**   93

Introduction to Part II   95

5.   Mercury Case Study   103

6.   Perchlorate Case Study   126

7.   Ozone Case Study   150

PART III. **Cures**   171

Introduction to Part III   173

8.   A Question of Values   175

9.   New Government   195

Notes **215**

Bibliography **241**

Index **257**

# Acknowledgments

This book is the product of countless discussions with wonderful colleagues, many of whom are members of the Center for Progressive Reform (www.progressivereform.org), a virtual think tank comprised of forty-four member scholars that we founded in 2001. I especially appreciate the guidance of Katherine Baer, Margaret Giblin, Lisa Heinzerling, Tom McGarity, and Sidney Shapiro, who were kind enough to read and comment on the manuscript, and to Frank Ackerman, John Applegate, Alyson Flournoy, Catherine O'Neill, and Wendy Wagner, who discussed major themes with patience and insight. Linda Greer and Katherine Squibb, the two wisest scientists I know, helped me to get the technical details right, although any remaining mistakes are my responsibility. My two peer reviewers, Holly Doremus and Robert Kuehn, deserve enormous credit for helping shape the book into a more coherent piece of work.

Four classes of law student research assistants gave me invaluable assistance; they include Andrea Curatola, Natalie Havlina, Evan Isaacson, Anna Kuperstein, Jesse Martin, David McMurray, Andrew Schatz, Ray Schlee, Matt Shudtz, Jason Smith, and Michael Wright. David took ultimate responsibility for preparing the manuscript for submission, revising every footnote and painstakingly editing the text. Laura Mrozek, the administrator of the University of Maryland Environmental Law Program, was the talent-spotting matchmaker who put us all together.

I am grateful to Karen Rothenberg, Maryland's dean, and to the school's faculty for making it possible for me to take a research leave to work on this volume.

Bill Bishel, my editor at the University of Texas Press, can take as much credit as anyone else for getting this volume into print, wanting from the beginning only to improve it rather than tone it down. Lisa Heinzerling shares those honors—this would not have happened without her encouragement.

Finally, I thank Alice Southworth, who made it possible for me to get to the place where I could undertake this project, and my children, Daniel and Hannah Espo, who made this project seem so important.

**Mother Earth and Uncle Sam**

# Prologue

America entered the twenty-first century on top of the world. We had the most successful democratic government, the strongest economy, and a national defense second to none. We were universally acknowledged as the most powerful, if not the most popular, nation on earth. And we got that way by combining hard work, unprecedented civil liberties, and extraordinary fortune in the natural resources that endow the country. Many of us rail against the country and its culture. Few would live any other place.

Yet just as a new millennium of prosperity got under way, we suffered the most spectacular and terrifying attack by a foreign enemy in six decades. The collapse of the World Trade Center's Twin Towers affected our national politics in ways we have only begun to comprehend. Preoccupation with the newly named "War on Terror" swamped the public's attention, and the decision to invade Iraq ensured that the nation remained preoccupied by a conflict that was both intractable and costly.

At this close historical distance, it is difficult to underestimate the impact of these events on the collective American consciousness. The dual traumas of September 11 and the Iraq war upset the country to the point that key elements of the body politic—Congress, the president, and the media—appear to have lost the ability to focus systematically on pressing domestic problems. Lack of focus has gradually evolved into chronic neglect. From health care to social welfare, from education to energy policy to pollution control, we find government dysfunction on a grand scale. These problems did not originate on September 11, 2001. But in the wake of those shocking events, the degeneration of federal government institutions has accelerated dramatically. The more dysfunctional those institutions become and the more alienated people feel, the higher the risk that government will simply stop delivering the services that people need most.

Despite short spells of patriotic unity, America's political leadership remains divided, or so the pundits tell us, making it difficult to envision common ground between "red state" and "blue state" ideologies. Harsh discourse exhausts the electorate. In the environmental arena, for example, right-wingers accuse the left of irresponsibly predicting damnation even though environmental quality in America has never been better. Left-wingers retort that the right is maniacally fiddling as the earth slowly cooks to death. The extreme ends of the spectrum include companies that hate regulation and activists who hate companies, along with ideologues who excoriate "big government" regardless of what government does or does not do.

Yet lurking beneath the surface are the faint outlines of possible compromise. These signs of movement reflect the reality that only a dwindling number of pundits think the status quo is either sustainable or appropriate. The full spectrum of constituencies—from local environmental activists to the chief executive officers of Fortune 100 multinationals—agree that existing government institutions are failing us, although they differ on the origin of this state of affairs. In the privacy of their own minds, all well-informed people are aware of the overwhelming pressure to improve quality of life in the developing world by accelerating industrialization. At the same time, people understand that the natural environment cannot sustain the pollution caused by existing populations, much less the billions added in the next fifty years. Political leaders are moving inexorably toward the realization that global warming must be abated, and several of America's largest companies have begun to design voluntary programs to get the jump on the mandatory controls that they now see as inevitable.

There are no easy solutions to these problems. Undoubtedly, any long-term solutions will involve incremental progress, taking two steps forward for every step back. On the other hand, most informed adults remember the 1950s and 1960s, when schoolchildren routinely participated in "duck and cover" drills in anticipation of a third world war that would annihilate the planet. Although we have not eliminated threats posed by nuclear weapons and the number of countries possessing nuclear capacity continues to increase, the world no longer faces an arms race between superpowers and the likelihood that a nuclear attack by either side would destroy life as we know it in a matter of hours. However daunting today's challenges appear, those memories should motivate us to believe that we have the capacity not only to pull back from the brink but to make real progress.

This book focuses on how our growing inability to get a grip on such problems affects children. One-quarter of the American population (73.5 million people) is comprised of children younger than eighteen; 7 percent are under five. The book argues that very few parents would feel anything less than great agitation if they were confronted with evidence that pollution threatened their children and the children of people they know. If this case could be made, it might shatter our complacency about the severity and immediacy of the problems we face. Today's adults may well reach the end of our lifetimes without facing environmental catastrophes. Yet it is vital that we raise our eyes and look further down the road toward the crises our children will confront as a direct result of what we did and did not do.

To deepen this analysis, the book presents three high-profile controversies that have not been resolved: controlling mercury air emissions that fall into water bodies and contaminate the fish that are an integral part of the human food chain; cleaning up drinking water contaminated by perchlorate, a component of rocket fuel used widely by the military; and reducing ozone, or smog, to acceptable levels, especially in America's largest cities. In each instance, exposure to unsafe levels of pollution is especially harmful to children.

Five ideas are at the heart of this book. First, we are neglecting our children's health to an extent that we would find unthinkable as individual parents. Second, the primary reason for this unacceptable outcome is the erosion of government's role in protecting public health and the environment. Third, this outcome is not where most Americans believe we should be heading. Fourth, as matters stand now, our children and their children will not inherit the legacy that we owe them: a healthy, sustainable planet. Fifth, we can arrest these developments but only if a critical mass of Americans becomes convinced that the problems are urgent and the solutions near at hand.

Some caveats are necessary before we get started. First and foremost, this book is confined to the ways in which the U.S. government copes with domestic environmental problems. These problems have international implications, but international solutions are beyond the book's scope. Second, the book concentrates exclusively on public health issues. Nature per se is also priceless and under siege. But the implications of human exposure to toxic chemicals are a more urgent moral concern.

Many fine books have been written about how environmental problems threaten children's health, and I am indebted to those experts for their research and their insights.[1] What is different about this book is its focus on the dysfunction of the federal government and the ramifications of that collapse for our children and their children. The book argues that hollow government is the central cause of the alarming status quo and that the resurrection of effective government is the only viable solution. Obviously, both propositions are controversial, with many influential commentators arguing that private institutions and the free market are far better alternatives.

This odyssey considers only in passing what people can do as individuals. If we want to leave our children a better world by getting the environment as clean as we can manage, we will have to make lifestyle changes, especially in the area of energy consumption. But for the time being, the fulcrum needed to shift us off dead center is collective action motivated by public opinion. If we can get government back on the job, employing better, more efficient, and more powerful strategies to reduce pollution, we have a shot at resuming the march forward and arresting the slide backward.

Throughout the book, I refer to the "right wing" and "conservatives" and to the "left wing" and "progressives." Readers may be surprised to hear the argument that neither end of the spectrum has a lock on environmental correctness. Conservatives with impeccable credentials, such as F. A. Hayek and Milton Friedman, recognize the imperative of controlling industrial "poisons," while progressives bear a significant measure of responsibility for creating the gerrymandered regulatory system that is failing us so spectacularly right now.[2] In the midst of these ideological struggles, constituencies with an economic stake in the stringency of regulation—namely, the entities that manufacture and use them—have muddied the debate and obscured the issues, both advertently and inadvertently. Although it is legitimate for corporations to advance the immediate financial interests of their stockholders, those considerations play far too large a role in how the government defines and protects the public interest. A major goal of this volume is to disentangle these threads.

**PART I**

# DIAGNOSES

# Introduction to Part I

Part I of this volume is analogous to an annual physical, with the "patient" defined as policies and programs designed to protect children from toxic environmental hazards. Chapter 1, "Predicates," evaluates the conditions that have contributed to the patient's poor state of health, including the excessive complexity of policy-making decisions, the erosion of scientific integrity, unrealistic statutory mandates, and the gross underfunding of government efforts to protect public health and the environment.

Chapter 2, "The Rise of Conservatism," traces the patient's cultural history, explaining how broader currents of social change have disabled and undermined its government caretakers. The chapter concludes that the zeal and effectiveness of the crusade against "big government" have wreaked havoc with programs designed to protect children from environmental harm. The irony of this outcome is that traditional conservatives who do not have a financial stake in the outcome of any particular dispute might well agree that environmental protection is a perfectly appropriate mandate for government. These views have been stampeded by a broad cross-section of special-interest groups, especially regulated industries, that have managed to cloak their short-term financial interests in the trappings of conservative ideology.

Chapter 3, "Battered-Agency Syndrome," takes the patient's vital signs by examining the state of affairs at its institutional host, the U.S. Environmental Protection Agency (EPA). Beset by conflicting pressure from liberals and conservatives in Congress, a suspicious judiciary, rebellious representatives of regulated industry, and outraged advocates from organized public interest groups, EPA has been brought to its knees, no longer able to function in the arenas where its intervention is needed most. The chapter concludes that it will take interdisciplinary reform by all of its constituencies to reclaim the Agency's strength and credibility.

Chapter 4, "Corporations and the Commons," examines the universally negative posture assumed by regulated industries toward EPA's mission, mandates, and implementation, summarizing the arguments they have made to Congress, the courts, and regulators. The chapter concludes that although "corporate environmentalism" is a strengthening and encouraging trend, most experts in the field recognize the importance of a regulatory framework in motivating voluntary initiatives.

## CHAPTER 1

# Predicates

## Overview

The adverse health effects caused by children's exposure to toxic chemicals are subtle. Often, they do not kill outright but instead undermine their victims' quality of life. Neurological damage, diminished intelligence, chronic respiratory illness, hormone disruption, birth defects, and infertility take a great, often hidden, toll. The damage we do to our children and their children's future is especially discouraging because we have made great progress in improving environmental quality. But those hard-fought achievements are slipping from our grasp.

By any ethical code, sense of morals, or religious belief, we have no right to impose such risks on our children. Nor do we have a moral right to consume natural resources to the point that they are not available for future generations. And yet, as we will see, the mode of analysis for all such momentous decisions is based on traditional economics, a discipline that does not effectively acknowledge present, much less future, harm. Even the damage toxic chemicals cause to children who are alive today gets short shrift in such obsessive analysis, with its effects either ignored or steeply discounted.

The goal of this chapter is to pull the camera back to the point that the reader can achieve an overview of the predicates for the problems and solutions discussed throughout the book. Hopefully, this overview will provide a framework for issues that are as confusing as they are opaque. We begin with brief summaries of the circumstances surrounding three unresolved threats to children that serve as case studies later in the book: mercury, which contaminates the human food chain, threatening children's neurological development; perchlorate, which is dissolved in the drinking and irrigation water supplies of thirty-five states, potentially interfering with normal development of babies by cutting short their supply of thyroid hormones; and ozone, a common air pollutant that exacerbates an epidemic of childhood asthma.

The chapter then considers why the debate over pollution's effect on children has become complexified to the point that the public is unable to monitor, or even understand, these issues. These conditions have produced a policy-making netherworld where decisions are made on the basis of considerations that contradict fundamental, widely shared public values. The chapter examines the product of this netherworld—government agencies that are hollow, unable to fulfill the missions they were assigned by Congress. It concludes by mentioning the two most prominent alternatives to strong national government: devolution to ill-prepared, individual states or the "free market" alternative of buying and selling pollution rights.

### Clean Food, Clean Water, and Clean Air

#### Clean Food

As explained in Chapter 5, "Mercury Case Study," 15 percent of American women of childbearing age have blood mercury levels greater than amounts considered safe; this number doubles in Native American women living near the Great Lakes, which are heavily contaminated by this most toxic of metals.[1] The primary pathway of human exposure is the human food chain, specifically fish that have absorbed methylmercury, the most persistent and dangerous form of the pollutant, from water bodies contaminated by industrial sources. About 30 percent of mercury emissions occur naturally as a result of such events as volcanic eruptions. Anthropogenic, or man-made, sources produce the remainder.

Prenatal exposure to methylmercury at very low doses causes neurological and other developmental damage, even if the mother herself does not appear to suffer any ill effects. Exposure to mercury pollution, primarily through eating contaminated fish, means that as many as 637,000 babies born annually in the United States are put in jeopardy. This pollution is so widespread in forty-eight states that people are warned not to consume specific species caught in waters posted with "fish advisories" that now cover 35 percent of American lakes and 24 percent of American river miles.

Despite this startling evidence, the federal government's efforts to compel large chemical and power plants to use more effective pollution control technology have stalled for the foreseeable future. In a final rule that has yet to be put into effect, EPA adopted the weakest possible controls for nine outmoded chemical plants that were the leading domestic source of mercury pollution.[2] The next biggest source—power plants that burn off the mercury present in coal, sending it up the smokestack and into the atmosphere—also got a pass until 2018 at the earliest. Instead of requiring the installation of technology that could capture such emissions before they went into the environment, EPA will allow electric utilities to buy and sell pieces of paper that grant them mini-licenses to emit mercury, producing very gradual overall reductions and potentially concentrating contamination in states where water bodies already bear an unsafe load of contamination.[3]

Such "market-based" trading is considered exemplary by conservatives who abhor more intrusive "command and control" methods for reducing pollution. But the Clean Air Act does not contemplate trading as an alternative to more stringent controls in this context, and the courts are likely to overturn EPA's misadventure in lawmaking. The litigation will prove exhausting for all concerned, however, and it will be years before more effective reductions are accomplished.

## Clean Water

At six hundred square kilometers, Lake Mead on the Colorado River is one of the world's largest man-made reservoirs, providing potable water to Las Vegas. The Colorado River downstream of Lake Mead serves as the primary drinking water source for Los Angeles. Within the past few years, local officials have discovered that this vital resource was contaminated by perchlorate, a component of rocket fuel provided to the U.S. military by a Kerr-McGee plant in Henderson, Nevada. Similar instances of contamination have been discovered throughout the nation wherever chemical plants produced perchlorate or military bases undertook weapons testing and training.

Studies completed in the past decade show that perchlorate interferes with the uptake of iodide by the thyroid, disrupting thyroid hormone levels and causing developmental problems in fetuses, babies, and young children. These problems are especially acute when the mother also has insufficient thyroid function to give her fetus enough thyroid hormones for normal development during the early months of gestation. Pregnant and nursing mothers are exposed to perchlorate through consumption of contaminated water, milk, or vegetables.

Chapter 6, "Perchlorate Case Study," explains that, with its own back-of-the-envelope estimates of cleanup costs running into billions of dollars, the Department of Defense (DOD) elbowed its way into the interagency working group of scientists formed to develop a scientific research agenda that would address this emerging threat. The working group's quest for reliable science was effectively sabotaged by the military, which had no business joining an expert panel designed to be impartial.

Although the government and private manufacturers have spent several million dollars investigating the health implications of exposure to perchlorate—a very large sum of money for such an effort—the research did not answer fundamental questions about perchlorate's impact on children. Among other unanswered questions, we do not yet know how much perchlorate has infiltrated into the food supply through the use of contaminated irrigation water. Nor do we understand exactly what combination of circumstances—maternal thyroid condition and neonate iodide shortages—will produce irreversible damage.

Facing stalemate within the working group, EPA and the military decided to refer the controversy to the National Research Council (NRC), part of the National Academies (NAS), the country's premier scientific institution founded to give informed advice to policy makers. A blue-ribbon panel of experts was convened and opened hearings on the science underlying the controversy. Among the witnesses offering testimony was an Army colonel named Dan Rogers, a lawyer by trade, who informed the scientists in no uncertain terms that they would jeopardize the nation's security if their conclusions reflected too much concern for public health. In a related vein, the *Wall Street Journal* reported in 2003 that the George W. Bush administration deflected pressure for a stricter standard by issuing a gag order barring government scientists from commenting publicly on a study showing dangerous levels of perchlorate in lettuce grown in California's Imperial Valley and consumed throughout the country.[4]

Ultimately, the NAS panel concluded that perchlorate exposure should not exceed 0.0007 milligrams per kilogram of body weight per day for babies and fetuses—a very small number in absolute terms.[5] Meanwhile, the battle has shifted back to EPA, which faces the daunting task of translating the NAS conclusions into tangible and practical cleanup protocols despite continued opposition by the military and its contractors. No one expects a decision any time soon.

## Clean Air

Families in a dozen large cities are warned to keep their children inside on "Code Red" days, especially if the child is one of the 6.5 million Americans between the ages of five and seventeen afflicted by asthma. Childhood asthma rates have skyrocketed over the past twenty years; 85 out of every 1,000 children have the disease.[6] Compelling scientific research shows that air pollution makes the disease worse. Ground-level ozone, or smog, is among the primary culprits. It forms when emissions of nitrogen oxides and volatile organic compounds mix with oxygen in the presence of sunlight; these chemicals are known as ozone "precursors." The main sources of these emissions are large power plants, factories, and motor vehicles of all varieties.

Chapter 7, "Ozone Case Study," explains that Congress has made several abortive efforts to place the states on a schedule to ramp down the "ambient," or outside air, levels of the most common and harmful pollutants by regulating the sources that emit them.[7] The driving force to accomplish these reductions is listing polluted cities and their surrounding suburbs as "non-attainment areas" under the 1970 amendments to the Clean Air Act.[8] In theory, if a state fails to meet those targets, a series of stringent penalties should be imposed until air quality improves, including withholding federal highway construction grants from the state governments responsible for achieving attainment. In practice, the states with the worst problems have run right up to the deadlines without coming close to these public health goals. Each time a deadline looms, Congress has flinched, granting extensions as many as three times in some places. Early in 2005, as the fourth set of deadlines came due, EPA decided to simply abolish these requirements administratively without asking Congress, replacing them with new deadlines that will not expire in many places for a few more years. That decision, like most others of importance, was challenged in court and the case is still pending as this book goes to press.

## Cognitive and Political Dissonance

How did we get to the point where we accept as routine the bizarre injunction that children should not go outside on certain days? And why are we resigned to the notion that pregnant women should stop having tuna fish sandwiches for lunch? Would we be outraged if it was widely known that expectant mothers should also avoid eating salad or breast feeding their babies?

Has this troubling information been drowned out by the cacophony of other issues and preoccupations? Do people really not know anything about the risks that preoccupy environmentalists? Simple ignorance certainly explains some of our apparent quietude, but it is unlikely that a critical mass of people have avoided all of this information for so many decades.

If we know about these threats—in the big picture if not in detail—do we accept them as facts of modern life? Or do we recognize them, feel upset, but perceive that we are powerless to respond? Or, and this is the most discouraging alternative, do we know them and yet feel no responsibility to future generations, figuring that our kids will just have to fend for themselves?

There is, of course, a fourth alternative: we know on some level that we are in trouble but cannot come to grips with the realization because we have lost any sense of what to do. Psychologists define "cognitive dissonance" as a conflict between two cognitions, including knowledge, attitude, emotion, belief, or behavior.[9] Such conflicts mean that people can be troubled and angry, have difficulty maintaining these mental states, and revert to denial. There is an analogous dissonance in politics—people's concerns are directly contradicted by what the government actually does, and yet the public is not able to retaliate for such discrepancies at the polls. While public opinion and policy making in a government as large and complex as ours have always suffered from these discrepancies, environmental threats to children compel us to confront a new strain of what could be called "political dissonance," one that is highly resistant to the checks and balances established by the U.S. Constitution, including freedom of the press.

Polling shows consistently large majorities of people both support strong environmental protection and believe that the government is not doing enough to safeguard our natural resources. Chapter 8 discusses these polling results in greater detail. Yet the country has a president as well as dependable caucuses in both houses of Congress who are willing to ignore such sentiments. Most people deem fatal pediatric asthma and irreversible damage to babies' neurological development unacceptable. And most people suspect that these outcomes exist and that they are linked to pollution. But the public has yet to send a message to politicians that it wants these problems fixed.

Conservative commentators assert that such polling is deceptive because survey questions distort results by, for example, asking people whether they are concerned about pollution in the abstract without explaining how much they would have to pay to address these risks. Pollsters have tried to respond to these criticisms by incorporating questions about the public's willingness to "pay more" for a cleaner environment. Such surveys show that a strong majority is worried and would pay more, although the answer to the questions of how much more money to address which specific environmental problems remains elusive.

Whatever the polls say about what people think now, though, my goal here is to convince readers that conservatives are wrong in at least one crucial, overriding sense. If people knew what pollution could mean for children, and if they could see a path to a solution, they would compel the government to shift course dramatically, beginning real efforts to repay our debt to the future.

## Complexification

In large measure, the paradoxical gap between public support for environmental protection and government dysfunction is the inevitable by-product of how difficult it is to fully understand the causes, scope, and severity of environmental problems. Problems that seem obvious—you can see smog in the air and feel breathless if you jog on a bad ozone day—have multiple sources and affect different people in different ways. They are analyzed from every angle to the point that it takes a multi-disciplinary panel of experts from a variety of fields to grapple with the most significant problems. Much of the debate centers on scientific uncertainty: what does science tell us about pollution and its impact on the young? What don't we know? Should we act on the basis of what we know or wait for more information?

So, for example, we have some grip on why ozone is harmful, but we are unclear on how it interacts with other causes of respiratory illness: Does it trigger, or only exacerbate, asthma? Is it a more significant aggravating factor than indoor air pollutants? Does ozone affect certain children more than others? We also strain to understand how ozone forms once pollution is emitted into the air, how climate affects its transport to places long distances away, and similar questions. The more we know, the more we realize what we do not know and the more we are inspired to undertake better research. On the other hand, indulging our urge to search for the truth can exact a high price. If we wait to answer all these questions before curbing pollution, millions of additional asthma attacks will occur. Action in the face of uncertainty is essential if we want to protect people, as opposed to merely compensating them after they are hurt.

Ideally, independent government experts would be available to decide when to take action in the face of uncertainty. But the condition of government is far from ideal. As the government's resources diminish and the bureaucracy's political will grows weaker, the scientific debate is increasingly dominated by other voices, becoming far more confusing than it needs to be. Venturing into the thicket of conflicting views can be overwhelming for seasoned experts and far more so for the average television or newspaper reporter. Four distinct trends cause and exacerbate the phenomenon I call "complexification":

1. The insistence by regulated industries that only "sound"—as in comprehensive and complete—science be used to make decisions about problems that cost significant amounts of money to fix;
2. Government officials' efforts to placate regulated industries by creating more convoluted and intricate regulations;
3. Environmentalists' penchant to participate in these technical exercises rather than translating such esoteric efforts into language everyone can understand;
4. The mass media's extraordinarily short attention span, which does not lead to insightful reporting on decisions with long-term, subtle implications.

## The "Sound Science" Campaign

Ten or fifteen years ago, regulated industries decided that many government-mandated pollution controls were unnecessary. Rather than try to convince the public to forgo these protections because they cost too much or because the risks posed by the additional pollution should be acceptable, the companies leveraged concerns about scientific uncertainty, developing the strategy of insisting on "sound science" to document a direct, causal connection between a given form of pollution and illness. Once the debate shifted from a discussion of how much pollution people are willing to tolerate to a demanding, time-consuming evaluation of interdisciplinary, highly technical science, the public-at-large was hard-pressed to discern which side was right. The public's confusion shields politicians from the backlash that would occur if the debate had not become so convoluted.

Thus, for example, industry advocates argue that data are insufficient to prove that ozone is a primary cause of asthma, as opposed to heredity, indoor air pollution (for example, second-hand smoke or dust mites), and access to immediate medical assistance. They contend that even if ozone exacerbates asthma, science is too uncertain about which sources—power plants, factories, or cars—are the worst culprits and should be controlled first.

The sound science campaign also involves ferocious disagreements about the credibility of scientific data, slowing standard setting in a broad swath of the manufacturing sector. As explained in Chapter 6, "A Perchlorate Case Study," the most prominent example of this phenomenon is the widespread debunking of "animal studies" (experiments involving the dosing of rats, mice, and various forms of aquatic life) linking toxic exposures with disease. While animal studies, like every other form of research, can be performed badly, reputable scientists would never suggest that a well-run study is not worth adding to the mix of evidence they consider. Further, the only alternative to animal studies is the analysis of human exposures, either through deliberate dosing, an extremely controversial alternative from an ethical perspective, or through epidemiological studies of populations that are exposed to the threat.

Finally, the campaign on behalf of sound science relies upon the rapid mobilization of experts to challenge research results that suggest pollution is harmful. Industry-funded experts pick apart each individual study, fighting a battle of attrition that is designed to increase confusion and dissension in the scientific community. This approach is diametrically opposed to the traditional method for evaluating research, known as "weight of evidence" analysis, which depends on a review of the full body of data, including the weaknesses and strengths of individual studies, to arrive at a final judgment.

## Defensive Governing

Another source of complexification is EPA's reaction to the high stakes raised by many of its core statutory mandates, both for public health and for the economy. The pressure on the Agency is exacerbated by Congress' propensity to duck difficult issues, punting them to the bureaucracy to resolve without much guidance. This approach leaves Congress free to criticize when EPA fumbles its missions. As explained in Chapter 3, "Battered-Agency Syndrome," after a short honeymoon period, EPA was inundated by constituencies concerned about how it would implement broad mandates to control air and water pollution and identify and clean up hazardous waste sites. Buffeted by a steady drumbeat of criticism from Capitol Hill, dragged into court over most significant decisions, and demeaned by a succession of presidents, the Agency has been on the defensive throughout its three-decade history.

These conditions led to a series of mistakes made by bureaucrats who attempted to negotiate their way out of disputes with regulated entities by writing into environmental rules a series of arcane exceptions, variations, factors to be considered, and additional procedural requirements. Rather than fighting hard to keep its rules straightforward and understandable, the Agency's staff convinced themselves that if the rules were convoluted enough, they would satisfy industry and gain some breathing room. Unfortunately, the regulations were complexified to the point that even sophisticated companies are unclear which requirements apply to them. A 1993 survey found, for example, that only 30 percent of corporate counsel for large companies believed it was possible for their companies to achieve compliance with all the environmental laws that applied to them.[10] Not only did EPA have the daunting challenge of enforcing the law in the face of such confusion, it had lost the attention of its public constituency.

## Inside Ball Versus Public Relations

Propelled by a groundswell of grassroots activism, as exemplified by the first Earth Day, the 1970s were a heyday for the passage of breathtakingly ambitious laws. The Clean Water Act, for example, announced a goal of "zero discharge" of pollution into surface waters such as rivers, lakes, and streams by 1985, and this provision is still included in the statute.[11] When EPA and the states floundered in their effort to implement this first generation of relatively simple laws, environmentalists and their congressional allies successfully pressed for a second generation of far more detailed legislation, laced with literally hundreds of mandates.

As legislative activism receded in the early 1990s, and public attention drifted away, the environmentalists' orientation as highly skilled insider experts left them poorly prepared for a re-energized industry public relations campaign. The public interest community always depended on public opinion to give it an influential seat at the tables where decisions are made. Before environmentalists knew it, those meetings had become increasingly technical debates over complexities the public could not hope to understand, and environmentalists had fallen far behind in rebutting the far more visible public relations war against regulation. Regulated industries had the resources to play on both fields. Environmentalists did not.

## The Media's Attention Span

The general atmosphere of overload, hype, and extreme rhetoric that characterizes all public policy-making disputes these days has only served to exacerbate the public interest community's problems. A twenty-four-hour news cycle has pushed reporting on public affairs toward staccato sound bites. The media appear to believe that the best way to compete is to avoid intricate technical disputes within government, however important they may be, in favor of following scandals and other shocking events. These trends do not produce complexification per se, but they give an enormous boost to those who promote it.

## Policy-Making Netherworld

Most Americans do not follow the intricate details of policy-making in Congress, much less the bureaucracy, on a daily basis. Yet American democracy works because citizens assume what Professor Michael Schudson calls a "monitorial role," staying enough in touch with the broad outlines of what government is doing to correct its course as necessary.[12] By far the most important implication of complexification is its devastating effects on the public's ability to play this monitorial role. The result is the creation of a policy-making netherworld where decisions are made on the basis of principles, values, and rules that are obscure to the public.

"Cost-benefit analysis" is the preeminent example of such invisible policy making. On its face, this approach makes a lot of sense: We need to figure out how much money we will need to pay to clean up pollution—the "cost" side of the equation—and then make sure that the "benefits" we will gain are worth it. Each day, all of us make numerous analogous decisions: How much does it cost to heat our houses and how high should we turn the thermostat? Should we purchase less, high-quality food or more, less nutritional food? Will it cost more to drive than to take public transportation and what is the additional cost worth in terms of time saved and convenience?

But shift the questions a bit, and the supposedly simple calculation becomes much more difficult. A child gasps for breath in a hospital emergency room while a power plant a thousand miles away sends a letter to its congressional representatives urging them to vote against legislation that would require the installation of smokestack scrubbers. If the legislation passes, the power plant executives warn, the cost of electricity will rise enough that the elderly poor in a nearby inner city cannot afford to keep their air conditioning operating during the worst days of summer. A pregnant factory worker sits down to a fish dinner caught by her husband in a nearby lake; years later, her daughter has learning disabilities that block the child's progress in school. But the owners of the mercury-cell chlor-alkali factory down the road explain that if the factory was converted to a cleaner technology, it might raise the cost of laundry bleach. Clearly, one person's costs are another person's benefits, and translating, much less weighing, the cross-currents of ethical responsibility raised by these scenarios cannot be easy.

Proponents of cost-benefit analysis claim with remarkable temerity that they have all these questions worked out. In cost-benefit analysis everything has a price tag, at least in theory, and justice is served by balancing the two sets of numbers against one another. Economists begin by quantifying—or translating into monetary terms—the amount it will cost polluting firms to prevent or reduce their emissions, usually on the basis of industry estimates. In areas where no readily marketable technology exists to accomplish those reductions, these estimates typically overestimate actual costs by large margins. Once a final rule creates a market for the development of pollution control equipment and competition kicks in, these costs drop dramatically.

Having tallied inflated costs, economists turn to the benefits side of the equation, monetizing the value of the lives harmed by pollution or, conversely, the value of the lives that would be saved if the pollution at issue were reduced. The going rate of a human life is about $6 million. But economists do not leave the process of monetization there. The $6 million is what a life would be worth if the person drops dead on the spot. But if people suffer from illnesses like cancer that do not become apparent for twenty or thirty years or more economists use a different formula. They argue that in the case of these "long latency diseases" that take many years to emerge after exposure, the relevant question is: How much money would have to be invested today to come up with $6 million in twenty or thirty years? This math, commonly referred to as "discounting," reduces the value of human life to a fraction of the $6 million in current dollars, making it far more difficult for life to compete with costs in the neat equations that emerge from such analyses.

While they have little trouble working out the value of life in comparison to death figure, economists struggle with the value of a decreased quality of life that falls short of death, such as the loss of a few intelligence quotient, or IQ, points by children exposed to toxics in utero. As explained in Chapter 5, "Mercury Case Study," the current going rate for a single IQ point is about $8,800. Or, in other words, the *monetary value* of the injury suffered by a child who lost five IQ points as a result of lead poisoning or exposure to any other toxin that causes comparable brain damage would be less than the down payment on the average small house in many major cities. Low-balling the "price" of such short-term health effects usually means taking no action because the benefits side of the equation comes up short in comparison to industry cost projections.

We cannot afford to ignore the costs of taking action. The United States may be the richest country on earth, but resources are finite and many expensive problems confront us. But acknowledging these realities means we have to find a better way to discuss these difficult trade-offs, not resort to a deceptively precise methodology so obscure that only a few thousand people understand it.

## Hollow Government and the
## "Tragedy of Distrust" Syndrome

As mentioned earlier and explained further in Chapter 2, "Battered-Agency Syndrome," EPA has had a very difficult time interpreting the lengthy and at times internally inconsistent statutes that Congress has asked it to implement, not least because Congress has deferred many of the most contentious decisions to the Agency. These difficulties are exacerbated by severe shortfalls in EPA's budget. Statutory mandates not only tell EPA how to write implementing regulations but often set strict deadlines for the issuance of a final product. The Agency misses most of these numerous deadlines because it simply does not have the staff to get them done.

Ongoing, increasingly effective conservative arguments against big government as the ultimate enemy of the people have accelerated these trends. As explained in Chapter 3, "The Rise of Special-Interest Conservatism," the election of President Ronald Reagan was a triumph for the conservative vision of an enlightened republic: the national government should limit its role to defending the country's interests abroad and ensuring a stable climate for business, with its intervention into daily domestic affairs sharply limited. Conservatives argue that the Great Depression was triggered by misguided government interference with the banking system. The Great Depression's legacy, the New Deal, started the country down the road to damnation, and the New Deal's successor, the Great Society, hastened this decline. Conservatives believe we must restore the founding fathers' constitutional vision of strong states and a small federal bureaucracy.

Of course, this pure strain of conservative ideology is almost always sidetracked by political pressures. The relative size of government under Reagan and all subsequent Republican administrations has grown exponentially despite conservative claims that the people want government out of their lives. And traditional conservatives are only one group on the right-wing end of the spectrum. The other, equally powerful participants either have very different agendas (consider the Christian right, multinational corporations, and small business) or disagree with the simplistic view that limited government is an overarching value (consider the so-called "neoconservatives" who have successfully pushed the country into the role of engineering regime change to bring their version of freedom to the rest of the world).

The Republican Party has managed to transform this melting pot of divergent ideologies into a powerful movement that now controls the executive branch of government. That coalition blurs the motives of pure conservatives, self-interested corporations, evangelicals, and international militarists. The portion of the Republican coalition that is by far the most invested in environmental issues is big business, which has skillfully lost itself in the crowd of a more broadly based conservative movement, obstructing environmental protection far more effectively than it could ever hope to accomplish on its own.

Exacerbating this confusion is the uncomfortable fact that the left-wing end of the political spectrum is as enamored of condemning government as the right, albeit for distinctly different reasons. Beginning with the New Left in the 1960s, government was demeaned as a "military-industrial complex" that was as corrupt as it was hypocritical. While it is certainly true that the left strongly supported the birth of EPA as well as the expansion of federal health and safety regulatory authority over food and drug safety, consumer and worker rights, and the preservation of natural resources, deep distrust of government compromised these creations almost as soon as they were initiated.

In sum, government has been subjected to a double-pincer attack, and it remains under fire. Decried by the right wing as unnecessary and the left wing as untrustworthy, the federal civil service today is increasingly dysfunctional. Professor Richard Lazarus has written eloquently about the "tragedy of distrust" that undermines EPA at every turn.[13] Its most important implication is that even when we decide as a society that something must be done about serious environmental problems, the institution available to do the work has no credibility. We will be hard pressed to find a shortcut to the goal of renewing the people's faith in government. Yet nothing less is likely to generate reliable and permanent change.

## Devolution

On the rare occasions that government intervention is deemed necessary, conservatives argue that the power and responsibility for taking action should be devolved to levels of government closer to the people. This approach is most often introduced with the claim that federally imposed "one-size-fits-all" regulation is an economically inefficient method for controlling pollution that the people would not want if anyone ever asked them.

Conservatives contend that centralized federal decision making is not what the Constitution's framers had in mind, in large measure because it is affirmatively undemocratic. They criticize the irresponsible behavior of Congress, which writes elaborate laws that impose unfunded mandates on state and local governments and then washes its hands of the expenses that arise during implementation. When these unfunded programs prove a failure, federal lawmakers largely escape accountability. Conservatives add that the most effective way to guarantee public choice, or full democracy, is to devolve most domestic decisions to the state and local level, where voters can understand problems more easily and evaluate the trade-offs involved in taking action.

It should come as no surprise that all states are not created equal, with some far more capable than others to stand in for the federal government in protecting their most vulnerable citizens. But EPA has become so weak that it has no means to force the worst states to do a better job. The result is grossly disparate levels of protection depending on geography, not environmental health. To address these obstacles, EPA must not only be revived but have enough resources and credibility to get recalcitrant states back into line.

### "Free Market" Alternatives

On the relatively rare occasion when cost-benefit analysis justifies intervention and the science is sufficiently clear, decision makers must select the appropriate approach to reducing pollution. Conservatives are similarly well prepared for that turn in the road. With great effectiveness, they have argued that the government is going about protecting public health and the environment all wrong. Rather than browbeating American industry into compliance by forcing every plant in an industrial category to install pollution control equipment, say these critics, we should concentrate on harnessing the technological brilliance of corporate America to deliver better results for much less. Awarding industrial sources the opportunity to freely trade rights to emit pollution is always a better approach than requiring them to install scrubbers on their smokestacks regardless of cost.

In a trading system, every plant is awarded a set number of pollution credits or allowances, generally based on its past emissions. So, for example, a plant that emitted one hundred tons of pollution in the year 2000 would get one hundred tons of credits or allowances annually under a trading plan. If the plant chooses to install pollution control equipment and reduce its annual emissions to fifty tons, it can sell the extra fifty tons to cover emissions at a plant that does not have such technology. However, as we shall discover in Chapter 5, "A Mercury Case Study," the fatal flaw of trading systems is that plants can buy extra credits, increasing the pollution they emit, regardless of what is going on around them. In areas where public health is vulnerable to the increased pollution load, the formation of such hot spots is a powerful argument against trading, especially of toxic substances like mercury.

### Conclusion

The right-wing gadfly and popular author P. J. O'Rourke once described environmental protection as a "luxury good" available only to those who are able to pay for it.[14] So outrageous is this statement that it is difficult to imagine a public spokesperson for any organized entity—from Dow Chemical Company to the Heritage Foundation—ever embracing it. Yet far below the water line that demarcates national news, the criteria used to make decisions have the result of restricting the benefits of a clean environment to those either lucky enough or rich enough to live in areas of the country that are relatively pollution-free.

While the content of government decision making for the most part is not secret, crucial details rarely emerge in the popular media and therefore remain obscure to most people. The public has little idea that such decisions are being made, much less the arguments offered to validate them. Decision makers are increasingly isolated and inbred, offering justifications that might well prove unpopular, even embarrassing, if brought into public view.

The federal government's efforts to deliver environmental protection are in more trouble than they have been since the Reagan administration. The entire policy-making debate revolves around extraordinarily complex arguments over relatively dry subjects. The public harbors cynicism about the government's effectiveness, and obscure controversies do nothing to inspire renewed confidence. Even where they concede action might be necessary, conservatives argue that the states are best able to take care of the problem or that industries should be given the opportunity to buy and sell rights to emit pollution. Today's adults may escape the worst effects of this situation, but our children will surely reap the consequences of our complacence.

The pages that follow argue that the environmental risks to our children are real, have unacceptable consequences, and are increasing. These problems harm children of all races, ethnic groups, and class backgrounds, no matter where they live. For the most part, the nation has stopped making progress on these problems, and if we do not take action soon, we will fall further behind. Most maddening, unlike world hunger or peace in the Middle East, these are all problems that can be solved with a modest investment of money and political will.

CHAPTER 2

# The Rise of Special-Interest Conservatism

*I don't want to abolish government. I simply want to reduce it to the size where I can drag it into the bathroom and drown it in the bathtub.*
GROVER NORQUIST

## Overview

Political dissonance—defined as the contradiction between what people want and what government does—dominates our troubled efforts to protect children from pollution. It is safe to assume that the vast majority of parents would never accept the idea that their children will be significantly harmed by pollution, either in the short or long term. Almost the same number would not sanction harm to anyone else's child. Yet U.S. government policies routinely fail to address these concerns. Not only is government intervention largely ineffective, the underlying policies responsible for these outcomes would offend most people if brought to light. Few people are naïve enough to hope for a perfect match between what people want and what government ends up delivering. But the integrity and stability of a democracy depends on their close alignment. Especially when an issue is grounded in a universal sense of moral values, as protecting children from environmental hazards must be, governments that stray too far from broadly endorsed goals should get into trouble.

Chapter 1 presented an overview of the reasons why these policies have evolved to this point. One of its major conclusions was that people do not really understand what is being done in their names and that, if they did, many of these policies would change drastically. This second chapter explores why U.S. politicians have escaped accountability for our neglect of environmental threats to children. Across the spectrum, politicians have embraced the conservative notions that "big government" is bad and Americans do not want it. This mantra, repeated over and over again in multiple contexts, leaves most people feeling frustrated and angry, in large measure because political leaders do not seem to have any constructive ideas about how to solve these worsening problems.

The chapter begins with a brief taxonomy of political positions discussed throughout the book. It explores the historical roots of conservatism, which has emerged as the dominating ideology of the last three decades. It discusses the evolution of the conservative movement from Ronald Reagan to George W. Bush. The chapter concludes with a further examination of political dissonance and the reasons it must be minimized if we are to have any realistic hope of protecting children's health from environmental hazards.

## A Brief Taxonomy of Ideology and Interests

Two factors inspire political actors as they array themselves along the political spectrum: "ideology," meaning well-developed and coherent theories of government, and "special interests," meaning idiosyncratic positions that are adopted for opportunistic reasons. In common parlance, conservative ideologies occupy the right end of the spectrum, and progressive or liberal ideologies occupy its left.[1] Special interests are oriented toward the right or toward the left, but make sure to retain the flexibility to float along the axis as necessary to serve their short-term interests. Among the biggest problems in American politics today is that ideological bickering camouflages the design of policies that serve these special interests, and not the public's interests.

Traditional right-wing ideologues have always believed in limited— or minimalist—government, at least from a programmatic perspective, especially with respect to domestic programs. Adherents would abolish funding for everything from social welfare (or "safety net") programs to the enforcement of anti-discrimination laws to private-sector subsidies of any kind. They contend that an oversized public sector impinges on individual freedom and undermines the economy. They would cut the federal budget to the bone and curtail anything but essential expenditures, defined very narrowly. Although traditional conservatives are the public face of the conservative coalition that governs today, the coalition has expanded to include the Christian right and neoconservatives, two ideologies that do not embrace these core tenets with anything approaching the traditionalists' fervor.

The Christian right focuses almost exclusively on moral issues and, in a notable departure from traditional conservatism, demands that the federal government promote "family values" by intruding to a far greater extent in Americans' private lives. While this intervention does not inflate the federal budget, it is the antithesis of the individual liberty so prized by traditionalists.

Neoconservatives favor a large and costly military to control undesirable developments such as terrorism by proselytizing free-market democracy throughout the world. Achieving this vision has led neoconservatives to gain allies by looking the other way as the federal budget grows, provoking strident discord with their traditionalist allies.

As this coalition has matured, tensions have deepened, and the three groups are now in the midst of a noisy battle for the Republican Party's soul. Because this volume is focused on the government's role in protecting children from environmental hazards, the agendas of the neoconservative and Christian right movements need not detain us. They are important in this context primarily because they compete for public attention and obscure the causes of the problems that are the focus of this book.

The Republican Party's Herculean effort to keep these disparate interests contained under one large tent is offset by equally intense conflicts at the other end of the spectrum. Left-wing ideologues generally advocate using the public sector to provide a "safety net" for the poor through robust social welfare programs. Forged by the bitter experiences of the labor and civil rights movements, most progressives distrust the states' capacity to provide fundamental civil rights and embrace a strong federal government role in enforcing such protections. These beliefs sometimes run afoul of the left's equally fervent commitment to civil liberties and individual autonomy, causing fault lines within the loose group of intellectuals that struggle to define progressive ideology. In the wake of September 11, 2001, liberals were deeply ambivalent about the Bush administration's invasion of Iraq and other efforts to wage the war on terror but were unable to articulate an alternative vision of U.S. foreign policy, costing them a major opportunity to gain traction with the public.

There is little question that conservative ideologies have dominated the political landscape for most of the last several decades, as demonstrated by Republican victories in all but three of the last eight presidential elections. These trends have forced the left into a defensive crouch, compelling them—among many other things—to embrace conservatives' antipathy to big government. The most prominent example is President Bill Clinton's 1996 State of the Union address announcing that "the era of big government is over."[2] Clinton followed this pronouncement with an overhaul of the public welfare program and, amazingly enough, produced a budget surplus. Conservatives were understandably delighted by these aspects of Clinton's reign, interpreting his declaration and follow-up actions as strong evidence that their campaign to undermine government had achieved bipartisan momentum. Yet rhetorical hostility to government is not the same thing as devotion to limited government. Nor does it lead to much of an effort to reconceive government as a more effective institution. Without such affirmative proposals, progressives have little to offer in response to the problems at the heart of this book.

The special interests that float along the axis between the spectrum's opposing endpoints include organized entities—for example, industry trade associations, labor unions, or nonprofit advocacy groups—that have as their primary goal immediate benefits, whether measured in money or influence. The constant movement of special-interest groups along the trajectory between left and right is at the heart of the political dissonance that is so destructive to efforts to protect children from environmental hazards.

Special interests travel along this axis for opportunistic reasons. For example, large multinational corporations support the devolution of more authority to state and local governments. Paradoxically, they oppose any "patchwork" of state regulation that could impose substantial costs on business that is conducted across state lines. The only way to reconcile the two positions is to assume that these groups believe devolution is good if it does not generate regulation at the state level. That conclusion is motivated by self-serving and pragmatic considerations, as opposed to principled ideology.

In a similar vein, liberal interest groups oppose the preemption of state tort laws that impose liability for the harm caused by everything from corporate malfeasance to pollution to stock market fraud. But they support the creation of federal causes of action for such problems, especially if federal liability standards are more stringent than state standards. These positions are opportunistic because they are not based on a principled vision of federalism, which typically assigns to the state courts the responsibility for lawsuits seeking damages.

Obviously, there are multiple exceptions to these simplistic characterizations. They are offered here not as a finely tuned template for assessing the wide gamut of ideologies or political posturing but rather as a broad framework for understanding how we have reached the point of distrusting government across the spectrum from right to left, while at the same time relying on it to provide an incredibly diverse universe of services. There can be no question that ours is the largest, most ambitious, and best-funded national government in history, in absolute terms and probably also per capita. Paradoxically, we love to hate it. This conflict in attitudes blocks us from thinking about what government does best and when we need it most. And, like most other fundamental conflicts in American political life, this one is rooted in the country's historical origins.

## The Framers' Compromise

As any schoolchild knows, the colonists' victory in the American Revolution stood for the principle that an autocratic, lavishly funded, central government posed the greatest challenge to the liberty the colonists held dear. At the same time, the wild frontiers of the vast continent convinced the revolutionaries that they needed a unified defense against threats real and imagined. In response, the political leaders (or "Framers") who authored the Constitution developed the innovative compromise of a federalist republic, with responsibilities divided between national and state governments.

The endurance of the U.S. Constitution is taken for granted these days, although nothing would have surprised the Framers more. They considered themselves to be teetering on the brink of failure in the years leading up to its adoption. In fact, *The Federalist Papers*, a series of essays authored by Alexander Hamilton, James Madison, and John Jay, were written in a frenzied effort to persuade nine of the thirteen original states to ratify the draft Constitution, with the outcome very much in doubt.[3]

The final Constitution combined Madison's vision of a decentralized, federalist republic that would prevent the concentration of power with Hamilton's vision of a unified, central authority strong enough to keep enemies of the fragile new country at bay. In a victory for Hamilton, the national government was given the all-important power to raise taxes and promote the general welfare, giving it the means to fund its own expansion. In a victory for Madison, the power of the national government was divided among three branches. The federal government's powers were enumerated, with all other authority reserved for the states.

*The Federalist Papers* are considered the ultimate legislative history of the Constitution. Although Hamilton wrote the bulk of the essays and Jay went on to become a prominent justice of the Supreme Court, traditional conservatives focus on the writings of Madison, the only one of the three essayists to become president of the United States. Papers 10 and 45 are the most influential, explaining that Madison's fear of a tyrannical majority animated his vision of limited government:

> Among the numerous advantages promised by a well-constructed Union, none deserves to be more accurately developed than its tendency to break and control the violence of faction. The friend of popular governments never finds himself so much alarmed for their character and fate as when he contemplates their propensity to this dangerous vice. . . . By a faction [I mean] a number of citizens, whether amounting to a majority or a minority of the whole, who are united and actuated by some common impulse of passion, or of interest, adverse to the rights of other citizens or to the . . . interests of the community.[4]

Madison noted ruefully that "faction," that most destructive of political phenomena, was dependent on "liberty" as "air is to fire."[5] Recognizing that liberty was also indispensable to the new country, he searched for other ways to dissipate the influence of misguided majority rule, in the end settling on the idea of strong yet localized government. If faction did ignite at the local level, he reasoned, it would burn out more quickly and cause far less damage. Both results were acceptable to him.[6]

Madison acknowledged that government per se could advance the public good, but only if the weight of its authority resided with the states:

> The powers delegated by the proposed Constitution to the federal government are few and defined. Those which are to remain in the State governments are numerous and indefinite. The former will be exercised principally on external objects, as war, peace, negotiation, and foreign commerce. . . . The powers reserved to the several States will extend to all the objects which, in the ordinary sense of affairs, concern the lives, liberties, and properties of the people.[7]

There is much to be said for these insights, and viewed as one crucial element of balanced federalism, they have certainly stood the test of time. Localized authority over crime, education, zoning, family affairs, health care, and a slew of other concerns makes sense, even if politicians across the political spectrum, including many who claim the mantle of traditional conservatism, have insisted on a federal role to win short-term political advantage.

For traditional conservatives, however, the problem is not just one of usurping state authority. An equally urgent and compelling threat is the uncontrolled growth of the federal government, which threatens liberty at every turn. Traditional conservatives' commitment to a small and weak national government, limited in authority to the conduct of foreign relations, remains as fervent as it was in those far less complicated colonial times.

To judge from the country's actual history, this view of the Constitution is hopelessly quixotic as a practical matter. The federal government has grown to mammoth proportions, and there is no hope of stuffing this particular genie back in its bottle to the extent envisioned by traditional conservative ideology. Remarkably, traditional conservatives remain undaunted. Consider this manifesto from the Cato Institute, among the most prominent right-wing think tanks on the national scene:

> We can either amend the Constitution so that it authorizes all the government we now have. Or we can carefully roll back those programs and policies that Mr. Madison's Constitution, as amended, does not authorize. Those of us who cherish the right to be free, the right to plan and live our own lives, will prefer the latter course, to be sure.[8]

This strict construction of "Mr. Madison's Constitution" is the central animating theory of traditional conservatism in America today. Adherents believe that the creative tensions between federal and state government and between government and the governed are but a minor characteristic of the document. They categorically reject the argument that the Constitution's compromises bestow the flexibility to adapt the size and mission of the federal government to meet the challenges of a post-industrial, post-nuclear, and post–World Wide Web world. They urge that judicial candidates, especially appointees to the Supreme Court, swear allegiance to the principle of strict construction.

Few people outside the legal profession, political science disciplines, or the intelligentsia have any idea what *The Federalist Papers* say. This ignorance does not matter much on a day-to-day basis because the gist of the Constitution has been thoroughly absorbed into American culture. From a larger perspective, however, overlooking the details and nuances of the Framers' ambivalence, as well as the compromises they crafted, leaves largely unrebutted the conservative doctrine that the Constitution is a kind of holy writ. That assertion, reiterated again and again in debates over domestic issues, is used to justify deregulation of industrial activities in terms that are more palatable to the average citizen than an admission that business interests must be served by the politicians who owe their election to corporate financial support. With this historical background in mind, we are ready to fast-forward to the twentieth century, when Madison's vision was modernized and made relevant to the post-industrial world.

## Modernizing Conservatism

Perhaps the best-known proponent of modern conservative ideology is Milton Friedman, winner of the 1976 Nobel Prize for economics, who wrote the classic *Capitalism and Freedom.*[9] The book has been reprinted with an updated preface three times since it first appeared in 1962, most recently in 2002. Friedman saw what Madison could not have imagined: the staggering implications of industrialization, two world wars, the invention and use of nuclear weapons, the rise and fall of communism, globalization of the world economy, and the advent of the World Wide Web. Rather than couch his arguments in terms of faction, Friedman advanced capitalism and the free market as the guarantors of personal freedom and happiness. He spoke in language more nuanced than Madison's but with respect to the proper role of government ended up in fundamentally the same place:

> How can we keep the government we create from becoming a Frankenstein that will destroy the very freedom we establish it to protect? Freedom is a rare and delicate plant. Our minds tell us, and history confirms, that the great threat to freedom is the concentration of power. Government is necessary to preserve our freedom . . . yet by concentrating power in political hands, it is also a threat to freedom. . . . [T]he scope of government must be limited. Its major function must be to protect our freedom both from the enemies outside our gates and from our fellow citizens: to preserve law and order, to enforce private contracts, to foster competitive markets. . . . [G]overnment power must be dispersed. . . . If I do not like what my local community does, be it in sewage dis-

posal, or zoning, or schools, I can move to another local community. . . .
If I do not like what Washington imposes, I have few alternatives in this
world of jealous nations.[10]

Friedman was in no way kidding. He opposed "detailed regulation of
industries," social welfare programs, government controls on manufacturing output, price supports or other government subsidies for agriculture, tariffs, occupational licensing, public housing, national parks,
and the draft, except in wartime, contending that "the appropriate free
market arrangement is volunteer military forces [that hire] men to
serve."[11] Friedman would have abolished all forms of corporate taxation.
Instead, he would have required that companies attribute to individual
shareholders any earnings that are not paid out in dividends and that
shareholders report "attributed but undistributed" earnings on their tax
returns.[12] He blamed the Great Depression on government mismanagement and deeply regretted the growth of the public sector triggered by
those mistakes.[13] In fact, it is not an exaggeration to say that Friedman
believed the country began a long slide downhill with the New Deal,
landed with a jolt in the middle of the Great Society, missed an opportunity to resurrect itself under Ronald Reagan, and has hung in the balance
ever since.[14]

Friedman's enthusiasm for the free market as the best alternative to
government knew few bounds. "Underlying most arguments against the
free market is a lack of belief in freedom itself," he declared.[15] Only by
preserving the autonomy of the individual—and organized groups of
individuals—to buy and sell goods and services through a plethora of
means and arrangements, he argued, can we forestall the concentration
of power that produces dictatorships, oligopolies, communist states, and
even genocide. Friedman not only recognized but extolled the government's role in providing "a stable monetary framework for a free economy" and a legal system that enables the free market to grow.[16] He supported publicly financed dams and expressways, the public schools (at
least kindergarten through high school), and the Sherman antitrust laws,
and he conceded that "public health measures have contributed to the
reduction of infectious disease."[17] He recognized that government has a
role to play in addressing the problems of "neighborhood effects," specifically in the context of pollution:

> The man who pollutes the stream is in effect forcing others to exchange
> good water for bad. These others might be willing to make the exchange

at a price. But it is not feasible for them, acting individually, to void the exchange or to enforce appropriate compensation.[18]

As we shall see in Chapter 4, "Corporations and the Commons," a different articulation of the same theory—Garrett Hardin's famous 1968 essay on the "tragedy of the commons"—is the bedrock of modern environmental law.[19]

Further confirmation of Friedman's "neighborhood effects" theory is found in the work of an earlier scholar, F. A. Hayek, whose book *The Road to Serfdom* was of great importance to the development of Friedman's ideas.[20] Hayek, writing in the aftermath of World War II, was as fearful of communism as Madison was of anarchism. He condemned "central planning"—that is, government—in almost any form, with very few exceptions. Nevertheless, he wrote:

> To prohibit the use of certain poisonous substances or to require special precautions in their use, to limit working hours or to require sanitary arrangements, is fully compatible with the preservation of competition. The only question here is whether in the particular instance the advantages gained are greater than the social costs which they impose.[21]

So, where are we left then, other than stunned by these world-renowned economists' extraordinary independence of thought? In essence, Friedman and Hayek, like Madison before them, feared big government as the greatest evil. In their worldview, everything has a price and can be traded so long as the government does not intervene. Bad doctors will be rooted out of practice by an irate public; farmers will succeed or fail regardless of the vagaries of nature; and the national government will collect what little money it needs to provide a legal and monetary framework for the free market through an individual tax.

And yet Friedman and Hayek understood that some problems—at the very least, epidemics and downstream pollution—demand public intervention because the free market cannot prevent or control them. Within this framework, it is obvious that today's children, much less future generations, do not participate in the free market. Children are only crudely represented by their parents and not at all by the vast remainder of the population. When natural resources are finite and people cannot buy their way out of difficulty, the free market is not the solution to these problems. Unfortunately, these concessions, as well as their crucial implications, were long ago lost in the shuffle because a broader coalition of right-wing special-interest groups intent on taking back the government from their left-wing counterparts was already on the march.

## Reagan

### Limited Government and Runaway Deficits

Few would disagree that Ronald Reagan's presidential career was a success, however much one might oppose the substance of what happened when he was president. Beloved by many Americans, elected by a landslide to his second term, and forgiven no matter what his transgressions, Reagan left an ideological legacy that resounds throughout American public policy to this day. For our purposes, the most important element of that legacy is that Reagan changed the reputation of government from benign social force to incompetent and bloated bureaucracy, all without substantially altering the federal budget's actual size.

Reagan came to office sounding like a traditional conservative, pledging to restore limited government and the people's liberty. As shown in Figure 2.1, he left office having cut taxes without significantly changing federal spending, leaving what was at the time an unprecedented budget deficit in his wake. To be sure, specific parts of government—social welfare spending and regulatory implementation and enforcement—were curtailed sharply. Yet Reagan did not demand any real changes in government entitlement and other popular programs, much less those that subsidize business, thereby dodging any measurable negative reaction from the Republican Party's traditional constituencies. Overall, the Reagan "revolution" was far more important for its ideological legacy than for its practical accomplishments in changing the direction of the country.

These contradictions remain an object of teeth-grinding frustration for traditional conservatives. Edward Crane, president of the Cato Institute, wrote in 2005:

> Three big mistakes have cut short any sustained downsizing of the federal government in recent years. The first mistake was Ronald Reagan's 1984 campaign. Reagan was enormously popular. . . . He had a great opportunity to seriously cut government, but his handlers decided to run a "Morning in America" campaign with lots of shots of pretty beaches, forests, and people having fun, but with no substance. He carried 49 states but had no mandate for further reforms. It would have been better

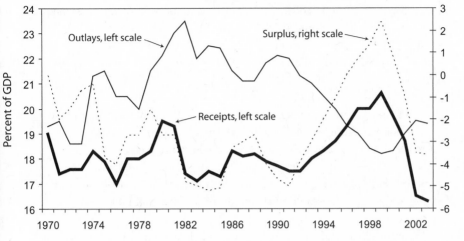

**Figure 2.1.** Budget Outlays, Surpluses, and Receipts as a Percentage of Gross Domestic Product. Source: Office of Management and Budget.

if he had carried 40 states and had a mandate for cutting the government. . . . [M]any in the Republican Party have focused exclusively on tax cuts and growing the economy without dealing with the tougher job of limiting government to its proper size.[22]

So if Reagan did not really cut the budget, how did he accomplish such success in demeaning government's reputation?

### Bully Pulpit

Reagan's threshold and brilliantly executed strategy was to use the bully pulpit to define government bureaucrats as an isolated and distrusted elite. In 1977, as governor of California, he declared that big government was a threat to what Americans hold most dear:

We fear the government may be powerful enough to destroy our families; we know that it is not powerful enough to replace them.[23]

He told the people that they already agreed with him in their hearts:

And today more than two-thirds of our citizens are telling us, and each other, that social engineering by the federal government has failed. The Great Society is great only in power, in size and in cost. And so are the problems it set out to solve. Freedom has been diminished and we stand on the brink of economic ruin.[24]

He pictured himself as a noble gladiator doing battle with this evil force:

> I had never in my life thought of seeking or holding public office and I'm still not quite sure how it all happened. In my own mind, I was a citizen representing my fellow citizens *against* the institution of government.[25]

And in 1980, as he accepted the Republican nomination for president, he engaged in a frontal assault on the credibility of bureaucracy itself:

> We must put an end to the arrogance of a federal establishment which accepts no blame for our condition, cannot be relied upon to give us a fair estimate of our situation and utterly refuses to live within its means. I will not accept the supposed "wisdom" which has it that the federal bureaucracy has become so powerful that it can no longer be changed or controlled by any administration. As President I would use every power at my command to make the federal establishment respond to the will and the collective wishes of the people.[26]

## Deregulation and the Advent of Cost-Benefit Analysis

Reagan's second strategy was to smother government activism at its inception. As explained by Susan Tolchin and Martin Tolchin in their comprehensive history of this aspect of the Reagan revolution, *Dismantling America: The Rush to Deregulate*, the president issued Executive Order 12291, which required agencies to submit their proposals to accountants and economists at the Office of Management and Budget (OMB) for approval.[27] The order further mandated that all regulations, from environmental protection to drug safety, be justified by cost-benefit analyses. Reagan seated his vice president, George H. W. Bush, as the chair of a task force designed to implement the order. He slashed the operating budgets of those agencies, making it more difficult for them to comply with his new procedural and analytical requirements. And he appointed deregulatory "true believers" to head the agencies he expected to cause the worst trouble.

The relatively new EPA and parts of the Department of Interior (DOI) that were responsible for protecting national forests and wild lands were the poster children for this campaign. Reagan appointed as heads of the two institutions Ann Gorsuch Burford and James G. Watt, respectively, both of whom had impeccable credentials as leading conservatives with intense hostility for government intervention in the private use of property and natural resources. For the most part, Reagan himself remained mild about these issues, speaking optimistically about the "beauty of our land" as "our legacy to our children."[28] But these benign statements were meaningless as a practical matter.

## Progressive Backlash

The Reagan era dealt a body blow to the morale and credibility of the federal workforce and was especially devastating to EPA. Ironically, the momentum and tenacity of Reagan's deregulatory campaign gained additional strength from the efforts of its progressive opponents to rescue the agencies. While doing their best to administer effective antidotes to Reagan initiatives, environmentalists on and off Capitol Hill inadvertently made matters worse.

Between the early 1980s, shortly after Reagan came to power and began his deregulatory campaign in earnest, and the end of 1990, during the presidential administration of former deregulatory task force chair George H. W. Bush, Congress passed a series of extraordinarily detailed and ambitious environmental statutes. Taking Reagan at his word that he meant to dismantle EPA's regulatory mission, legislators such as Senators Edmund Muskie (D-ME) and Robert Stafford (R-VT) and Representatives Henry Waxman (D-CA) and James Florio (D-NJ) were determined to hem in executive-branch discretion by making it illegal to roll back environmental protection administratively. They filled the second generation of environmental statutes with detailed, stringent, and nondiscretionary mandates, setting the Agency's agenda—at least on paper—for years to come.

Specific deadlines down to the day, month, and year were established for the promulgation of regulations with noncompliance enforceable by private attorneys' general citizen suits. Congress told EPA which chemicals to regulate and which regulatory approaches to use in controlling them. It imposed stringent liability on those who owned, operated, or sent hazardous substances to thousands of dump sites. And it commanded factories to disclose the quantities of toxic chemicals they were discharging into surface waters, sending to landfills, and emitting into the air on an annual basis.

The environmental legislators' intentions were clear: they sought to micromanage EPA to the point that it would have no choice but to regulate swiftly and aggressively, regardless of changes in its political leadership. But the statutes went too far in many cases, forcing the Agency to expend a large share of its increasingly scarce resources on specific chemicals that were the subject of newspaper exposés but that objectively posed less risk than other types and forms of pollution. Hundreds of statutory deadlines were imposed, but EPA met only a fraction of them. As Professor Richard Andrews has described it, "This failure triggered a self-reinforcing cycle of distrust."[29]

But the real tragedy of this difficult period was that the distrust came at EPA from all directions: it was at the root of the progressives' suspicion of EPA, and it fed the disdain of conservatives. Reagan and followers attacked the civil service for being too active, and environmentalists attacked it for being too passive. From the perspective of those who were not immersed in these daily skirmishes, however, EPA and other agencies just appeared incompetent.

By the end of Reagan's second term, environmental regulation was gridlocked. The implications of this situation for EPA's development are the subject of the next chapter. For the purposes of understanding the rise of conservatism, however, the most important point is that progressives in effect joined the Republican attack on the EPA bureaucracy, even if they approached their critique from the opposite end of the political spectrum and used micromanagement by statute rather than hostile rhetoric to achieve their goals. By failing to refute the claims that were the foundation of Reagan's crusade against the bureaucracy, progressives inadvertently made the crusade that much more effective.[30] In the end, this clash of forces launched a political boomerang for regulated industries that still persists. In a classic illustration of the old adage "Be careful what you wish for," Reagan's highly effective efforts to cripple government produced the ultimate nightmare for regulated industries: onerous laws and an irritable, erratic bureaucracy.

## Bush I

Although President George H. W. Bush was Reagan's anointed successor and Reagan remained a conservative icon, the Bush I administration began disillusioning right-wing ideologues almost as soon as the president took office. His most grievous offense, the decision to raise taxes, was interpreted as the abandonment of the dogmatic struggle against big government. He also strayed from the conservative script in the regulatory arena, announcing that he intended to be "the environmental president" and delivering on that pledge by supporting the 1990 Clean Air Act amendments. The 1990 amendments represented a dazzling finale to an extraordinary period of bipartisan legislative activism, even though its implementation was undermined by budget shortfalls.

Bush I pursued a moderate approach to the administration of EPA. As his first EPA administrator he appointed William Reilly, the chief executive officer of a relatively conservative environmental group, and as his second, Lee Thomas, a professional civil servant. Both men adopted a centrist approach to most difficult policy questions. EPA as an institution was not released from its statutory and funding constraints, but from an internal management perspective, the Agency definitely got a breather from the hostile takeover it had experienced in the Reagan years.

## Clinton

By the end of Bush I and the beginning of President Clinton's two terms, it had become obvious that EPA could not administer the elaborate statutes provoked by the Reagan era. Funding fell far short of what was needed to implement those mandates. EPA was awash in litigation challenging its tentative efforts to implement them. And on Capitol Hill, political warfare prevailed, especially after 1994 when Republicans achieved control of the House of Representatives.

The "Republican Revolution" led by Speaker Newt Gingrich was fueled by an extraordinarily powerful, skillfully selected coalition of traditional conservatives and business special interests. The Contract with America met the goals of both groups, and for awhile it looked as if the government would be revamped in ways that seemed inconceivable under Bush I.[31] In the final analysis, the movement did not accomplish much on Capitol Hill, failing after repeated efforts to pass a comprehensive regulatory reform bill and a comprehensive rewrite of the Clean Water Act, among other items.

In reaction to these disconcerting reversals, conservatives retained their substantive proposals but changed both their strategy and their tactics. Rather than attempting to push business-friendly legislative proposals past the media, through the Senate, and across the president's desk, conservatives and their allies in regulated industry worked to defund the programs the statutes created. Instead of excoriating environmental regulations in public, they learned the subtleties of indirection, retooling their rhetoric to attack EPA on the basis that its rulemaking proposals were not supported by sufficient data or would have unacceptable economic consequences. Conservatives argued that America had achieved great progress in environmental quality, and they advocated celebrating these victories rather than becoming preoccupied with the last small increment of such problems. Over time, these new arguments, couched as they were in careful and affirmative language, permeated the media.

Republican strategist Frank Luntz, best known for inventing the Contract with America, has polished the tactics of indirection to perfection. In a memorandum to Republican candidates, he advises:

> Provide specific examples of federal bureaucrats failing to meet their responsibilities. . . . Do not attack the principles behind existing legislation. . . . Describe the limited role for Washington. . . . Emphasize common sense. In making regulatory decisions, we should use best estimates and realistic assumptions, not the worst-case scenarios advanced by environmental extremists.[32]

As a veteran political adviser, Frank Luntz is an adept, highly competent participant in the latest iteration of political communication theory: the interest group that is best at framing the issues wins, regardless of the merits of its positions and the public's reaction if people better understood those arguments. Luntz recognizes the popularity of the idea that every child should have an equal opportunity to share in the American dream. He understands that most Americans would react with hostility to the elitist notion that a clean environment is a privilege to be enjoyed only by people who can pay for it. Consequently, Luntz counsels his clients to pursue deregulatory policy objectives with as much enthusiasm as they can muster but to explain what they are doing as a more effective way to protect public health and the environment.

Largely because he was forced to contend with divided government, the two terms served by President Bill Clinton had little impact on these destructive trends. The Clinton administration adopted the same moderate management practices as Bush I, appointing as EPA Administrator Carol Browner, a former Florida regulator and grassroots environmental organizer. Browner took less interest in internal management and more interest in EPA's public image. She became enmeshed in constant guerrilla warfare with EPA's congressional critics and their industry allies. Thrown off balance, she spent far more time defending the Agency than either designing or pursuing an affirmative agenda.

## Bush II

Elected after an exhausting fight that was a leading catalyst for America's ongoing political polarization, President George W. Bush began his presidency in flush economic circumstances, with a small surplus and a strengthening economy. Rather than proceed with caution, however, the president and his advisors were determined to pursue two distinct, albeit overlapping, domestic agenda items: solidifying bonds with all three elements of the Republican Party's ideological base and simultaneously repaying supporters in the business community.

The tragedies that began on September 11, 2001, gave Bush II an unexpected infusion of political capital, not least because these events and the nation's lengthy response distracted attention from a whole slew of domestic problems, from race and labor relations, to a deteriorating social safety net, to the hollowing out of regulatory programs. The escalating cost of the war in Iraq soon undermined the progress Clinton had made, and the federal budget headed rapidly back into the red. Focused primarily on success abroad, Bush II abandoned any serious effort to initiate meaningful budget cuts and responded only mildly to bipartisan congressional earmarking of billions of dollars for local pork-barrel projects. The administration's single-minded pursuit of tax cuts completed the deficit-building pattern. By the fifth year of his presidency, traditional conservatives expressed disappointment with this performance as intense as the views of the most avid liberal, decrying government's growth and intrusiveness, escalating deficits, and overweening foreign policy.[33] *The Economist*, the unofficial journal of that movement, sarcastically labeled the administration's approach "big government conservatism," an apt if oxymoronic description.[34]

The president and his top officials insist that their approach to governing will dominate for the foreseeable future. But these extravagant claims are undermined by volatile polling results. Although the American public remains divided on most important domestic issues, it is united in dissatisfaction with the status quo. Unfortunately for America's children, this commitment to change has yet to emerge as an effective political force. Instead, the subterranean agenda set up during the 104th Congress is proceeding full speed ahead, a product of the political dissonance regarding these issues that remain unresolved.

## Conclusion

When our children's children look back on this era, they will be hard-pressed to identify any coherent principles in either political party's attitudes toward government, especially with respect to how much government does—or does not do—for the people. The constriction of government's role with respect to public health, safety, and environmental protection began long before President George W. Bush took office. Indeed, it is not hyperbolic to suggest that over the last two decades, the role of government has eroded to the point that agencies are "hollow" in functional terms. In theory, this erosion should please conservative ideologues because it means that government is limited as a practical matter. The flaw in this logic is that the legal infrastructure that created the bureaucracy, as well as large numbers of harassed and demoralized bureaucrats, remain in place. From the perspective of traditional conservatives, it is as if a hole has been punched in the ship of state, but there is sufficient crew to keep bailing so the vessel never quite goes down.

How did we get to the point that government is sharply curtailed in some areas but operates with grandiose intrusiveness and largesse in others? After three decades of developing these ideas and building institutions that promote them in all aspects of political life, advocates of limited government can claim spectacular successes in getting government off the back of business. Yet they have accomplished little in terms of dismantling the elaborate legal infrastructure erected by their ideological and political opposition and designed to impose pollution controls on large segments of the manufacturing sector. This battle—between those who want EPA to take a backseat and those insistent that it should drive forward—is the subject of the next chapter.

## CHAPTER 3

# Battered-Agency Syndrome

*Man's ability to alter his environment has developed far more rapidly than his ability to foresee with certainty the effects of his alterations. It is only recently that we have begun to appreciate the danger posed by unregulated modification of the world around us, and have created watchdog agencies whose task it is to warn us, and protect us. . . . [U]nequipped with crystal balls and unable to read the future, [the agencies] are nonetheless charged with evaluating the effects of unprecedented environmental modifications, often made on a massive scale. Necessarily, they must deal with predictions and uncertainty, with developing evidence, with conflicting evidence, and, sometimes, with little or no evidence at all.*

JUDGE SKELLY WRIGHT, 1976

*The Environmental Protection Agency is now staggering under the assault of its enemies—while still gravely wounded from the gifts of its "friends." . . . [T]he image of the agency as an overweening bureaucracy is miscast. In fact, if anything, it is an* underweening *bureaucracy. Any senior EPA official will tell you that the agency has the resources to do not more than 10 percent of the things Congress has charged it to do.*

FORMER EPA ADMINISTRATOR WILLIAM RUCKELSHAUS, 1995

*The EPA, the Gestapo of government, pure and simply has been one of the major clawholds that the government has maintained on the backs of our constituents.*

FORMER U.S. REP. TOM DELAY (R-TX), 1995

## Overview

In 1973, a mere three years after it was founded, EPA took the extraordinarily courageous step of setting limits on the amount of lead allowed as an additive in gasoline. Lead served as an "anti-knocking" agent to prevent engine damage. But disturbing scientific evidence regarding the health implications of lead exposure, especially for children, was beginning to emerge. The initiative was courageous not only because EPA was so new, but because it inspired a tsunami of negative reaction from the oil and automobile industries, among the most powerful special-interest constituencies doing business with the Agency. The young Agency was fortunate enough to gain affirmation from the influential Federal Court of Appeals for the District of Columbia Circuit, in the opinion by Judge Skelly Wright quoted at the outset of this chapter, and overcame this strong resistance. To this day, getting the lead out of gasoline is widely considered to be among EPA's most momentous achievements. Blood lead levels among children declined precipitously, especially for those living in urban areas, and an entire generation of children was saved from the largely symptomless but nonetheless devastating neurological effects of such exposure.

Subsequent scientific research has completely vindicated EPA's decision. At the time the Agency acted, public health experts thought that blood lead levels above *forty* micrograms per deciliter were potentially dangerous. Today, levels at or above *ten* micrograms per deciliter are considered dangerous, especially for children under the age of six, including babies in utero. According to the U.S. Centers for Disease Control and Prevention (CDC), lead poisoning can cause children to have lower gestational ages, reduced weight at birth, smaller stature, decreased intelligence, and hearing problems.[1]

EPA's experience with the science of lead poisoning has been repeated over and over again in the three decades since the opinion. Toxic substances targeted as posing a potential threat at routine exposure levels turn out to cause harm at levels far lower than first suspected. In fact, it is difficult to think of more than a small handful of situations in which EPA revised its estimates of acceptable exposure *upward* from its initial concerns.

Despite unanimous agreement among EPA's broad spectrum of constituencies that its lead-in-gasoline decision was brilliant, it is difficult to imagine today's EPA taking anything remotely similar to such bold and prescient action. A different institution stands before us, one that would almost certainly dive for cover when presented with the same evidence it had available in 1973. How did this bold toddler of an agency evolve into such an insecure and timid young adult? (EPA is only thirty-seven years old as I write these lines, a relatively youthful age for a federal government agency of its size and importance.) Like many analogous biographies in the social science and fictional literature, unrealistic expectations, demanding parents, economic hardship, and a series of crippling disabilities provide the keys.

The central reasons two-time EPA Administrator William Ruckelshaus was right to lament EPA's plight in the article quoted at the outset of the chapter are considered below. The chapter begins with a brief review of EPA's gestation and birth, setting the stage for the high expectations that have caused such difficulties in its later life. It then considers the yawning gap between funding and mandates that stymie EPA's efforts to control its destiny as an institution. The chapter examines management problems that have further undercut the Agency's performance, including the overwhelming influence of regulated industries on its day-to-day activities and its counterintuitive and overly rigid statutory organization. It then analyzes two closely related, cross-cutting "reforms"—risk assessment and cost-benefit analysis—that have imposed such a heavy burden of proof on the Agency before it acts to protect public health that it often cannot manage to eke out the pollution controls that are mandated by the law. The chapter closes with a review of EPA's relationship with the courts and the states, outside institutions that have played a central role in the Agency's development.

## Bright Beginnings

EPA was created during a period when the balance of power in the nation was definitely tilted toward the left. The 1962 publication of Rachel Carson's *Silent Spring* triggered the birth of modern environmentalism, adding concerns about the effect of toxic chemicals on public health to the agenda of conserving nature that was formed during the presidency of Teddy Roosevelt.[2]

Republican President Richard Nixon established EPA by sending Congress a plan for the "reorganization" of the government that combined all the disparate programs dealing with environmental and public protection into one centralized institution.[3] No innate environmentalist, Nixon took this momentous step in response to his well-founded fear that the

Democratic Party would get far out ahead of Republicans on environmental issues if he did not act. Professor Richard Andrews argues that the lack of statutory authority for the creation of EPA set the nascent bureaucracy up for failure because Nixon essentially moved existing programs together on paper and announced his decision by press release, rather than taking the time to win congressional approval of the new enterprise.[4] If the president and Congress had spent more time thinking through the new agency's goals, structure, substantive mandates, and legal authorities, EPA would have been more effective earlier in its tenure and might be sturdier today. But EPA's severe problems have evolved far beyond its lack of better parentage.

The most telling aspect of the Agency's early years is that its creators appeared oblivious to the controversy its evolving mission was likely to cause. President Nixon was grandstanding, a noble political tradition, but in this case he undertook the exercise without much comprehension of the economic and social implications of controlling industrial pollution for the first time in a systematic way at the national level. This naïveté was a double-edged sword, of course. If Nixon had realized the implications, he might well never have acted, and the momentum achieved by the first Earth Day in 1970 would have been lost in the wreckage of Watergate. The powerful industries that became EPA's first targets were caught flat-footed by the political hoopla of this launch and supported President Nixon's proposal. Within a few years, however, corporate executives, especially in the oil and chemical industries, realized that, from their perspective, a bureaucratic Frankenstein had been born. EPA soon lost the advantage of catching its regulatory targets by surprise.[5]

## Raising Cain

As EPA matured, Congress quickly adopted the Agency as its own, constructing an intricate statutory framework for EPA's operation. Every major trade association in the manufacturing sector developed staff and internal procedures for coping with the new bureaucracy, and several national environmental groups were formed to counter industry influence. Perceiving that environmental issues attracted the media's attention and were at the forefront of the agendas of powerful special-interest groups, multiple committees in Congress, especially in the House of Representatives, tried to grab a piece of the EPA action. Rather than concentrate its legislative and oversight authority in a single committee, as it does in other highly technical areas such as national defense and security, Congress spread jurisdiction over a dozen committees and subcommittees, each of which had its own views of the Agency's mission.

Throughout the 1970s and 1980s, despite the many cooks trying to squeeze into an overheated kitchen, environmental legislation and oversight were largely bipartisan affairs. Moderate and liberal Democrats and Republicans supported aggressive regulation, while conservative Democrats and Republicans opposed it. Battles remained hard-fought and exhausting, but took place across regional and ideological, as opposed to political party, lines. As explained in Chapter 2, "The Rise of Special-Interest Conservatism," much of this balance was upset when Ronald Reagan was elected president. Not only did Reagan demean the value of government at every turn, he appointed polarizing figures like Ann Gorsuch Burford and James Watt to run EPA and the Department of Interior. Reagan was ultimately forced to accept the resignations of both officials because they had become lightning rods for one of the worst public relations fiascos of his presidency—the perception that most Republicans were affirmatively opposed to environmental protection.

In the aftermath of those strident battles, the Reagan administration was determined to take EPA controversies off the front page, sending EPA's first administrator, William Ruckelshaus, back to the Agency on a rescue mission. Ruckelshaus, who had initially served on the special committee appointed by President Nixon to design EPA by executive order, was dismayed to find demoralized staff, confused and gerrymandered organizational structure, copious statutory mandates, and grossly inadequate funding. With bitter humor, Ruckelshaus diagnosed the problem as "battered-agency syndrome" and predicted that the pendulum of politics that had rocked the Agency would ultimately prove destructive for all of its constituencies.[6] As Professor Andrews describes it, the "politics of pendulum" meant that EPA did not get enough resources to cope with its dense thicket of statutory mandates.[7] Paradoxically, it also meant that supporters of the Agency's mission never wavered in their high expectations of what it could do.

Although it has existed for much of its life under siege, EPA's great achievements are incontrovertible. Despite rapid growth in population and industrial activities, air emissions of the most common pollutants have been cut in half. The nation's rivers, lakes, and streams are significantly cleaner than they were two decades ago, and some water bodies (for example, Lake Erie) have literally been rescued from the dead. EPA has removed thousands of leaking barrels of toxic waste from hundreds of abandoned dump sites and finished cleanup at about one-fifth of the nation's priority sites. These achievements were facilitated by remarkable technological progress.

Yet resting on its laurels is not an option for the Agency. New technological discoveries enable us to detect and evaluate pollution caused by an expanded universe of toxic chemicals at significantly lower levels than before. The incidence of environmentally related diseases like asthma is on the rise. Accompanying those developments is our growing realization that we are affected not just by the national environment, but by global pollution cycles. Confronted with these new challenges, EPA has spent much of the past fifteen years running in place, maintaining its earlier achievements without making much more progress, as the effectiveness of the conservative deregulation campaign gained traction and the Agency's congressional friends lost their legislative power. Institutional growth also has been arrested, with the Agency's budget shrinking in comparison to the nondiscretionary mandates it must implement and efforts to reform those laws thwarted by congressional gridlock.

## Chronic Underfunding

The cost of implementing EPA's statutory mandates exceeds its appropriations by billions of dollars. This problem is the single most important explanation of why EPA has faltered so badly. It means that the Agency is always a day late and a dollar short in fulfilling all of the extensive, nondiscretionary mandates it has been assigned by Congress. It also means that outside parties, especially those that can afford litigation, have control over the priorities EPA sets among these duties because they are able to sue the Agency and obtain court-ordered schedules for completion of whatever mandates are at stake in the case.

Because EPA is subject to the jurisdiction of numerous congressional committees, it cannot easily consult with Congress on how to prioritize its statutory mandates in any coherent fashion. Budget shortfalls leave very little money available to address emerging problems not yet considered by Congress. As its authorizing statutes age—the last major set of amendments was passed in 1996, revamping the Food Quality Protection Act[8]—and legislative gridlock deepens, this aspect of EPA's budget woes becomes increasingly important.

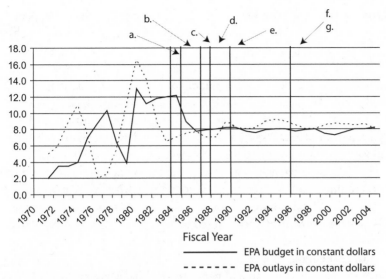

a. Hazardous and Solid Waste Amendments of 1984
b. Safe Drinking Water Act Amendments of 1985
c. Water Quality Act of 1987
d. Federal Insecticide, Fungicide, and Rodenticide Act Amendments of 1988
e. Clean Air Act Amendments of 1990
f. Safe Drinking Water Act Amendments of 1996
g. Food Quality Protection Act of 1996

**Figure 3.1.** EPA Budget in Constant Dollars, 1970–2005. Figure by Matthew Shudtz.

## The Budget in Constant Dollars

Figure 3.1 shows two aspects of the EPA budget: appropriations (money awarded by Congress) and outlays (money actually spent). The two are different because the Agency does not always spend funds in the same year that they are appropriated. These figures are presented *in constant dollars* for the years 1970 to 2005 to compensate for the effects of inflation.[9] As the graph illustrates, the budget in constant dollars has been pretty much flat since the mid-1980s despite the passage of multiple amendments to the major environmental laws that have dramatically increased the scope and difficulty of the Agency's workload.

## The Budget in Relation to the Mandates

EPA implements nine environmental statutes, with some dating back to the period immediately after World War II.[10] By 1980, the year the Reagan administration took office and EPA's budget peaked, the federal government played a major role in regulating air and water pollution, evaluating pesticide hazards, and supervising drinking water systems. But even those ambitious efforts pale in comparison to the dramatic expansion of the federal role that began in the middle of that decade, during Reagan's second term. As discussed in Chapter 2, "The Rise of Special Interest Conservatism," a backlash against the administration's hostility to EPA fueled a period of remarkable legislative activism. Congress overhauled the most important statutes once and in some cases twice.[11] The unifying theme of all these changes was to expand EPA's mission exponentially and to circumscribe its discretion, directing its activities at an unprecedented level of detail. By 1989 more than 800 specific deadlines were on the books, 86 percent of them aimed at EPA, as opposed to regulated industries. By 1991 the Agency had succeeded in meeting only 14 percent of this overwhelming total.

For example, the 1987 amendments to the Clean Water Act (CWA) enlarged the scope of EPA's authority over "direct dischargers" (facilities that discharge wastewater—or "effluent"—directly into rivers and streams).[12] Congress instructed EPA to establish standards for a lengthy list of contaminants according to a rigorous schedule. It told the Agency to develop a program for controlling municipal stormwater discharges and to issue regulations specifying management practices for sewage sludge. The statute further required EPA to launch ambitious new research on the harmful effects of water pollutants, especially as they might affect aquatic ecosystems.

The 1990 Clean Air Act (CAA) amendments for the first time required EPA to establish a system for establishing, tracking, and trading allowances to emit sulfur dioxide, the cause of acid rain.[13] Recognizing that EPA had become paralyzed in its struggle to control toxic air pollutants, the amendments established an actual list of 188 substances that had to be considered for regulation and put EPA on a rigorous schedule for establishing priorities among them and for regulating the manufacturing plants that emit them. Congress required that EPA revamp the system used to write permits under the act. It also made a series of changes in EPA's implementation of the act's core pollution control programs concerning attainment of National Ambient Air Quality Standards (NAAQS) and the regulation of mobile sources, further complicating the Agency's already delicate relationships with state and local governments. Lastly, the 1990 amendments required EPA to establish new programs covering such problems as deposition of toxics in the Great Lakes and coastal waters and the need for more effective emergency planning at facilities using hazardous chemicals.

Amendments to the Resource Conservation and Recovery Act (RCRA) passed in 1984 extended EPA's regulatory authority to so-called "small quantity" generators, bringing thousands of "mom and pop" businesses within the ambit of the act's hazardous waste treatment, storage, and disposal requirements.[14] If EPA failed to meet these deadlines, the amendments specified that a statutory hammer would fall, subjecting these small companies to the same regulations that apply to much larger firms. The 1984 amendments also required EPA to revise its regulations defining the "characteristics" of hazardous waste. Congress put EPA on a strict schedule for issuing permits to commercial disposal facilities. Among other tasks, EPA was required to write regulations controlling the disposal of hazardous waste by deep-well injection (pumping waste into wells of brackish water located thousands of feet underground) and incineration, two increasingly popular disposal methods. Last but not least, EPA was required to issue a series of reports and studies analyzing the desirability of regulating a wide range of "special" wastes, including those derived from mining coal, uranium, and other metals; burning fossil fuel; operating cement kilns; and extracting oil and gas.

Safe Drinking Water Act (SDWA) legislation enacted in 1986 placed EPA on a schedule to issue regulations covering a prioritized list of eighty-five specific contaminants within three years of the date of enactment.[15] The new law commanded the Agency to develop complex new regulations concerning the filtration of surface water supplies. But in 1996, Congress changed gears in this crucial area, removing the numerical quota for regulatory output and instructing EPA to apply different standards when writing new regulations.[16]

Last but not least, Congress acted in 1988 and 1996 to address EPA's slow progress in reviewing the safety of widely used pesticides by amending the Federal Insecticide, Fungicide, and Rodenticide Act (FIFRA) to require that EPA reregister pesticides still in use and instructing the Agency to review each pesticide on a fifteen-year schedule for the duration of its market life.[17] The 1996 amendments further required EPA to reevaluate pesticide-residue tolerance standards, taking into account the sensitivities of such vulnerable groups as infants and young children.

### An Agency Overwhelmed

EPA was overwhelmed by this demanding and complex agenda. Not only was it compelled to undertake tasks that were extremely difficult from a scientific and technical perspective, it found itself confronting seemingly endless squadrons of better-paid experts hired by potentially regulated industries. As Agency staff struggled to wend their way through the advice offered by these "stakeholders" (in the lexicon, any entity or person directly affected by an Agency action or formed to advocate the interest of those directly affected), they were second-guessed by opposing stakeholders, congressional oversight committees, the courts, and the White House. EPA had few resources to conduct its own, original scientific research and became overly dependent on research sponsored by the industries it was commanded to regulate.

While all these challenges were daunting enough, staff at every level in the Agency believed that they had to pick their battles very carefully if they wished to get much of anything accomplished. Sensing the Agency's weakness, special-interest groups that had opposed the statutes when they were legislation pending before Congress soon discovered that they could live to fight another day by working to expand EPA's "burden of proof"—that is, the amount of information it would need to write the implementing regulations required by Congress. They achieved success by persuading the White House, the courts, and EPA's senior political leadership to adopt two ostensibly sensible but absolutely draining analytical methodologies: risk assessment and its fraternal twin, cost-benefit analysis. These lengthy analytical regimens became the coins of the realm, sealing the fate of an Agency that by then had evolved from "the little engine that could" to a spent locomotive dragging miles of boxcars behind it with a fuel tank one-quarter full.

## Management Problems

### Stockholm Syndrome

Throughout the history of administrative law, a major preoccupation of political scientists, management experts, and regulatory lawyers is that agencies will be "captured" by their outside constituencies, producing decisions that are responsive to those views, as opposed to the public interest.[18] As a corollary, agencies that are perceived as captured are robbed of their credibility in the eyes of the constituencies who do not enjoy a favored position. The problem is so dangerous that it can even be analogized to "Stockholm Syndrome," the vivid psychological term for victims (for example, hostages, battered wives, abused children) who perceive that their lives are dependent on their captors' goodwill. Large portions of EPA are now in the throes of this phenomenon.

Capture proceeds in several stages. Congress passes largely symbolic laws containing numerous challenging mandates, setting EPA up for failure. Congress then refuses to appropriate the funds the Agency needs to make a credible attempt to obey its commands. EPA is beleaguered by business interests trying to forestall implementation of what they see as devastatingly stringent regulations, inundating the Agency with technical materials regarding the scientific, legal, and economic implications of its proposals. As EPA does its best to wade through these objections, environmentalists sue to enforce statutory deadlines. Most of the cases are settled, with EPA and the plaintiffs agreeing on a new rulemaking schedule. Yet when the Agency attempts to implement the schedule, it is once again inundated by regulated industries. Throughout, numerous committees of Congress subject the Agency to withering and contradictory oversight. Too often, EPA's role degenerates into taking the action that is least offensive to the most people.

As discussed in Chapter 1, "Predicates," the remarkable success of regulated industries in complexifying environmental regulation, combined with the failure of the public-interest community to combat this campaign effectively, exacerbate each stage of the capture process. The environmentalists were prescient enough to build their own cadre of scientists, economists, and lawyers. But they have always been grossly outnumbered by the far larger universe of industry experts. Once the public and the press perceived that environmental policy had become a highly technical battle, their interest in getting to the bottom of any dispute waned.

Rulemaking became so attenuated that it bred opportunities for special-interest groups to intervene inappropriately, for example by asking congressional allies to pass obscure riders on lengthy appropriations bills withholding funding for a controversial program. In this way, the mandate remains on the books, sparing members of Congress the political heat that would be generated by an outright repeal but rendering implementation moribund. Most often, such midnight lawmaking escapes any public attention. On other occasions, riders are recognized as controversial but remain in the legislation until it reaches the president's desk, giving him the impossible choice between signing into law the must-pass legislation, and therefore the rider, or threatening to shut down the government over one program someone does not like. Once signing is complete, the controversy disappears in the next day's news cycle.

As a result of all these developments, the regulatory playing field has tilted decidedly toward the right over the past few years, giving regulated industries unprecedented private access to EPA decision makers. Among the more troubling examples is a series of some fifty private meetings between EPA regulatory staff and two of the country's largest pesticide manufacturers, Syngenta and AMVAC Chemical Corporation. The purpose of the meetings was to negotiate specific terms of the Agency's registration and disapproval process for two toxic pesticides: atrazine, the country's most popular herbicide, which has become controversial in recent years because of the discovery that it disrupts the endocrine system of frogs at very low doses, and Dichlorvos, a widely used insecticide that is an organophosphate, a class of chemicals developed as neurotoxins for use as weapons in World War II. Upon discovering this resurrection of the proverbial smoke-filled room, the Natural Resources Defense Council (NRDC) sued EPA for violating open-government laws. The environmentalists lost the first round of their lawsuit, and at this writing the case is on appeal.[19]

No democracy that honors the rule of law as one of its central organizing principles should tolerate agencies that develop policies behind closed doors in close consultation with the industries it is supposed to regulate. Excessive statutory mandates and funding shortfalls are major external sources of EPA's problems, but Stockholm Syndrome is something the Agency largely brings on itself.

## Stovepipe Organizational Structure

Any diagnosis of EPA's institutional condition must consider its internal organization, which is based on individual offices, each devoted to a single medium: air, soil, or water. As we learn more about the diversity of pollution sources, the intricacies of how pollutants interact with each other, and the nuances of how pollution travels through the environment, restricting the analysis of a problem to a single medium makes less and less sense. EPA's "stovepipe" management structure, which organizes by environmental media—air, water, and land— induces a woefully shortsighted mentality: once pollution is diverted from one medium, it is someone else's problem.

As Terry Davies and Jan Mazurek explain in their important book,

*Pollution Control in the United States,* "the physical law of conservation of matter is replaced by the political law of narrow jurisdictions."[20] For example, a smokestack scrubber removes harmful chemicals from gaseous combustion waste before it is released into the air. The chemicals drop to the bottom of the stack, where they become fly ash that is sent to a landfill, where it may leach into groundwater, becoming a problem for a different group of regulators. Similarly, mercury emissions released from power and chemical plant smokestacks fall into rivers, lakes, and streams. Yet the EPA staff charged with responsibility for cleaning up such water-based pollution says they have no authority to do anything about air emissions and environmentalists should go try to convince another office to take care of the problem.

If we had the past thirty years to do over again, there is little doubt that the threshold decision to organize the Agency's various components by the medium they are assigned to protect—air, water, land—would deserve extensive debate and might well come out another way. The real question at this juncture is whether attempting such radical restructuring would amount to killing the Agency in order to save it.

## Paralysis by Analysis

### Risk Assessment

Paracelsus, the sixteenth-century alchemist who is widely recognized as the father of toxicology, was the first scientist to observe that "the dose makes the poison," that is, the greater the amount of toxic chemical that one ingests, the more harm one will suffer, until the body shuts down completely, either in the short or the long term.[21] Conversely, the more toxic a chemical, the smaller the dose needed to trigger such a chain reaction.

It took centuries for humans to perfect the methods needed to predict the effects of the deliberate dosing of the body with drugs that were designed for their benefit. Environmental hazards require scientists to take these difficult problems one giant step further to the point of predicting what level of exposure to literally thousands of chemicals traveling through the ambient air or water will cause any one of multiple harms. The science—really a mixture of science and science policy—that sorts through these complexities is called risk assessment.[22]

Over the past two decades, risk assessment has gone from an experimental tool to the methodology of choice for making decisions. It is uniformly embraced by regulated industries, mainstream lawyers and economists, and leading government officials. (William Ruckelshaus, who served twice as EPA Administrator and is quoted at the beginning of this chapter, is a great fan.) Whatever its merits in the abstract, risk assessment is undoubtedly the single greatest source of complexification in environmental policy. EPA has tied itself in knots attempting to implement versions of this evolving methodology.

To assess risk, EPA must surmount several major hurdles. First, regulators must gather enough information to understand the amounts of potentially harmful pollutants that are emitted by industrial sources. Such estimates are complicated by the fact that sources often are not obligated to monitor their emissions and do not have a firm grip on how much pollution they produce. Once pollutants have left the smokestacks or pipes that transport them into the ambient environment, they change their composition and are further transformed as they travel through sunlight, water, soil, and air. Analyzing what happens during this period—what scientists call the "fate and transport" of pollution—necessarily involves determining the temperature of the air and water; the speed and directions of prevailing winds or water currents; the effect of structures (e.g., buildings, mountains, or underground rock formations) that stand in the path of such currents; the depth of the water table; the flow of aquifers hundreds of feet underground; soil composition above and below ground; and a slew of other factors. Because we do not monitor these transformations nearly thoroughly enough, scientists are often relegated to using models that attempt to predict such outcomes using a small number of real data points.

Once levels of pollutants are either monitored or modeled in the ambient air, water, and soil, scientists must guess what amounts of such substances are actually ingested (eaten), inhaled, or absorbed through the skin by people and ecosystems. This phase of assessing risk, known as "exposure assessment," is also quite challenging. People do not normally wear monitors so that experts can tell the dose of pollution that actually reaches them, and we are once again relegated to models that predict the point at which the pollution reaches the receptor. Development of biomarkers that indicate exposure—for example, the presence of mercury in blood or hair—is a promising new field but not yet refined or extensive enough to clarify these uncertainties.

The next phase of risk assessment requires an evaluation of the consequences of exposure. Even if they know what and how much of a substance people have inhaled, ingested, or absorbed through the skin, scientists may not have the data they need to predict how the chemicals travel through the body and how long they remain there. Some are easily excreted, while others lodge in bones or the lungs. Much of the material that informs this phase is derived from animal studies on rats and other species because researchers do not deliberately dose human beings, for obvious ethical reasons. Scientists can undertake epidemiological studies that measure what is happening or has happened to a population of people otherwise exposed to a chemical, in the workplace, for example, but those studies are also challenging to design and implement without bias.

Finally, research on the toxic effects of various chemicals is riddled with data gaps. A study by the Environmental Defense Fund, now known as Environmental Defense, estimated in 1997 that 70 percent of the most hazardous and ubiquitous chemicals did not have a basic set of toxicity data available.[23] A similar study done the next year by EPA showed that no basic safety information was available for half of the chemicals sold in the highest amounts.[24] The lowest estimate of this gap was produced by an industry trade association, the Chemical Manufacturers Association, which concluded that one-third of the one hundred high-production-volume chemicals it studied had insufficient screening data.[25] A high-production-volume chemical is one that is manufactured in or imported into the United States in amounts equal to or greater than one million pounds annually.

Because EPA has the burden of proving the likelihood of harm and its decisions are subject to court review, regulated industries that oppose regulation are cast in the relatively rewarding role of critic, challenging EPA's authority to issue final assessments without more information. Even when political or legal pressure has pushed manufacturers to explore the risks presented by their products, with a few notable exceptions (for example, registered pesticides), they are not obligated to share the information. Small wonder, then, that risk assessments are complexified and delayed.

## Cost-Benefit Analysis

### NUMBER CRUNCHING IN THE FACE OF UNCERTAINTY

Having run the gauntlet of risk assessment, EPA is far from finished with the long process of gaining approval for pollution controls. The scientists hand the matter over to the economists, who must conduct a cost-benefit analysis for the rule, predicting whether controls will cost more than they are worth, as measured in dollars. Outside those directly involved with the government and Wall Street, most people are not nearly as familiar with how economists influence public affairs as they are with the role of lawyers, the other profession that dominates public policy making. In the environmental arena, economics has grown in influence to the point that it is as important as law and is often used to trump legal requirements.

Adam Smith, the father of modern economics, defined the discipline as the "science of wealth."[26] Most prominent economists have followed the Smith tradition, which begins with the premise that government intervention in the "free market" in order to protect public health is only justified when the market—that is, unrestrained capitalism—has failed and cannot correct itself. Even assuming that the market we enjoy today is truly free (consider the contrary evidence of such constraints as trade barriers, subsidies for private industries, and the vagaries of the tax system), this formulation means that policy making never leaves the context of buying and selling goods. Everything, including health, is assumed to be available in return for money.

At first blush, this simple notion appears irrefutable: the owners and operators of industrial facilities should not have to pay to reduce or prevent pollution unless the benefits of those reductions exceed the costs of the remedies. Instinctively, people analogize this approach to a household budget: people know they cannot afford to spend more than they take in, and they must trim expenses to match revenues. To accomplish household budgeting, two columns are recorded and added up—expenses (rent, food, transportation, health care, etc.) on one side and revenue (salary, welfare payments, investments, and other income) on the other. If the two columns roughly match, the household is in good shape. If there is something leftover to save for the future, all to the better.

The reassuring analogy between household budgeting and cost-benefit analysis breaks down almost immediately in the context of environmental threats to anyone, especially children. Cost-benefit calculations involve elaborate numerical projections of how much it will cost to prevent or reduce pollution, as well as quantifications of whether those expenditures are worthwhile for society as a whole when they are offset against the monetary value of preventing certain children from getting sick. Unlike a household budget, these trade-offs involve people in no real relationship to each other—people responsible for sources of pollution and people who suffer ill effects from exposure—presenting economists and other decision makers with some profound social inequities that require moral and ethical judgments to qualify the number crunching. Or, to put it more bluntly, the parents of children exposed to neurotoxins do not tolerate such risks willingly because they receive money in exchange for their children's injuries.

The second problem with cost-benefit analysis is uncertainty, also masked by apparently precise numerical calculations. These uncertainties begin with cost-benefit's fraternal twin, risk assessment. Such assessments must rely on rough estimates of how many people will die or become sick as a result of toxic exposures, and scientists typically qualify their findings as limited to a best guess on the scope of harm. So, for example, a well-done risk assessment should give us some sense of which children are exposed to a pollutant, the possible levels of those exposures, and the adverse health effects that could occur as a result. But exposures are hard to quantify (because we do not have comprehensive monitoring of contamination in air and water); many types of harm are difficult to identify and measure (for example, subtle damage to a developing nervous system); and illness may become manifest years in the future (brain damage in utero may not limit development until a child goes to school). Nevertheless, economists use the results of risk assessments to quantify, with deceptive precision, the monetary value of the "benefits" that would be achieved by controlling pollution: fewer deaths and less illness.

As for the expense of controlling pollution—the other side of the cost-benefit equation—a decent risk assessment begins to identify facilities that emit pollution and to quantify the amounts they release. Many different categories of sources may emit the pollutant, or there may be sources that emit other chemicals that are transformed into substances that are most damaging as they are transported through the environment. Wind can blow these chemicals hundreds of miles away from their sources, and monitoring often is not required to determine where the chemicals originate. Building on the guesswork that occurs during a risk assessment, EPA engineers must then identify specific industrial facilities that should be subjected to pollution controls and investigate the pollution-control equipment and other technological solutions that either are available now or might be available in the foreseeable future. The companies that own these potential regulatory targets then weigh in, coming up with their own, often overstated estimates of how much it would cost them to comply with the government's requirements. The result can be inflated costs offset against deflated benefits, defeating rules that would in the long run have made overall social and economic sense.

No reasonable person would argue that, as a society, we can afford to eliminate all risk, even if we could imagine what such risks are and invent ways to prevent them. But weighing the costs of producing pollution against the benefits of stopping it cannot help but involve qualitative judgments. Regulators should evaluate imprecise estimates in conjunction with other, equally important values. Final decisions cannot credibly boil down to an open-and-shut comparison of numbers to the precise decimal point. Unfortunately, as we shall see in the case studies that comprise Part II, this description bears no relationship to cost-benefit analysis as it is now practiced within EPA. Instead, economists have conquered the process with such force that cost-benefit analysis translates most aspects of environmental threats to children into numbers that not only are unreliable but stack the deck against pollution control.

Although it sounds like the centerpiece of a plot for the TV series *The X-Files*, Circular A-4 is in fact a forty-eight-page document issued by OMB in September 2003 that explains the requirements for all cost-benefit analyses that must be conducted before any major rule is released in final form.[27] Formal cost-benefit requirements began under President Reagan with the issuance of Executive Order 12291.[28] President Clinton revised those requirements, issuing Executive Order 12866, which was retained by President George W. Bush.[29] Under Circular A-4, cost-benefit analysis proceeds in four steps: (1) identification and quantification (or monetization) of costs, (2) identification and quantification (or monetization) of benefits, (3) discounting of all these numbers if compliance is delayed or harm will not occur immediately, and (4) unflinching (but erratic) comparisons of costs and benefits.

## COSTS

The costs of preventing pollution include the obvious: how much money must a power plant pay to install equipment on its smokestack that prevents mercury emissions? Under Circular A-4, they also include the counterintuitive: how much money could the utility that owns the plant earn if it took the money or resources it would have committed to pollution controls and invested them in some other lucrative enterprise? This second category is called "opportunity costs."[30] Finally, economists take opportunity costs and attempt to extrapolate them to society as a whole: What items (jobs, other social welfare investments, etc.) would society have available if it did not force an industry to spend comparable sums of money on reducing environmental threats to children? As economists proceed from the relatively straightforward estimation of compliance costs to lost opportunity costs on a micro and macro level, the intricacy—and uncertainty—of the economic analysis grows.

Estimates of compliance costs are heavily dependent on information provided by industries that are candidates for regulation and are notorious for being inflated.[31] Agencies starved for resources, like EPA, have a sharply diminished ability to challenge predictions that pollution control equipment will not become available in time or at a reasonable price. The few retrospective, empirical studies that have been done document large decreases in such costs once a regulation has gone into effect, as the market for the equipment develops and competition for sales drives prices down.[32] Yet OMB has demonstrated little interest in working to improve the accuracy of such estimates by pursuing retrospective empirical studies on a larger scale.

BENEFITS

Cost-benefit analysis as it is practiced today attempts to place a *monetary* value on every benefit that counts. To be sure, Circular A-4 pays lip service to the idea that certain losses are not easily quantified in monetary terms, and it invites agencies to describe such outcomes qualitatively— that is, in language not in numbers.[33] But there is little evidence that such qualitative assessments have nearly the clout in final decision making as quantified values.

The going rate for a human life is somewhere between $6 million and $7 million. For adverse outcomes short of death, such as brain damage or respiratory problems, economists struggle to develop figures based on what people would supposedly be willing to pay to avoid such injuries. "Willingness to pay" has its own acronym, "WTP," which appears as a crucial factor in the equations that are the vehicle for these calculations.

So, for example, suppose you are the parent of a severely asthmatic child. Economists ask whether you would be willing to pay $190 to avoid ten attacks or $1,940 to ensure that your child will not have to go to the emergency room for asthma treatments. Would you, or more accurately, could you pay to avoid these outcomes? As we shall see in Chapter 7, "Ozone Case Study," both figures are derived from EPA's cost-benefit analysis of the Clean Air Act. What if a company said that it would *pay you* to allow your child to suffer such attacks so that the company could avoid the expense of installing pollution control equipment, would you accept the money? This version of the problem is known as "willingness to accept" (WTA), although it is used far less often than its WTP counterpart.

The justification for these approaches is that people in a democracy should get to choose what levels of risk they are willing to buy, as opposed to having the government decide for them. Of course, very few citizens of this society have any idea these kinds of calculations are actually going on, much less that they are used all the time to make decisions about whether and how much we should protect children from toxic exposures.

The economists brush aside the fact that your perspective might depend on how much money you have. So, if your income is low and you have little if any surplus money you might have a different reaction to the question about your willingness to pay thousands of dollars to avoid your child's asthma attack than if you were a wealthy person. You might or might not have a different reaction to the notion that you should "sell" your children's health, although it seems intuitively obvious that most parents would never make such a cold calculation.

Even if one likes the idea of letting people decide these questions rather than the government, the validity and reliability of the methods used to make such determinations is obviously key. How do economists get baseline figures for people's WTP, much less their WTA? For the most part they rely on what are called "wage premium studies," the vast majority of which were done in the 1970s and 1980s. Such studies examine the generally higher wages for risky jobs like construction or the manufacture of toxic chemicals and compare them to the generally lower wages for relatively safe jobs. The difference between high-risk and low-risk wages is assumed to be the measure of what people are willing to sacrifice financially for relative safety or, conversely, how much extra money they think their risk of injury is worth.

Problems with this approach are immediately obvious: Did the workers really have the information they needed to make the choice to do more hazardous work? Even if they were aware of the risks, did they make the choice freely, without regard to economic pressures? After all, we are ostensibly gauging willing choices, and if people were coerced by bad economic circumstances, they can hardly be said to have made a voluntary decision. Last but not least, what do the choices of healthy adults have to do with the risks faced by children, the elderly, or those who are already ill? Even if an able-bodied man is willing to take a risk, does this state of mind translate into willingness to put his young children in the same circumstances?

Wage premium studies are by far the dominant mode for calculating WTP and WTA, although economists occasionally go out and actually survey people's opinions on these subjects. For example, economists at

Resources for the Future recruited a group of 930 adults in Ontario, Canada, who ranged in age from forty to seventy-five and had an average annual income of 58,000 Canadian dollars.[34] The researchers asked the subjects to take a complex, self-administered computer survey designed to gauge how much they would be willing to pay in order to avoid certain risks. The researchers' goal was to see if people's willingness declined as they grew older. They concluded that such willingness did not begin to decline in any noticeable way until people reached seventy-five years old, at which point people apparently felt they could more easily afford to die. No one asked how they would evaluate risks to their children. Moreover, many respondents became so entangled by the questions that they could not answer the survey effectively. For example, when asked to compare what they would pay to avoid a five-in-one-thousand chance of dying versus what they would pay to avoid a one-in-one-thousand chance of dying, they did not agree to pay five times as much to avoid five times the risk.

On relatively rare occasions, economists permit other methods to enter the monetization process. They evaluate a child's lost IQ points as a result of lead exposure by looking at studies that show how much less the child would earn over her lifetime if she was stupider. Certain diseases are monetized by looking at how much it would cost to put a person in the hospital for treatment of the illness. All of these approaches are "objective" in the sense that they pay absolutely no attention to the values people might place on avoiding these results—values that might or might not be translatable into money.

## DISCOUNTING

Once they have established the monetary value of the costs and benefits of a proposed protection, economists proceed to a final, crucial phase known as "discounting." They reason that because people will not suffer the adverse effect of exposure to a pollutant for many years, the monetary value of the benefits they will receive should be "discounted" to reflect what the money is worth in today's dollars. Or, in other words, economists compute how much one would have to invest at a specific interest rate *today* to come up with the dollar value of a life or of a disease (for example, non-fatal neurological damage that diminishes intelligence or fine motor coordination) at a designated point in the future, when the problem actually manifests itself. Similarly, if compliance costs (for example, the money spent to operate and maintain smokestack scrubbers) will be paid at a point several years in the future, those amounts are also discounted. OMB advises agencies to use a 7 percent discount rate, although they may do an additional run of the numbers at a 3 percent rate if they wish and include those alternative calculations in their analyses.[35]

Discounting has the effect of reducing both sides of the cost-benefit equation, although its diminishing effects on benefits are by far the most important because so many environmentally caused health problems take so long to become evident. For example, if a regulation would save one hundred lives in thirty years, the *current* valuation (the number used for cost-benefit analysis) at a 7 percent discount rate would be 13.14 lives, or 13.14 multiplied by $6 million, for a total of $78.8 million, as opposed to the $600 million the lives would be worth if we considered their present value. One hundred lives discounted at 7 percent for fifty years equals 3.39 lives at the point when damages are manifested; in seventy years, the value has dwindled to 0.88 lives.

Depending on how far it is carried into the future, discounting eventually swallows the benefits that might be achieved for our children and their children by controlling pollution, meaning that we take no action because costs exceed benefits. This outcome occurs despite the fact that some toxic chemicals and metals are persistent and build up in the environment to the point that they eventually overwhelm nature's ability to repair itself. Mercury and perchlorate, the subjects of the first two case studies, are prime examples. Economists rationalize inaction even though species that become extinct are gone forever. And costs could exceed benefits under this methodology with respect to climate change, though scientists warn that at some point the holes we have made in the stratospheric ozone layer will be (if they are not already) irreparable.

The OMB economists who authored Circular A-4 are untroubled by these interactions. They acknowledge in passing that it is rarely feasible to gauge a child's willingness either to pay or to accept. They admit that adult wage premium studies may not accurately reflect the correct valuation of a child's life. They are aware of a few studies showing that parents may value their children's health more than their own. Despite these concessions, Circular A-4 says that monetizing the benefits of saving a child's life should proceed under all the usual rules, beginning with $6 million, applying a 7 percent rate, and discounting into the future. The analysis should result in "monetary values for children at least as large as the values for adults (for the same probabilities and outcomes) unless there is specific and compelling evidence to suggest otherwise."[36] They give no examples of what might constitute specific and compelling evidence.

As for future generations who may well be harmed by long-term damage to natural resources because the current generation decides it is not willing to pay to preserve them, the OMB economists acknowledge that such situations raise "special ethical considerations."[37] After all, "future citizens who are affected by such choices cannot take part in making them, and today's society must act with some consideration of their interests."[38] The solution the economists offer is to proceed with standard valuation and discounting but to acknowledge at some point in the analysis that the proposal could bestow potential intergenerational value. Again, it is hard to see how our children's children can win at this game if the pollution at issue is widespread and will be costly to clean up.

How do the economists justify these results? In perhaps the most chilling passage in Circular A-4, they rely on inflation and economic prosperity to get them off the hook. Citing "the expectation that future generations will be wealthier" than we are today, they contend that a few dollars in lost benefits will not mean as much to children born in 2010, 2030, or 2050.[39] Using a lower discount rate or otherwise giving future generations an economic advantage "would in effect transfer resources from poorer people today to richer people tomorrow."[40] Or, in other words, the only way to give today's poor people air conditioning in the summer is to expose our great-grandchildren to the risk of irretrievable environmental damage.

THE FINAL SUM

The culmination of a cost-benefit analysis is to take costs and compare them to benefits. Most often, because of the complexity of the assumptions that go into the calculations of monetized costs and benefits, these numbers are stated in ranges. If costs are a significantly larger number than benefits, the government is supposed to back off. If benefits are significantly larger, the government is supposed to plow ahead, intervening in the market in the name of economic efficiency. OMB requires that a cost-benefit analysis accompany every proposal for intervention, although it has issued several decision documents cutting back on regulatory protections without bothering to make agencies jump through this hoop. OMB requires cost-benefit analysis even where the statute mandating issuance of the rule says that EPA should stay focused exclusively on the benefits of health protections.

The obvious influence of cost-benefit analysis on the outcome of EPA decisions is troubling enough in itself. As important as its substantive effects, however, is the enormous burden it puts on the Agency. Unlike many other federal agencies and departments, EPA is not an institution that is sitting around staring at broad, generic mandates trying to decide which of hundreds of possible problems to address. Instead, the Agency's priorities, overly demanding as they may be, have been set by Congress in a group of statutes that is thousands of pages long. Cost-benefit analysis reexamines all of these mandates, in effect second-guessing decisions already made by Congress. Instead of asking how we can control environmental threats to children in the most cost-effective or efficient way possible, Circular A-4 asks whether the problem should be regulated in the first place.

## Days in Court

### Checks and Balances

The federal judiciary was created under Article III of the Constitution to serve as one of three pillars of the checks-and-balances system of government, the others being the executive branch and Congress. In theory, judicial review provides an important antidote to an executive branch that instructs agencies to ignore Congress and, vice versa, a legislative branch that impinges on executive-branch prerogatives. The federal courts are organized on three levels: district courts, which try cases in which the facts are in dispute (for example, criminal charges under federal statutes or civil cases when money is in dispute); appellate courts, which review district court opinions and take cases challenging industry-wide regulations in the first instance; and the Supreme Court, which—unlike the lower-tier courts—does not consider every case that is filed but rather has the discretion to choose the cases it deems the most important.

Federal judges are appointed for lifetime terms and confirmed by the Senate.[41] The appellate (or circuit) courts are populated by some of the finest legal minds in the country. In theory, these judges are as dispassionate as they are brilliant, applying the law without regard to their views on how the statutes should have been written or—as important—how EPA should have interpreted them. In practice, as in any other human endeavor, personal policy preferences, political orientations, and deep-seated values shape judges' decisions, for better or for worse.

The federal courts hear two kinds of cases involving what EPA has done or failed to do. The first category, mentioned above, encompasses cases that involve the way the Agency implements its extensive statutory mandates by writing industry-wide rules. These cases are decided by *appellate* courts as soon as the EPA decision is made final and may be reviewed by the Supreme Court. Second, as insurance that EPA would implement the law faithfully, Congress equipped almost every major environmental statute with "private attorney general" or "citizen suit" provisions that allow any person (or group or organization) to sue EPA for not meeting its statutory deadlines for taking action and to sue companies if they violate the law.[42] If plaintiffs win such lawsuits, the government must pay their attorneys' fees and costs. These cases are filed first in federal *district* courts and then appealed if one of the parties does not like the outcome and thinks it can persuade an appellate court that the district judge was wrong. Because the second category of cases is much less important than the first to the Agency's overall failure to act to protect children from environmental hazards, we will not pursue it any further here.

The federal judiciary has come under enormous strain in the past two decades because the numbers of cases the judges are asked to decide have multiplied beyond their capacity to hear them.[43] The total number of appellate judges authorized for all thirteen circuits (twelve regional courts and the federal circuit) is 179, and the number allocated to the District of Columbia Circuit, which hears most cases against EPA, is 12. Since 1995 the number of cases pending in the U.S. appellate courts has risen 28 percent making the courts' intrusiveness in agency business still more puzzling.[44]

## Can't Get No Respect

In the years since EPA's creation, appellate judges have approached review of EPA decisions from both ends of the political spectrum at the behest of national, regional, and even local environmental groups as well as diverse members of regulated industries. Although there are notable exceptions to each of the following generalizations, during the first decade and a half of EPA's existence, the judiciary viewed EPA from a liberal or pro-environmental position, as illustrated by the *Ethyl* case discussed at the outset of this chapter. From the late 1980s to the present, however, judges have steadily become more conservative, demanding that EPA provide more evidence to justify decisions that impose major costs on industry and interpreting the Agency's authority more narrowly.

Petitioners asking the courts for relief typically argue that EPA has misinterpreted its statutory authority and done something Congress did not intend for it to do; the Agency has failed to compile an adequate record of information supporting its decision; and/or the Agency has failed to explain convincingly why it made the decision on the basis of the record it compiled and the statutory authority it was implementing. The courts are supposed to give EPA deference in such cases on the theory that an expert agency should know better than others what its statutes require and what to do in response to available information. In several notable cases, however, it has been difficult to discern any such politeness or even much respect.

Statutory language is often opaque and internally inconsistent, reflecting the elaborate compromises Congress makes to get them passed. Ambiguity gives judges the opportunity to impose their own views regarding what Congress told EPA to do, as opposed to deferring to EPA's understanding of those mandates. It is no small irony that judges who take this approach are often quite conservative and decry judicial activism in other contexts.

As problematic are cases in which petitioners challenge a decision because EPA lacks a "reasonable basis" for the outcome and therefore has acted in an irrational, or "arbitrary and capricious," manner. Sometimes the problem identified by the judges is insufficient information in the "administrative record" (akin to a case file) that supports the decision. Or the judges may say that regardless of the record, EPA has not explained well enough why it did what it did. These decisions cause trouble because, unlike a relatively straightforward disagreement about what statutory language means, they provoke endless second-guessing, anxiety, and defensive behavior with respect to *future* cases. Two opinions decided a decade apart illustrate why such cases have these repercussions; the first involved workplace exposures to benzene, and the second involved asbestos used in consumer products.

## Hard Cases and Bad Law

The first case addressed a decision by the Occupational Safety and Health Administration (OSHA) to lower the tolerable level of workplace exposures to the chemical benzene to 1 part per million (ppm) in the air.[45] The case was decided in 1980, only five years after the landmark opinion upholding EPA's decision to ban lead in gasoline,[46] by a closely divided Supreme Court voting 5 to 4 to overturn OSHA's new standard. Although the decision applied specific language of OSHA's authorizing statute, as opposed to the statutory schemes applicable to EPA and other health and safety agencies, it sent shock waves throughout the community of public health, safety, and environmental agencies, causing them to think, rethink, and think again before imposing pollution controls that would be as vehemently opposed by the manufacturing sector.

The Supreme Court held that OSHA's authorizing statute only allowed it to regulate in the event of a *"significant* risk of harm."[47] The burden of proving harm is on OSHA, which must "show, on the basis of substantial evidence, that long-term exposure to [higher levels] of benzene presents a significant risk of material health impairment" and that lowering the acceptable levels of exposure was therefore necessary.[48] The Court then proceeded to comb through the administrative record compiled by OSHA, finding that its interpretation of the available, highly technical data was fatally flawed and that it lacked a considerable amount of the information it needed to make a final decision.

In a passionate dissent, Justice Thurgood Marshall wrote that "risks of harm are often uncertain, but inaction has considerable costs of its own. The agency must decide whether to take regulatory action against possible substantial risks or to wait until more definitive information becomes available—a judgment which by its very nature cannot be based solely on determinations of fact."[49] He accused the majority of usurping power from Congress, which was democratically elected by the people precisely to make such hard calls. As a tragic postscript, in 1987, seven years after Marshall's prophecy, OSHA assembled considerable, additional scientific data to support a workplace standard for benzene, even lower than the one rejected by the Supreme Court. OSHA found that at the higher levels left in place by the Court's decision for those seven years, leukemia and other cancers as well as chromosomal aberrations were more prevalent among thousands of workers.[50]

The second case that continues to chill EPA's regulatory initiatives was decided in 1991 by the Fifth Circuit Court of Appeals but never reviewed by the Supreme Court.[51] After more than a decade of deliberation, in a decision called *Corrosion Proof Fittings v. EPA*, the appellate court rejected EPA's decision to ban virtually all uses of asbestos, with "friction products" such as brake drums singled out as the greatest threat.[52] Once again, the court did not confine itself to reviewing how EPA interpreted its statutory authority. Instead, the judges took a long and punctilious tour through the rulemaking record, challenging both the Agency's interpretation of the facts and the methodologies it used to make judgments about the costs and benefits of the proposed rule. Among other things, the court said that EPA had to go through the arduous process of calculating the potential costs and benefits not only of the rules it had chosen but of all possible "less burdensome" alternatives. The moral of the story from EPA's perspective? Move toward a decision even more slowly and carefully, bolstering the record in any conceivable way, to avoid reversal by the courts.

Professor Thomas McGarity, among others, has characterized these results as the "ossification" of rulemaking.[53] This phenomenon severely undermined EPA's effectiveness. The judges making these decisions have no special qualifications to second-guess either EPA's or OSHA's interpretations of science. By pouncing on agencies like EPA and OSHA in such highly technical areas after the fact, the courts exceed their appropriate role, substituting their judgments for the agencies' expert decisions rather than policing the blatant abuse of administrative authority.

### Arranged Marriage with the States

The vast majority of federal environmental laws divide the authority to implement programs between federal and state governments.[54] States are given the opportunity to apply for a federal delegation of authority giving them responsibility for implementing a given program, with EPA remaining accountable for writing the regulatory standards that guide such implementation. States must promise to maintain a program at least as strong as the program defined by EPA. If the states do not live up to their commitments, EPA can withdraw the delegations, an outcome state officials regard as both politically damaging and humiliating. EPA's increasingly acute budget problems have meant that it threatens withdrawals but does not execute them, diminishing but not eliminating the effectiveness of EPA's threats. The Environmental Council of the States, the association that represents the heads of state environmental agencies, estimates that 75 percent of federal programs have been delegated.[55] EPA administers programs in states that do not apply for delegated authority. However dependent the Agency is on state administration and enforcement, it is clearly the senior partner in these arrangements, both by law and by practice. As state environmental agencies grow in size and competence, this arrangement becomes increasingly strained. And, like most marriages, turmoil increases when finances get tight.

President Reagan came to Washington pledging big change.[56] In addition to excoriating "big government," Reagan proposed a "new federalism" that would devolve most power back to the states.[57] Ultimately, the Reagan administration was far more successful in cutting grants and shrinking bureaucracy than in devolving authority. Aid to states and local governments was cut sharply at the outset of the administration, but its efforts to expunge ambitious federal regulatory programs foundered early on. As the federal budget deficit ballooned to record levels, "cooperative federalism" and "regulatory federalism" gave way to coercive or fend-for-yourself federalism, at least from the states' perspective. Reagan's loyal opposition in Congress continued to enact ambitious social programs but gave up any pretense of providing substantial aid for the implementation of such mandates at the state and local levels.

When conservative Republicans took over the House of Representatives, mandating slowed somewhat, but the money was never restored despite a period of economic growth and deficit reduction during the Clinton administration. In 1995 state and local government frustration boiled over. In short order, the Unfunded Mandates Reform Act became law.[58] The statute allows members of Congress to raise a point of order on the House or Senate floor if a piece of legislation is missing an analysis of its unfunded impact on state and local governments. Likewise, federal agencies are required to prepare such analyses to accompany new regulations. A point of order can be waived by majority vote, and the statute says nothing about the quality of such analyses. As its authors should have expected, the statute has not proved terribly effective, and some states and their Republican allies are now declaring that it must be amended to give it teeth.

Beyond financial woes, the federal-state partnership has also suffered from severe management problems. The states are not a monolith, either politically or administratively. Some states are led by conservative Republicans and others by liberal Democrats. States in the West, such as Montana, Wyoming, and Utah, want to control the land without anyone from Washington interfering. States on either coast, whatever the politics of their governors, put pressure on EPA to be more aggressive. As explained in Chapter 7, "An Ozone Case Study," northeastern states' demands that the Agency crack down on polluting power plants in the Midwest and join international efforts to address global warming have escalated to the extent that some states have sued the Agency and each other.

Just as they differ politically, the competence of state agencies runs the gamut from impressive to awful, raising the possibility of gearing the degree of federal micromanagement to the states' track records. But EPA has never managed to craft delegation policies that distinguish meaningfully between the states on the basis of their competence and their politics.[59] On paper and in practice, states that perform well are treated the same as those who cannot cope. The Agency's regional offices are very hesitant to approve variances in national standards that might be justified by individual state factors, such as geology or climate, further frustrating the states. EPA's tacit decision to manage state programs on an ad hoc basis means that it has never set any meaningful, objective, and uniform benchmarks for the investments states should expect to make in administering and enforcing delegated programs. Without such criteria, state regulators are hard-pressed to persuade their legislatures and governors to increase their funding.

## Conclusion

Halfway into the first decade of the new millennium, EPA is at a crossroads. The Agency is underfunded, understaffed, subject to debilitating badgering by regulated industries, disdained by the White House and the courts, and stuck with mandates so ambitious and numerous that it cannot help but continue to fail.

Regulated industries have become so arrogant that they literally set up shop inside the Agency, consulting with its staff on a constant basis and even drafting the language that goes into rulemaking documents. Alarmed by the evidence of capture, the environmental community has retreated to the courts, where it hopes to persuade judges that ignoring the law simply is not an option. EPA cannot possibly choose between approaches on the basis of protecting public health, as it is supposed to do, but instead must consider whether it can compromise enough that neither side stalemates progress by bringing it to court. Such quests are increasingly fruitless.

In addition to compelling EPA to cannibalize other programs to pay for the new ones under a flat budget, EPA must contend with the use of risk assessment to select regulatory targets and determine final standards and the application of cost-benefit analysis to justify proposed and final rules. These methodologies, which are rapidly on their way to becoming institutionalized without statutory authorization, significantly increase the length and expense of the regulatory process. Can EPA be revived without major surgery? Before answering that question, we must first ask if there is an alternative to reviving it.

## CHAPTER 4

# Corporations and the Commons

## The Tragedy of the Commons

In 1968 Garrett Hardin, a microbiologist by training, wrote an essay titled "The Tragedy of the Commons," which was published in the influential journal *Science*.[1] This brief, beautifully written piece provided the conceptual foundation for modern environmental statutes. Hardin's hypothesis, based in part on work by Thomas Malthus, a political economist in nineteenth-century England, was stark and compelling. Hardin began with the proposition that the world's natural resources were finite. If human populations consumed resources without restriction, no amount of human ingenuity in the invention of technology would prevent the eventual destruction of the planet's environment. Only the government could avert such disasters by enforcing laws that compelled individuals to recognize the public good and change their behavior. Using the metaphor of an English "commons," Hardin wrote:

> Picture a pasture open to all. It is to be expected that each herdsman will try to keep as many cattle as possible on the commons. Such an arrangement may work reasonably satisfactorily for centuries because tribal wars, poaching, and disease keep the numbers of both man and beast well below the carrying capacity of the land. Finally, however, comes the day of reckoning, that is, the day when the long-desired goal of social stability becomes a reality. At this point, the inherent logic of the commons remorselessly generates tragedy.
>
> As a rational being, each herdsman seeks to maximize his gain. Explicitly or implicitly, more or less consciously, he asks, "What is the

utility *to me* of adding one more animal to my herd?" This utility has one negative and one positive component.

1. The positive component is a function of the increment of one animal. Since the herdsman receives all the proceeds from the sale of the additional animal, the positive utility is nearly +1.
2. The negative component is a function of the additional overgrazing created by one more animal. Since, however, the effects of overgrazing are shared by all the herdsmen, the negative utility for any particular decisionmaking herdsman is only a fraction of −1.[2]

Hardin's theory of the commons is consistent with the observations of Milton Friedman and F. A. Hayek that are quoted in Chapter 2, "The Rise of Special Interest Conservatism," to the effect that when jointly necessary resources are polluted by an upstream user, the result is an "externality" that the free market cannot resolve.[3] In the case of the environmental legacy we will leave our children, the dilemma of the tragedy of the commons is intensified because harm is not immediately visible and pollution builds up over time.

Hardin's frame of reference was rural herdsmen using the most basic natural resources, soil and water. The frame of reference for the pollution that threatens children is the modern, multinational corporation, enlarging and exacerbating the scope and severity of potential harm to the commons. A corporation's record in producing profits is the overriding measure of its success. All other aspects of corporate behavior—the exercise of social conscience, an interest in preserving ecology, the fear of losing the public's esteem, even corporate compliance with regulations that may be enforced with penalties—most often run a distant second to this primary goal. To expect that corporations will embrace motivations other than making profits is to misunderstand the dynamics of capitalism. Viewed from this perspective, Hardin's deep concern about what people do to the resources of the commons if their self-interests are not moderated by the public interest applies even more forcefully to corporate conduct than to individual behavior.

## Free Market Environmentalism

The tragedy of the commons is not the only idea fighting for traction in today's environmental policy debates. As Hardin readily acknowledged when his essay first came out, his views are in irretrievable conflict with the "invisible hand" doctrine propounded by eighteenth-century philosopher Adam Smith, who argued in *The Wealth of Nations* that an individual "intend[ing] only his own gain . . . [is] led by an invisible hand . . . to promote the public interest."[4] The modern, most relevant iteration of the invisible-hand theory is "free-market environmentalism," a school of thought that would take government out of the business of protecting the environment.

In their book *Free Market Environmentalism*, Terry Anderson, an economist, and Donald Leal, a mathematician, propose replacing centralized and compulsory regulation with a carefully designed system of property rights that would allocate all commons resources to private-sector entities to manage.[5] Owners would buy, sell, and use such rights at will. Common law liability ("If you dump hazardous wastes on my land, I can sue you for damages.") would serve as the sole remedy for egregious abuses.

Free-marketers contend that Hardin was wrong to forecast a tragedy of the commons because he failed to take into account "how human ingenuity stimulated by market forces finds ways to cope with natural resource constraints."[6] Or, in other words, technological prowess will allow us to find innovative alternatives to dwindling natural resources. Anderson and Leal acknowledge that depending on a free market might mean full consumption of a resource before any alternative is developed. Their response is that unless people are willing to pay to preserve natural resources, and work to develop technology capable of conserving those resources, then the resources will disappear until and unless the free market inspires people to embrace different approaches voluntarily. This result, they argue, merely reflects the preeminence of the human race in the natural world. The concept of formulating public policies on the basis of individual economic preferences—or, in other words, people's willingness to pay for clean air or clean water—is a cornerstone of mainstream economic analysis and plays a major role in cost-benefit analysis, the methodology used to make decisions on regulatory proposals by the George W. Bush administration.

Taken to its logical conclusion, free market theory means that the commons should be up for sale to the highest bidder. Although we have limited experience with auctions of the commons—that is, opportunities to buy intangible goods like clean air or clean water at auction—free-market environmentalists propose this approach as the favored vehicle for democratic decision making. Allowing present generations to give full rein to their preferences for today may not always result in equity for future generations. But, free-market environmentalists would counter, the question should not be whether the reliance on the market works perfectly. Rather, we must ask ourselves whether it is better than the overly intrusive, inordinately expensive regulatory system we have now.

With an intensity that has built steadily over the past decade, right-wing think tanks have declared that the time for free market environmentalism has arrived, citing as support the profound disillusionment with government caused by the institutional dysfunction. These predictions reflect the wishful thinking of ideologues, to be sure, and it is very difficult to imagine a government-sponsored auction of the Grand Canyon or the airshed over Harlem any time soon. However, many proponents of a free-market approach, especially the most powerful members of the large and diverse corporate community that are the primary targets of regulation, apply the theory in far more pragmatic and incremental ways. As a direct result of their advocacy, we already see instances in which free-market environmentalism has been brought into the mainstream as an alternative to traditional regulation. For example, proposals to control mercury from power plants are based on trading of licenses to pollute, a close variation on the idea of buying and selling opportunities to use up natural resources.

In the final analysis, readers must determine for themselves which of these theories—tragedy of the commons or free-market environmentalism—is a more accurate description of the world as they wish it to be. The central premise of this book—that strong government has a vital role to play in protecting children's environmental future—clearly embraces Hardin's theory and rejects the alternative proposition. For those who may need to hear more about this position, however, we must consider two additional questions: How have organized corporate interests justified their largely successful campaign against traditional regulation? Given this rhetoric and its underlying ideology, is it realistic to expect that if traditional regulation receded, it would be replaced by a robust and reliable infrastructure of voluntary corporate programs that could substitute for government controls?

## The Case Against Regulation

The conservative revolt against regulation is based on five distinctly different arguments, at times inconsistent and at times overlapping:

1. The comforts of modern life are well worth the disadvantages of pollution.
2. The environment is in much better shape than people think. Whatever the problems may be, government intervention through regulation will only exacerbate them and diminish the overall well-being of society.
3. We cannot afford to spend large sums of money on environmental protection because we have so many other, pressing problems to address.
4. Self-regulatory efforts by corporations address any problems of significance.

## Chemicals Are Not So Harmful

Regulated industries and their conservative allies argue that the overall value of chemicals to society far outweighs the advantages of further controls on pollution. The corporate-funded and very conservative Competitive Enterprise Institute (CEI) has a division devoted to environmental policy that has written a paper titled "Chemical Risk":

> The average worldwide human life span has increased from around 30 years at the beginning of the 20th century to more than 60 today . . . The freedom to develop and put to use thousands of man-made chemicals has played a crucial role in that progress by making possible such things as pharmaceuticals, safe drinking water, pest control, and numerous other items.[7]

From here, it is only a few short steps to a series of other arguments.

Because chemicals are necessary to maintain the quality of life, we must reject the exaggerated and self-serving claims of environmental "extremists" who urge us to reduce pollution from their privileged position as upper-class elitists. For example, the best way to combat malaria, conservatives argue, is to spray DDT, a pesticide banned in the United States, in homes in the developing world. "Thirty years ago this month the government launched an assault on a basic liberty—the liberty to protect one's own health using a pesticide," writes CEI's Angela Logomasini.[8]

Environmentalists are not only elitists whose influence over pesticide policies can be directly linked to millions of unnecessary deaths abroad, they are unrelenting pessimists intent on ignoring the tremendous progress in controlling domestic pollution over the last thirty years.

Because environmental quality is much better, proposals to impose more stringent regulations present a significant risk that we will spend disproportionately large sums to go after the relatively small remnants of the worst pollution. Conservatives are enormously frustrated by what they see as the media's propensity to enlarge viewing audiences by emphasizing bad news, as sensationalized as possible.[9]

Like most informed generalizations, these observations make sense in some contexts. Chemicals are important to the progress we have made as a civilization. Making drinking-water disinfectants widely available in the developing world could save millions of children's lives. People do need to recognize the progress we have made. On the other hand, one does not need to harbor an irrational hatred of all chemicals to be concerned about pollution. And letting everyone exercise their "freedom" to do what they like to protect themselves or protect their quality of life leads us back to where we began: a tragic outcome for the commons.

As in other areas of public debate, the perceived self-interest of the entity proclaiming a position is often determinative of whether the argument is heard, much less believed. If the Chamber of Commerce, the National Association of Manufacturers, or the industry-funded Competitive Enterprise Institute decry the need for environmental controls, their views are disbelieved by people on the left, just as the views of the Sierra Club or Greenpeace are dismissed out of hand by people on the right. Accordingly, the campaign against regulation got a tremendous boost from popular books written by independent commentators: *A Moment on Earth* by American journalist Gregg Easterbrook, published in 1995, and *The Skeptical Environmentalist* by Danish statistician Bjorn Lomborg, published in English in 2001.[10] Despite their length and extensive footnoting, the two books caused minor sensations when they were released because the authors challenged the fundamental premises of most national and international environmentalists that we must redouble our efforts to protect the earth's fragile ecology. Instead, Easterbrook and Lomborg argued, the planet is in excellent shape compared to where it stood in the immediate aftermath of industrialization. Having made this much progress, we should place our faith in man's capacity for innovation to continue this progress for the indefinite future. As a corollary, the warnings of doomsayers in the environmental community, international and domestic, should be dismissed by the public-at-large.

Easterbrook predicts that "in the Western world pollution will end within our lifetimes, with society almost painlessly adapting a zero-emissions policy."[11] He adds that "most feared environmental catastrophes, such as runaway global warming, are almost certain to be avoided." And, he announces with enthusiasm, that "far from becoming a source of global discord, environmentalism, which binds nations to a common concern, will be the best thing that's ever happened to international relations."

Lomborg essentially agrees with Easterbrook that the world is in much better shape than we think, declaring in his opening paragraphs that "mankind's lot has actually improved in terms of practically every measurable indicator."[12] But he adopts a far more aggressive stance against institutionalized environmentalism and the news media, accusing both of focusing on the negative because they have economic incentives to do so.[13] He argues that this negative focus leads us to solve "phantom problems while ignoring real and pressing (possibly non-environmental) issues."[14] And he urges us to stop worrying about the legacy we are leaving our children because all we owe them is "knowledge and capital, such that they can obtain a quality of life at least as good as ours *all in all*."[15]

Will we run out of oil and other fossil fuels? Of course, Lomborg acknowledges, at some point we will, but we have adequate resources for "the long-term future," and by the time the resource runs out, we will have found a source of energy that "makes us even better off."[16] As for global warming, our worries "could be seen as a search for a nemesis, to punish our over-consumption, a penalty for our playing the Sorcerer's apprentice."[17]

In the summer of 2005, a few weeks before a summit of leaders of developed countries, Dr. Bruce Allen, the head of the elite U.S. National Academy of Sciences, and his counterparts in the other seven G8 nations (Canada, France, Germany, Italy, Japan, Russia, and the United Kingdom) as well as those in Brazil, China, and India, issued the following statement:

> The scientific understanding of climate change is now sufficiently clear
> to justify nations taking prompt action. It is vital that all nations identify
> cost-effective steps that they can take now, to contribute to substantial
> and long-term reduction of net global greenhouse gas emissions.[18]

This statement was remarkable because scientists of high stature are averse to participating in political debates. If and when they enter the realm of public affairs to urge world leaders to take action, scientific consensus regarding a problem must be virtually unassailable. Easterbrook's and Lomborg's misstatements about global warming speak volumes about the two authors' penchant for exaggerating facts to shape fundamentally non-factual, and certainly unscientific policy arguments that offer scant proof one way or the other regarding the actual condition of the global environment.

## Regulation Does More Harm Than Good

Closely related to the observation that industrialization—and chemicals—bring enormous benefits to people is the argument that government interference through regulation will do far more harm than good. Advocates of this point of view contend that regulation imposes excessive costs and, adding insult to injury, these costs are passed directly on to the poor, depriving them of other necessities and impairing their overall quality of life. They say that these costs result because the government bureaucrats who craft regulation are astoundingly incompetent.

### OUT-OF-CONTROL COSTS

According to the U.S. Chamber of Commerce, the cost of *all* federal regulations to small businesses is as high as $7,000 per employee.[19] John Graham, at the time of his testimony the influential administrator of the Office of Information and Regulatory Affairs (OIRA) in the Office of Management and Budget (OMB), told Congress in May 2004 that manufacturing firms face a regulatory burden that is five times higher than firms in other sectors, largely because of environmental regulations.[20]

Since neither set of numbers is accompanied by an explanation of methodology, it is unclear how the Chamber or Graham accomplished the monumental task of tallying such a complicated universe of numbers in anything approaching an accurate way. After all, this figure includes everything from rules put out by the Internal Revenue Service and the Immigration and Naturalization Service to rules governing employee pensions and health benefits to rules designed to safeguard consumers, workers, and the environment. There are undoubtedly some wasteful regulations in this mix, but presumably neither the Chamber of Commerce nor Graham would go so far as to suggest that all the rules or even a majority of them should be repealed.

Another highly influential measurement of regulatory costs was initiated in 1986 by John Morrall, an OMB career economist, in the form of a table purporting to show how much money per life saved, or death avoided, we spent on public health, safety, and environmental regulation. Among other things, the table showed that OSHA required the nation to spend *$72 billion per life saved* to control formaldehyde exposures in the workplace. EPA controls on burying hazardous and municipal solid waste in the ground supposedly cost *$3 billion per life saved*. Of course, no informed person can read these figures without thinking costs are disproportionate to benefits and that we could save more lives using the money another way, making Morrall's table an extraordinarily powerful weapon in the campaign to deregulate.

Since the release of Morrall's table in 1986, dozens of iterations of it have circulated, including many that do not attribute the work to Morrall and some that contain arbitrary changes to his original text. Its most famous appearance was in the 1993 book *Breaking the Vicious Circle: Toward Effective Risk Regulation* by Supreme Court Justice Stephen Breyer.[21] In the book Breyer contends that America squanders excessive amounts of money pursuing ephemeral risks and that we should appoint a group of scientific and other technical experts to reorder the regulatory system. The Morrall table was the prime exhibit in support of these arguments.

In researching their insightful book *Priceless: On Knowing the Cost of Everything and the Value of Nothing*,[22] law Professor Lisa Heinzerling and economics Professor Frank Ackerman investigated the background data Morrall used and discovered that, in all its iterations, the table had three fatal flaws:[23] first, it incorporated figures on rules that were never issued and therefore have not cost anyone anything. Far from being a precise numerical evaluation of actual mistakes, the table misleadingly implied that federal agencies went ahead with bad ideas when in fact they did not. Second, to derive the cost per life saved, Morrall divided the total costs of rules by estimates of lives saved, thus ignoring most nonfatal health effects and understating benefits. Third, the table significantly understated the benefits of controlling pollution because it was based on steep discounting. Again, discounting is a mathematical methodology that computes how much one would need to invest today at a given interest rate to come up with the value of a death or disease caused by environmental pollution that does not occur until some point several years from now.

Morrall has never addressed these problems, and his table continues to circulate through policymaking circles, without modification. The idea of wasting money on runaway regulatory costs is offensive, but more so, say the deregulators, because these unjustified costs are passed directly on to consumers, imposing a premium on the costs of consumer goods and services, and leading to job loss in particularly fragile industrial sectors. They add that excessive regulations impose the greatest burden on the poor, many of whom live so close to the margin of economic viability that extra costs for such essentials as electricity could be life-threatening. As we shall see in Chapter 7, "Ozone Case Study," some go so far as to claim that costly regulations actually kill people by depriving them of the money they need for other necessities.

### STUPID BUREAUCRATS

Former U.S. Senator (R-ME) and Secretary of Defense Bill Cohen once said, "Government is the enemy until you need a friend."[24] Because regulated industries and their conservative allies have been highly successful in convincing policy makers that most serious environmental problems have been resolved, it is relatively easy for them to extend their logic one more step: government is the enemy, and no one needs it to be a friend. This argument has two contemporary pillars.

As earlier chapters have explained, traditional conservatives have worked for several decades to establish government bureaucrats as the central scapegoat for all that ails the regulatory system. Among the most prominent examples is *The Death of Common Sense: How Law Is Suffocating America* by Philip Howard, according to the book jacket a "practicing" lawyer.[25] Howard mercilessly chides the legal profession for engaging in a fruitless effort to make laws and regulations precise in order to offer people "protection through certainty" from bad drugs, bad food, unsafe products, and pollution.[26] The result is the creation of arbitrary power held by bureaucrats who have become lost in their own intricate webs of red tape, losing judgment and wisdom in the process:

> Avoiding arbitrary authority is a wonderful idea. Instead we have handed it out: When laws cannot be complied with, individual officials, who supposedly have no discretion, have complete power. Why do you think lawyers, who more often act like assassins, are generally so polite when they go down to the SEC or some other government agency? Because they know that no matter how precise the rules, the regulators can find a way to do them in.[27]

Howard does not try to make his case through statistics but rather tells story after story about bureaucracy run amok. The stories are not footnoted. Instead, the book contains several pages of sources at the end, along with the author's assertion that the incidents described in the book come from interviews conducted in 1994 and 1995 as well as accounts in popular print media. A deeper probe of the anecdotes reveals important factual errors and not a little exaggeration.

Perhaps the most relevant example for our purposes is Howard's allegation that misguided regulation of lead paint in Massachusetts housing has proved lethal.[28] Howard acknowledges that lead poisoning can be very serious for children. But, he argues, blanket requirements that lead paint be removed wherever it is located only put the children in greater risk because "scraping away lead paint can be a messy process" exposing children to more lead than if the paint had been left alone. Using their "arbitrary power" and not their common sense, bureaucrats in Massachusetts decreed that "lead paint must be removed in any household where there is a child under the age of six; no exceptions permitted." Howard claims that "horrible stories of children's blood lead levels worsening after abatement began to appear in the press," all attributable to the mindless, rigid, even evil bureaucracy.

As we saw in Chapter 1, "Predicates," the elimination of lead from gasoline was a marvelous success for EPA, given lead's toxicity and persistence in the environment (it does not degrade) and the grave risks very low exposures pose for children. The primary remaining source of lead poisoning is the contact children and their mothers have with lead in paint sold before 1978. EPA estimates that as many as 900,000 children have blood lead levels above those considered safe.

This type of paint, used for its lasting color, is extraordinarily toxic because it is composed of as much as 40 percent lead. The dust produced by the normal wear of the paint is the primary pathway for childhood exposure, and painting over original coats of the paint does not solve this problem, making removal the safest course of action. However, because removal is expensive, Massachusetts *never* required that all lead paint be removed no matter what. Rather, lead paint must only be removed if it is chipping, peeling, or flaking or it is present on certain surfaces such as window frames and window sills where normal abrasion produces hazardous dust or where toddlers might mouth the surfaces.[29] Children and their families must be removed from the premises before cleanup begins, to return only after certified, trained workers have finished remediation.

No one could reasonably dispute Howard's observation that bureaucracies, like any other human endeavor, produce instances of harmful excess. Yet his book reads more like a call to arms to destroy government than a thoughtful analysis of where it should go from here. In effect, Howard has opened a new battlefield in an ongoing war in which he and his fellow combatants believe they can only prevail by vanquishing existing bureaucracies, leaving regulation to lawsuits brought after people have already suffered damage.

### Bigger Fish to Fry

Because they believe that chemicals are of great value and that the most significant environmental problems are solved, regulated industries contend that the country shoulders huge lost opportunity costs as a direct result of excessive regulation. Or, in other words, the excessive costs of regulatory compliance would be better spent to solve far more pressing problems such as reducing U.S. dependence on foreign oil by subsidizing exploration at home, bringing democracy to the Middle East, or reforming public education. This argument begs the crucial questions of who benefits from further progress on environmental issues and why that progress is any less important than other policy goals.

In any event, even assuming that those other goals are more important, we have one, and only one, way to set important national priorities in America: except in cases of extreme national emergencies, the executive and legislative branches confer with a broad range of interested parties and develop proposals, the most important of which are written into legislation, considered by Congress, passed, and then sent to the president's desk for signature. Congress has not repealed the sturdy framework of environmental laws, and until it does, arguing that government should simply bypass mandates is not just illegal but fundamentally antidemocratic.

## Corporate Environmentalism

### Rhetoric and Reality

As the above review indicates, advocates of deregulation have developed a strong, well-integrated framework of arguments against the system as we know it. Of course, it is possible that Washington posturing by think tanks and trade associations has little to do with how regulated industries behave. The fact that companies large and small have enthusiastically enlisted in the campaign against regulation may not affect whether they comply with the regulations or take additional steps to protect the environment. If corporations confine their bitter complaints about government overreaching to the political arena but cooperate in the implementation of regulatory requirements, so-called "corporate environmentalism" might be a real candidate to replace more rigid controls. One test of this possibility is how companies position themselves during the rulemaking process, when few headlines are made and they have an opportunity to make rules better without sacrificing their broader political message that government is too intrusive.

It is hard to overstate the astonishing diversity of the industrial sectors and types of firms that are regulated by environmental laws. They run the gamut from multinational corporations of tremendous sophistication to small, single-proprietor businesses that provide services such as car repair, dry cleaning, or metal refinishing. Regulated industries include public institutions that generate pollution, from sewage treatment plants in small towns to military bases covering tens of thousands of acres. The largest private-sector companies were the first to be chosen for regulatory controls, and they have been living with EPA mandates for more than three decades. The Agency's relatively recent efforts to push regulatory controls down to mid-sized and small businesses have been arduous, to say the least.

Like all rules imposed on industry, environmental protection creates winners and losers and gives winners a high stake in maintaining the status quo. For a variety of reasons, some companies may comply with costly regulations early and thoroughly while their less prominent or stable competitors drag their feet, gaining short-term economic advantage until and unless government enforcement officials step in. This situation undermined the Superfund toxic waste program when the most visible deep pockets were compelled to pay for cleanup early, while less prominent companies that made the same contribution to the problem refused to contribute. Alternatively, industrial sectors comprised of large companies may be only partially responsible for an environmental condition but because of their size and visibility could be the primary group that is regulated, with categories of smaller sources left free to pollute. This phenomenon has occurred with respect to some air pollution problems when EPA staff just did not want to go to the trouble of rounding up these minor entities. Both scenarios are deeply disturbing to the large companies that bear the brunt of such outcomes.

Now it would be logical to think that on the basis of pure self-interest, the great diversity of regulated industries would respond to rulemaking proposals in equally diverse ways, with some sectors or individual companies supporting a proposal and others opposing it, depending on perceptions of their companies' financial interests. Yet with rare exceptions, this outcome does not occur. Instead, despite competing interests and multiple underlying tensions, the business community manages to appear as a monolith opposed to regulation in any form.

More than just Washington lobbyists are involved in the advancement of this unified front. Down to the plant manager in a town whose representative holds a swing vote in Congress, industry opposition has contributed in large measure to the gridlock that has prevented passage of most major environmental legislation since 1990. In fact, since conservative Republicans emerged as the House of Representatives majority in 1994, regulated industries have rarely negotiated any kind of consensus with environmentalists and federal and state regulators on protective regulation.[30]

There are several likely explanations for this phenomenon. Despite their diversity, regulated industries were united in a defensive posture by the moralistic approaches environmentalists took to regulation from the early days of the modern environmental movement, circa 1970. During this period, environmentalists routinely compiled "dirty dozen" lists of companies that produced the most pollution.[31] Similarly, the Superfund toxic waste cleanup statute was passed in 1980 and reauthorized in 1986 with the help of the slogan "polluter pays," suggesting that companies deliberately spoiled the environment and must compensate the government for these transgressions, even though the use of landfills to dump hazardous waste was legal at the time.[32] These characterizations worked well in garnering public support for stringent legislation, especially during the period of congressional backlash in response to the Reagan administration's deregulatory agenda. But they also provoked the undying enmity of their primary targets, especially executives in the oil and chemical industries, who felt offended not just in institutional terms but as individuals.

Regulated industries are interrelated horizontally as well as vertically, in a complex web of manufacturers of feedstock chemicals, suppliers of fabricated parts, customers for intermediate and end products, and service providers such as insurers and bankers. Allowing their united front against regulation to splinter, especially in controversies with a high profile, could cause unanticipated reverberations and lost business across and down all of these lines.

Finally, unified opposition to environmental regulation has worked very well. Despite efforts by environmentalists in Congress and EPA officials to find allies among the business community for large-scale initiatives, it is extremely rare to find business groups on both sides of such debates. Individual companies may privately report to their elected representatives regarding whether a proposal would benefit them, but at the trade association level, opposition appears uniform.[33]

In sum, from every visible angle, it appears that the business community, in all its diversity, is more hostile to proactive environmental proposals now than at any previous time since EPA's creation in 1970. From the grassroots to the boardroom, the people who make decisions for these corporations have embraced the cause of deregulation. But does this surprisingly widespread phenomenon mean that they also refuse to engage in practices that are helpful to the environment? And, even if they do engage in such activities, what is likely to happen if regulation and the threat of penalties disappear?

## Incentives and Disincentives

Over the past fifteen years, university-based business school academics have developed a rich literature regarding "corporate environmentalism."[34] Relying primarily on anecdotal evidence, these experts have argued persuasively that corporate environmentalism is a real phenomenon inside a significant number of prominent companies and is likely to be a strengthening trend. As important, perhaps because they excel in the study of corporate management as opposed to national policy-making polemics, not one of these experts argues that this trend would continue in the absence of a regulatory system. Instead, they acknowledge that strategizing to avoid government intervention is a major incentive for corporations to establish voluntary programs to prevent pollution.

Andrew J. Hoffman, a professor at the University of Michigan's Ross School of Business, has produced the best and most comprehensive body of work, exemplified by *From Heresy to Dogma: An Institutional History of Corporate Environmentalism*, originally published in 1993 and reprinted in 2001.[35] Hoffman and his colleagues argue that corporations should have ample incentives to develop voluntary environmental programs because such initiatives are a cost-effective way to avoid regulatory enforcement. They add that good environmental practices are capable of generating a large financial return because they reduce consumption of expensive raw materials and energy. Finally, like the rest of the human race, corporate employees have a large stake in solving environmental problems like global warming that could prove catastrophic if left unaddressed. Several of the nation's largest corporations have begun voluntary initiatives to control carbon emissions, a main contributor to climate change, both because corporate leaders believe it is the right thing to do and because they believe that internationally arranged, government-sponsored controls are inevitable.

All of these incentives are powerful in their own right and in combination. The question, however, is not whether there are incentives for doing well by doing right but whether in the absence of a mandatory regulatory system these incentives are powerful enough to override the drive for short-term profits. Even advocates of free-market environmentalism do not argue that a wish to do good is sufficient to motivate socially responsible corporate behavior. Rather, they assume that a free marketplace will spawn sufficient wealth controlled by nonprofit entities to create economic value for clean air and water. A leading example is the Nature Conservancy, which buys land in order to keep it pristine. If free-marketers are wrong, and even if they are only partially right, an unfortunate dynamic could be established. At least in theory, government regulation levels the playing field for companies in the same industrial sector, forcing them to spend roughly equivalent sums on compliance. With regulation gone, and especially if no strong market for environmental quality develops, firms that take the high road will suffer competitively, unless it is also true that the high road saves them money.

It seems intuitively apparent that engineering innovations that reduce the consumption of raw materials and, improve process efficiency, reduce waste, and conserve energy should also reduce corporate costs. The problem is that such investments must compete with other uses for corporate profits that have higher rates of financial return. In an economy that is fast-paced and undergoing equally rapid globalization, environmental investments, which often pay out over a longer time period than other investments, may lose more often than they win. There is surprisingly little public information or academic research on whether this hypothesis is true. The most prominent experiment involved an extremely unusual collaboration between Dow Chemical Company and the Natural Resources Defense Council (NRDC), one of the nation's most effective and aggressive environmental groups.[36]

In a nutshell, NRDC, Dow, and a group of local environmentalists agreed to investigate "pollution prevention" opportunities at the company's Midland, Michigan plant. As a term of art, "pollution prevention" means eliminating emissions as discharges, not treating or managing them after release. The Dow plant handled some very toxic chemicals when it manufactured Saran Wrap, the insecticide Dursban, the herbicide 2,4-D, and a host of other pesticides and industrial chemicals. In the end, the investigation was a stunning success, achieving a 43 percent cut in emissions and saving Dow some $5.3 million per year, balanced against one-time expenses of $3.2 million. Despite this success, Dow has never repeated this kind of collaboration.

What makes this admittedly anecdotal piece of evidence troubling is that Dow is considered one of the most progressive companies environmentally. It was among the first Fortune 100 companies to "go green," in part to compensate for the extraordinarily negative reputation the company had as a result of its manufacture of napalm and Agent Orange for U.S. military use in Vietnam. If the corporate-environmentalism-is-profitable experiment failed at Dow, it is even more likely to fail at other companies. This particular episode had a happy ending. But if exhaustive, plant-by-plant work with constant prodding by local activists and national environmental groups is what it takes to make similar initiatives succeed, the development of corporate environmentalism in the absence of enforceable regulation will unfold very slowly if at all.

The Dow case had a ripple effect in the larger corporate community, motivating a deeper examination of corporate motivations and effective external incentives. Among the most promising reforms is a body of research and commentary known as "green accounting."[37] Green accounting is an effort to reorganize corporate methods of accounting for profit and loss so that environmental costs are attributed to the unit of the company responsible for creating them or, conversely, the managers able to prevent their occurrence. Often, environmental costs (e.g., cleanup of Superfund sites, investments in pollution control, and payment of government penalties and associated legal fees) are attributed to corporate overhead rather than to the profit centers that could act to avoid such costs. If companies do not have a good grip on how much they spend to either dispose of hazardous waste or clean up the legacy of past disposal, the savings realized from pollution prevention investments will always appear deflated.

Another beneficial outcome of the Dow experience and the widening discussion of corporate environmentalism is a new emphasis on "environmental management systems" (EMS).[38] Large companies have long had environmental departments to ensure compliance. Too often, however, these departments were isolated from line managers and from chief executive officers. Integrating environmental experts into the chain of command and giving them adequate authority to change internal practices in a proactive way could remedy these bad dynamics.

## Conclusion

Hoffman and other proponents of corporate environmentalism argue that few chief executive officers of the largest corporations would willingly and consciously risk significant exposure to cleanup costs and penalties and that the multiplication of creative corporate programs should give us great hope for the future. These conclusions may well be right. But it seems clear from Hoffman's work and other information that corporate environmentalism would not exist in anything approaching today's scale, much less continue to grow, unless government plays a central role in setting the rules for behavior.

Especially during a period when protecting the environment is not just out of fashion but openly derided, the argument that we will gain more progress from the carrot if we forswear the stick simply does not hold together. Being solicitous of corporate sensitivities may be a wise and effective tactic in many contexts, but corporate volunteerism is not enough to justify tearing down the infrastructure of regulatory protections we have gone to such pains to erect.

**PART II**

# SYMPTOMS

# Introduction to Part II

Because efforts to protect children's health from pollution have produced a welter of conflicting information, it is no small task to produce convincing evidence that the diagnoses made in Part I are correct. Should the case be made using a raft of statistics assembled into patterns that appear utterly compelling, as Gregg Easterbrook and Bjorn Lomborg have done? How about well-selected anecdotes modeled on Philip Howard's best-selling work? Or would it be better to interview eminent experts to see if there is some kind of consensus about aspects of what I have said?

In the end, I decided to present three detailed case studies of the government's efforts to control pollutants that pose special hazards for children: mercury, perchlorate, and ozone. The case studies examine the scientific, legal, and economic issues that arise as government struggles to address these threats. My goal was to explain the disputes as clearly as possible to illustrate the most important flaws of the existing system. Clarity proved at least as big a challenge as analysis.

Use of the word "detailed" must be qualified. To expert observers and participants in the debate over any of these issues, the following three chapters are likely to appear superficial, omitting crucial facts and interpretive nuance. After all, the government's travails in formulating policy regarding any one of these three toxins could fill an entire book that would still miss many interesting points. But in this case, as it is so often, the perfect is most definitely the enemy of the good. Reams of materials are available to those who wish to pursue these topics in greater depth, and some of it is suggested in the endnotes.

Some readers may already be persuaded by the analysis presented in Part I. Others will never be persuaded, believing either that there are no serious problems with current efforts to protect children from pollution or that there is little more we can or should do. And then there will be a third group, unfamiliar with the territory, intuitively concerned about the future, but uncertain about which of the polarized perspectives clamoring for their attention should be believed. The case studies will be of most value to this last group, providing the opportunity to sift through a set of facts in context, applying common sense and value judgments to reach their own conclusions.

Because each case study takes place in the same context—the federal government's response to evidence that exposure to a toxic chemical poses risks—a summary of their common elements may be useful to readers not familiar with the ways business is transacted in the nation's capital.

## The Players

### The Executive Branch

Government officials appear in several roles. Under the category of "regulator" are two distinct groups—political appointees and career staff—who often conflict with each other. Both groups sometimes lay claim to the "white hat" or the "black hat" in the three case studies. Most importantly, however, EPA is increasingly in the grip of political appointees who are dismissive, even hostile, toward career staff.

The regulators are overseen by the White House OMB, which has authority to review and reject all regulations before they become final and which is responsible for negotiating agency and department budget requests. The OMB staff is dominated by economists who see their role as riding herd on overly aggressive regulators. Their power is second to none, and their role is almost entirely hidden from public view. OMB answers to the White House, where high-level staff members monitor environmental policy from a distance, doing their best to keep the president's fingerprints off controversial decisions.

The executive branch also encompasses federal institutions that have caused pollution on a staggering scale: the military, the Department of Energy (DOE), and the National Aeronautics and Space Administration (NASA). This group is central to the perchlorate story.

## The Legislative Branch

One of the most significant paradoxes in the nation's political life is the absolute refusal of congressional conservatives to pay any deference to the decisions made by past congresses. These rank-and-file conservatives are as deeply frustrated by legislative gridlock as they are angry that they cannot repeal all the laws they do not like. But they are perfectly capable of defunding the laws' implementation, amending statutes by appropriations riders, and continuously challenging the goals the laws were intended to achieve. As discussed in Chapter Two, "The Rise of Special Interest Conservatism," Congress has assumed different stances toward regulation over the years, from enthusiastic concern about the effect of pollution on public health in 1970s and early 1980s to cautious retreat from these ambitious and expensive initiatives in the late 1980s and early 1990s to full-blooded attack on environmental programs ever since. In large measure, the latest shift in direction has taken place quietly, with most legislative leaders reluctant to provoke a backlash among the public, which by large margins remains supportive of strong environmental protection.

## The Judicial Branch

Once EPA has eked out a rule or other "final agency action" (guidance, toxicological profile, permit, etc.), environmental statutes provide avenues for challenging the Agency's decision in federal court. Judges hearing such cases are asked to decide whether EPA interpreted its statutory mandate correctly; exceeded its statutory authority; made a decision that has a "reasonable basis" in the record it compiled during the rulemaking or other procedure; was "arbitrary" or "capricious" in its decision making; or took action inconsistent with the U.S. Constitution. The U.S. Department of Justice represents EPA in court, opposing teams of industry or environmental organization lawyers. Such litigation is very expensive to pursue, involving years of effort and hundreds of thousands, even millions, of dollars in legal fees.

Reviewing courts do not gather evidence independently but rather stick to an examination of the rulemaking or other record compiled by EPA, also known as a "docket." It is not uncommon for dockets to include tens of thousands of pages of material. Judges do not attempt to rewrite the rules or other decisions they have overturned; instead they remand the decisions to EPA for proceedings consistent with the opinions.

The federal courts are drifting steadily to the right as the Reagan, Bush I, and Bush II administrations' judicial appointments fill the seats available in most districts. But this trend is slow and stately in comparison to the rapid evolution of the executive branch. Above all, the courts take precedents and the implications of overruling them very seriously. They may be critical of Agency decisions, but they do not overrule them without thinking of the long-term consequences.

### The National Academies

The National Academies are a group of independent, nonprofit institutions supported by contributions from individuals, foundations, and corporations. They have an impeccable reputation as collegial, self-governed institutions run by eminent scientists, economists, engineers, doctors, and other technical experts. The academies leverage their funding by persuading the best experts in the country to sit on interdisciplinary panels convened to resolve controversial questions. The experts donate their time in exchange for the prestige of working with eminent colleagues to write influential reports on high-profile controversies. The academies encompass four separate entities: the National Academy of Sciences, the Institute of Medicine, the National Research Council, and the National Academy of Engineering. In the past few years, referral of regulatory controversies to National Academies peer-review panels has become a standard tactic used to resolve controversies about the public health risks posed by toxics.

The scientists who agree to serve are reimbursed for travel expenses but are not otherwise compensated for their time. Their incentives to participate in what is inevitably a time-consuming enterprise are the prestige of being associated with the Academies and their interest in affecting the outcome of the issue the panel was considering. Unfortunately, these nonmonetary incentives also tilt the playing field in favor of scientists who are paid, usually by industry or, in this case, the military to take a specific interest in the chemical at issue.

### Regulated Industries

Industries affected by environmental regulation and associated activities run the gamut from small to large businesses and from the manufacturing to the financial and service sectors. Their interests are amazingly disparate, but their opposition to environmental regulation has remained virtually monolithic. Trade associations and conservative think tanks with large staffs of experts represent their interests before Congress and the agencies and provide the intellectual foundation for their advocacy.

## Public-Interest Organizations

Generally supported by individuals and foundations rather than corporate funding, these organizations can be divided into two categories: grassroots advocacy groups that stress political work and groups that focus on matching the expertise of industry and government with their own comparable professionals.

## The Media

National news media cover the environment only sporadically. Even when reporters do venture onto this clamorous battlefield, few have the support of their news organizations for in-depth reporting. Notable exceptions are publications like *National Journal*, *Washington Monthly*, *Congressional Quarterly*, *American Prospect*, *The Nation*, and *Mother Jones*, but even those publications wait for stories that are controversial and that can be unraveled in weeks, not months. Far more extensive coverage is provided by a robust trade press, including the Bureau of National Affair's *Environment Reporter*, the Environmental Law Institute's *Environmental Law Reporter* and *Environmental Forum*, and *Inside EPA*. This last set of publications is read by the vast majority of people who participate in environmental policy making.

## The Process

### Legislation

Over the past fifteen years, Congress has been gridlocked on environmental issues, passing just a handful of new laws and leaving EPA to work under existing statutory authorities. Congressional gridlock in the statutory arena has not meant that Congress entirely avoids environmental issues. In addition to lending sporadic oversight, members of Congress have become adept at attaching riders to EPA appropriations bills that forbid it to use money appropriated by Congress to pursue a controversial course of action. While this last development is particularly damaging to any semblance of a reasoned and accessible rulemaking process, it is likely to continue until Congress manages to extricate itself from the political standoff it has created.

## Rulemaking

Environmental policy making is not for the impatient. It can take many years to:

1. enact a statute containing a detailed mandate for affirmative action;
2. formulate a rulemaking proposal, which includes vetting the proposal within the executive branch by submitting it to OMB and other affected agencies and departments;
3. print it in the *Federal Register*, the official record on administrative activities;
4. consider the public comments received in response to the rulemaking notice;
5. revise the rule in response to the comments;
6. have the final rule vetted within the executive branch;
7. publish the final rule;
8. withstand congressional oversight that is usually instigated by disappointed participants in the rulemaking process;
9. defend subsequent lawsuits challenging the rule, with the option open to the court to remand it for further agency consideration; and
10. at the end of this very long road, implement the rule with limited resources.

Bogged down in rulemaking, EPA has tried to make policy through informal "guidance documents" that set standards for industrial behavior. Its authority to take bold steps in that format has also been challenged in court, although the Agency continues to use this approach.

The three case studies that follow are at differing stages of development. The controversies over mercury and ozone have reached the courts, where vigorous challenges to final rules are pending at this writing. Perchlorate is still at a pre-rulemaking stage, mired in a debate over what reductions of the chemical will adequately protect public health.

All three case studies were chosen because they involve direct threats to children. Mercury poisoning of pregnant women through the consumption of contaminated fish causes neurological damage in their unborn children, including loss of IQ points and impairment of other cognitive abilities and fine motor skills. Perchlorate interferes with the formation of thyroid hormones by blocking the uptake of iodide, consequently causing problems with normal development of the nervous system in utero and after birth. Ozone is responsible for exacerbating an epidemic of asthma that afflicts growing numbers of America's kids.

## CHAPTER 5

# Mercury Case Study

*The population at highest risk is the children of women who consumed large amounts of fish and seafood during pregnancy. The committee concludes that the risk to that population is likely to be sufficient to result in an increase in the number of children who have to struggle to keep up in school and who might require remedial classes or special education.*

NATIONAL RESEARCH COUNCIL, 2000

*The push to regulate mercury emissions from power plants is an attempt by extreme environmental groups to hinder economic growth and force jobs overseas. Recent science shows that fish consumption, the only major cause of mercury exposure is not harmful to Americans and should be an integral part of a healthy diet. . . . These anti-job, anti-growth extremists need to quit scaring the public with bogus information.*

BILL KOVACS, U.S. CHAMBER OF COMMERCE RADIO ACTUALITY, 2003

## Overview

The Mad Hatter in *Alice in Wonderland* is the first well-known, if fictional, victim of industrial mercury poisoning. Mercury was used to make hats stiff in the days when Lewis Carroll picked up his pen, and hatters were poisoned to such an extent that they suffered irreversible dementia. Fortunately, the acute poisoning that drove hatters mad is relatively rare today. Unfortunately, scientific research has revealed that far lower doses of mercury can cause irreversible neurological damage not in workers handling the toxin, but in the very young and the unborn. The Industrial Age has produced such widespread infusion of mercury into the environment that we must now cope with dangerous levels of mercury in fish, a major component of the human food chain.[1]

The National Research Council (NRC), which is part of the National Academies—the nation's foremost scientific institution, concluded in 2000 that when pregnant women eat fish contaminated by mercury on a regular basis, their children are at risk for permanent neurological damage.[2] The federal Centers for Disease Control and Prevention (CDC) has assembled statistics showing that as a result of this consumption, 5.6 percent of American women of childbearing age have levels of mercury in their bloodstreams that could harm their unborn children. On the basis of those statistics, CDC estimates that as many as 300,000 babies are born each year with blood mercury levels above the maximum recommended by NRC. Faculty members from the nation's leading medical schools say that even these disturbing statistics understate the problem because venous (from the vein) blood tests of pregnant mothers *understate* the levels of mercury in their babies' blood by 70 percent.[3] Taking the higher concentrations of mercury in babies' blood into account, the scientists estimate that as many as 637,000 babies are born annually with blood mercury levels above the standard.

EPA regulations accomplished significant reductions in mercury pollution from batteries and from incinerators that burn municipal and hospital waste.[4] As required by the Clean Air Act, EPA then turned its attention to the two largest remaining sources of mercury air emissions: nine antiquated "chlor-alkali" plants that use mercury cells to manufacture chlorine and coal-fired power plants.

EPA issued its final chlor-alkali rule in December 2003.[5] After receiving comments suggesting that those facilities have "fugitive," or uncounted, emissions of up to sixty-five tons of mercury annually, as compared to the estimated forty-eight tons of mercury produced annually by some 1,100 coal-fired power plants, EPA nevertheless decided to forgo any binding numerical limits on such emissions. Instead, it required that workers do periodic visual inspections of equipment that holds hundreds of tons of pure mercury, largely a fruitless exercise since mercury vapor is colorless and odorless. Two years later, after a decade of study and bureaucratic hand wringing, EPA announced that it had adopted a rule to reduce mercury emissions from power plants but that these requirements would not go into effect until 2018. Eleven northeastern states and assorted environmental groups immediately challenged the Agency in court, alleging that the rule was far too weak to comply with the Clean Air Act's mandates.[6]

So audacious are these outcomes that they have pushed the polarization of environmental issues to new heights, shocking moderates and progressives and emboldening conservatives. The blatancy of these heavily politicized decisions is troubling enough as a precedent for future controversies. But the real crime is that it will be years, if not decades, before government initiatives to prevent mercury poisoning get back on track. The harm to public health caused by these delays will be compounded by what the *Christian Science Monitor* has called the "new coal rush."[7] According to the Department of Energy, 140 new coal-fired electric power plants with the capacity to power 85 million American homes will be built by 2025 in as many as forty states. The push toward coal is exacerbated by the war in Iraq, rising gasoline prices, and the damage that Hurricane Katrina caused to the nation's oil and natural gas production infrastructure.

The mercury controversy has played out on all three fronts in the larger war over deregulation: science, law, and economics. Regulated industries and their right-wing allies argue that the science on the threat mercury exposure poses to children is not definitive. In the alternative, they say that even if there is a risk, it cannot fairly be attributed to domestic plants but rather is caused by international sources that make far less effort to control pollution. Any portion of the risk that is caused by American sources would be too expensive to address. And if there is a risk caused by domestic sources that we could afford to address, the law allows adoption of the least expensive and least effective approaches. This chapter considers each of these inconsistent arguments in turn.

## The Science

### Implications for Public Health

Mercury is an extremely toxic heavy metal that causes major neurological problems even at low doses in fetuses exposed through their mothers' bloodstream and in babies exposed through breast milk, drinking water, and other sources. Mercury is extraordinarily "persistent" in the environment, meaning that it does not break down into less harmful substances. Mercury contamination in water and fish originates largely as air emissions that fall to the ground and into the water. Methylmercury (MeHg), the form of the metal that is most toxic to people, results from the interaction between elemental mercury and microorganisms in soil and water.

The metal is an essential element that occurs in nature, but industrialization over the past century has raised the anthropogenic share of the planet's circulating mercury to 70 percent, largely as a result of manufacturing, coal-fired energy generation, and the combustion of solid waste.[8] The mercury circulates and recirculates from air to water to soil and back again, traveling thousands of miles in the process and causing what scientists call the "global mercury cycle." EPA estimates that worldwide air emissions sources total 4,400 to 7,500 metric tons per year (TPY), with 3,080 to 5,250 TPY deriving from anthropogenic sources and the remainder from nature.[9] Consequently, like greenhouse gases and climate change, resolution of the problem will require international cooperation on an unprecedented scale.

Among the first steps in EPA's abortive attempts to reduce industrial mercury emissions was the establishment of a "reference dose" (RfD) for methylmercury. A reference dose is the estimated amount of a chemical that people can absorb on a daily level without a risk of adverse health effects over their expected lifetime. Exposures *above* the RfD over a lifetime may pose a risk and should be avoided, with risk rising in proportion to increased exposure. EPA's RfD for methylmercury is 0.1 microgram (one-tenth of one-millionth of a gram) per kilogram body weight per day (microgram/kilogram/day), or 5.8 parts per billion (ppb) in the blood, which translates into a tiny fraction of an ounce per pound of total body weight.

EPA's low number sparked such a firestorm within the utility industry that Congress directed EPA to request that the National Academies' NRC convene an expert panel and review all the available science. Although NRC does not do original research, its peer-review reports of available data are considered the gold standard for such work. In the last several years, virtually any significant controversy over EPA's efforts to regulate toxic chemicals has landed in the lap of either the NRC or the National Academy of Sciences, a sister institution that is also part of the National Academies. On the basis of this comprehensive review of the available science, the panel, composed of scientists from all the relevant disciplines, formed a unanimous consensus judgment supporting the EPA reference dose, delivering its analysis in a 335-page report titled *Toxicological Effects of Methyl Mercury*.[10] The panel's conclusions deeply dismayed regulated industries: "On the basis of its evaluation, the committee's consensus is that the value of EPA's [reference dose] is a scientifically justifiable level for the protection of public health."[11]

The 2000 NRC report was a defining moment in the battle over mercury. Because right-wing commentators have made National Academies referrals a hallmark of their crusade to restore "sound science" to regulatory decision making, they were faced with the Hobson's choice of either ignoring the NRC findings or attempting to refute the conclusions of no less authority than their own science court of last resort. They chose to reinterpret the report and, whenever possible, to simply overlook its existence. This reaction suggests that the quest for sound science is neverending and that its proponents are motivated more by the results of the research than its quality.

The NRC panel used the most widely accepted mode of scientific inquiry: an evaluation of the "weight of the available scientific evidence." Such evaluations involve exhaustive efforts to assemble all available, published scientific information regarding mercury's toxicity, derived from a range of scientific disciplines and methodologies. The NRC panel therefore considered: animal studies on the effects of mercury exposures; laboratory investigations into mercury's cellular and subcellular impacts; models that predict the amount of mercury emissions and what happens as they are transported through the environment; "pharmacokinetic modeling" to analyze how the chemical affects the human body once it is ingested or inhaled; and epidemiological studies designed to discern actual patterns of illness in exposed populations.

The electric utility industry approaches the available data from a very different perspective. It disputes the validity of the scientific evidence that does not directly measure the effects of methylmercury exposure on people, arguing that epidemiological studies on actual populations are the only reliable form of testing. Epidemiological studies examine how often the adverse health effect occurs in actual human populations. As the NRC approach to the data indicates, the position that only epidemiological studies suffice as evidence of a link between exposure and illness does not reflect the consensus in the scientific community, which instead follows an approach of looking at all available evidence.

Moreover, in urging that scientists focus exclusively on epidemiological studies as the only reliable evidence, the utility industry does not acknowledge that such studies are notoriously hard to conduct. Often the size of the exposed population to be studied is too small, leading to underpowered studies that cannot reach statistically reliable conclusions. Many confounding factors such as smoking, diet, and heredity can affect and confuse the results, leading scientists to conclude either that a chemical is harmful or that it is not harmful when in fact there is another explanation for these outcomes. The actual levels of exposure experienced by study subjects are extremely difficult to estimate. Finally, as in any study that involves talking to people over time, administrative problems plague such investigations. Study participants move without leaving forwarding addresses; subjects either do not remember or deliberately misreport their behavior; and people change habits of smoking, diet, and so forth in the middle of the study.

Even if one was willing to focus on epidemiological studies, three such investigations have focused on the harm to children caused by their mothers' consumption of mercury-contaminated fish while pregnant. The studies were done in remote locations with indigenous populations that consume very large quantities of fish and do not move around much.[12] Two of those studies—one conducted in New Zealand and the second conducted on the Faroe Islands—found significant neurological effects at low doses. A third study found that with similar exposures, Seychelle Islanders experienced no discernible effects. Although the NRC panel said that all three studies were well designed and carefully conducted, it ultimately concluded that the Faroe Islands study was the most reliable, in part because it was verified by the New Zealand study and in part because the results of the Seychelles study were a clear outlier in the larger body of available scientific information.

Given their focus on epidemiological studies, the opponents of mercury regulation now faced a new challenge: only one of the three epidemiological studies that have been done showed no adverse health effects at low doses, and the NRC concluded that this study, while well conducted, was not rich enough in data to contradict the other two studies. Undaunted, right-wing and industry advocates quickly pressed Dr. Gary Myers, lead author on the Seychelles study, into service in the political realm. Three years after the NRC panel issued its report, Dr. Myers told the U.S. Senate Environment and Public Works Committee: "We do not believe that *there is presently good scientific evidence* that moderate fish consumption is harmful to the fetus."[13] In this simplistic sound bite, Dr. Myers did not limit himself to the results of the Seychelles study. Nor did he acknowledge the existence of contrary scientific evidence. Instead, he was dishonest about the limits of his research and the prevailing view in the scientific community regarding the hazards of low-dose exposures.

Dr. Myers received considerable funding for his study from the U.S. National Institutes of Health (NIH), the Food and Drug Administration (FDA), and the U.S. Department of Health and Human Services (HHS). He also received $486,000 in funding from the Electric Power Research

Institute, the scientific arm of the utility industry.[14] In none of his scientific publications, public statements, and testimony before the Senate did Dr. Myers disclose this funding source. It is certainly possible to do credible scientific research under the sponsorship of industry sources. However, for ethical reasons, it has become standard practice for scientists to disclose their funding sources whenever they publish new research. Dr. Myers' failure to disclose this funding was a mistake in judgment that suggests he is not an objective participant in either the scientific or public policy debates.

So where does all this leave us? The nation's most eminent scientific body has conducted an independent review of the data on the toxicity of methylmercury at low doses and concluded that EPA's reference dose is correct. There is a clear and unacceptable risk, and it is growing. Not only are blood mercury levels elevated in 6 percent of women of child-bearing age and as many as 637,000 newborns annually, the number of states issuing warnings to the public about the danger of ingesting fish caught from local rivers, lakes, and streams has risen from twenty-seven in 1993 to forty-eight in 2004.[15] Fish advisories for mercury now cover 35 percent of lake acres and 24 percent of river miles. These trends are disturbing and suggest that something must be done. But what? Where is the mercury coming from and can we control those sources effectively?

## Tracing the Problem Back to the Source

Of the estimated 3,080 to 5,250 TPY global total of mercury emissions from anthropogenic sources, U.S. sources contribute a relatively small share—according to EPA estimates, approximately 158 tons annually.[16] The relatively small amount of mercury that American sources contribute to the global cycle is the leading edge of industry arguments against further controls. There are factual, logical, and ethical problems with this argument.

Although certain forms of mercury can travel thousands of miles, other forms are deposited locally, in the vicinity of the sources that emit them. Approximately 60 percent of the total mercury deposited in the United States comes from *American*—as opposed to worldwide—*anthropogenic* sources.[17] In fact, a recent study done in Florida contains the one piece of optimistic news about mercury from a scientific perspective: cleaning up local sources—in this case municipal and medical waste incinerators—results in immediate improvement in the amount of mercury in largemouth bass, one of the species most affected by contamination.[18]

This outcome means that we could make significant progress by cutting future mercury emissions despite the continuous slow release of so-called "legacy" mercury that has been stored in the soil and water over several decades and continuing contributions to the global pool by international sources.

There is no dispute that American power plants are far cleaner than sources abroad. But this observation can be taken too far, especially when the speaker ignores the facts on local deposition. Consider the following assertion by the Cato Institute's Patrick Michaels:

> The United States, with about 25 percent of the world's total economic activity, should logically emit about 1000 of these mega grams [of mercury]. But we only throw out, according to the EPA, 144 mega grams, or 3.6 percent of the world's total. That's a pretty good bang for your mercury buck. . . . All of this means that there are plenty of densely populated places on earth . . . that are exposed to one heck of a lot more mercury from power production and other economic activity.[19]

This argument appears to be grounded in a form of economic rough justice: so long as the United States is relatively clean and it is people in other countries who are suffering the most, we are justified in refusing to take action to curb pollution until dirtier countries go first. Of course, as discussed above, right-wing advocates do not concede that mercury poses a public health risk, making this kind of circular reasoning easier to advocate.

But on second thought, this "do not do unto others as you would have them do unto you" inversion of the Golden Rule has some frightening implications for future efforts to resolve international environmental problems. Rather than lead the world by protecting our own citizens, in the process developing technologies that the developing world can use, American industry argues that the United States should ignore the mercury problem until other countries—most notably China—go first. Applied to global warming, however, the other grave international problem that we now confront, this position ricochets: because developed countries contribute the lion's share of the chemicals that cause the problem, no one else should do anything until we go first.

In any event, the electric utility industry is now in the process of refining these arguments by sponsoring a series of new studies designed to trace with more precision where power plant emissions land and whether they are in fact converted to methylmercury deposits in fish after they get there. If performed objectively, these studies could help target pollution reduction efforts at home and abroad, but they come years after Congress told EPA to investigate the need for such controls and to take action. Far from intending an endless quest for perfect information, the Clean Air Act was the lawmakers' best effort to shove the Agency up to the plate.

## The Law

Serious efforts to clean up hazardous air pollutants like mercury began with the enactment of the 1977 Clean Air Act, which directed EPA to figure out what amount of hazardous pollutants in the ambient air that people could safely breathe. The result would be a "health-based standard" that depends on EPA making an explicit finding regarding what specific level of a given pollutant in the ambient air is tolerable from a public health perspective. In order to determine what number is acceptable, the Agency must engage in the complex process of risk assessment described in Chapter 3, "Battered-Agency Syndrome." Prospective regulatory controls raised high economic stakes for a variety of powerful industries, and EPA and the states soon became enmeshed in intricate calculations of ambient mercury levels and—most difficult of all—whether and how those levels of exposure harmed people. The regulatory process broke down so completely that EPA managed to regulate only a handful of hazardous air pollutants in the decade after the 1977 act.

The 1990 amendments to the CAA charted a radically different course.[20] In an effort to cut through EPA's institutional paralysis, Congress went so far as to list 188 specific chemicals, including mercury compounds, deemed hazardous air pollutants. It instructed EPA to stop wringing its hands over safe levels and health-based standards. Instead, Congress adopted a technology-based approach, meaning that EPA was to find the best pollution control equipment available for each category of sources—the maximum achievable control technology (MACT)—and set limits on emissions of hazardous air pollutants on the basis of what was emitted by plants that used the technology. For example, if the category of sources was a group of power plants that could reduce a given pollutant by using a smokestack scrubber, EPA would find the best scrubber in use and require its installation on all new and existing plants. For new plants, the law defined MACT as the best technology used by the cleanest plant. For existing plants, MACT was defined as the technology used by the cleanest 12 percent of sources in the category. The new statute put EPA on a rigorous schedule for completing the standards.[21]

With so many chemicals and sources to address and chronic shortfalls in funding, EPA struggled to keep up with these mandates and inevitably fell behind. By the time it was ready to cope with the chlor-alkali factories and coal-fired power plants, the political backlash against regulation at the national level was in full swing, as demonstrated by the final decisions in both contexts.

## Coddling Nine Old Dirties

Three technologies are used to manufacture chlorine: mercury cell, diaphragm cell, and membrane cell. The second and third technologies, installed at thirty-two plants nationwide, do not use mercury and are significantly more energy efficient than the nine plants that depend on mercury cells, which hold hundreds of tons of pure mercury. These facilities are so outmoded that a new one has not been built in thirty years, and their market share of chlorine production has dwindled to 10 percent of the nation's supply.[22] In fact, some of the Fortune 500 companies that own the nine antiquated plants have the newer, cleaner technologies operating on the same property. Table 5.1 presents a list of the companies that own these facilities, the nine plants' locations, and the water bodies they affect.[23]

Chlor-alkali plants produce chlorine by passing a brine solution through closed cells, compartments thirty to forty feet long and ten feet wide, that are filled with pure mercury. They are voracious consumers of mercury even though only trace amounts of the highly toxic metal end up in their final products. Industry sources estimate that the nine plants use or store approximately 3,000 tons of mercury in any given year. Chlor-akali plants' purchases of mercury depend on fluctuations in the market; they bought 219 tons of the virgin metal in 2003 but were down to 32 tons in 2005. Despite these relatively large numbers, the chlor-akali industry admits to official, or deliberate, emissions of between 6.7 (in 2004) and 8.2 (in 2002) TPY. These discrepancies are stunning, especially compared to the total emissions of the 1,100 facilities in the electric-utility industry, which account for approximately 48 tons annually.

What happens to the mercury that is "lost" in the sense that it is purchased, stored, used but apparently never escapes into the ambient air? The companies claim that the missing mercury is safely trapped in their

**Table 5.1. U.S. Mercury Chlor-Alkali Plants**

| Company | Location | Water Bodies |
|---|---|---|
| Ashta Chemicals Inc. | Ashtabula, OH | Lake Erie, Ashtabula River |
| Occidental Chemical | Muscle Shoals, AL | Pond Creek, Tennessee River |
| | Delaware City, DE* | Red Lion Creek, Delaware River |
| Olin Corp. | Augusta, GA | Savannah River |
| | Charleston, TN | Hiwassee River |
| PPG Industries | Lake Charles, LA | Bayou d'Inde, Calcasieu River Estuary |
| | New Martinsville, WV | Ohio River |
| Pioneer Americas LLC | Saint Gabriel, LA | Mississippi River |
| Vulcan Materials Co. | Port Edwards, WI | Wisconsin River |

*A Chlorine Institute Inc. report released May 15, 2006, states that the Occidental Chemical Company Delaware plant closed in 2005.

plants' piping. Environmentalists say the mercury is discharged as "fugitive" air emissions through leaky pipes and valves. And EPA acknowledges, without a hint of irony, that as far as it can tell, the fate of these missing tons "remains something of an enigma."[24]

On December 19, 2003, EPA announced that chlor-alkali plants could continue to operate indefinitely under a system of regulatory work practices.[25] The centerpiece of those requirements is visual inspection by cell-room workers on a periodic basis. The efficacy of such inspections is so uncertain that EPA refuses to estimate the amount of reductions its rule might achieve. In fact, these requirements are so minimal that EPA admits they will impose "plant-specific annual costs" ranging from $130,000 to $260,000; these figures amount to somewhere between 0.01 and 0.22 percent of their owners' annual revenues. The Agency has made no effort to quantify the benefits of a stronger rule, as it is required to do, dodging the dicey issue of why it is a better idea for the public to assume this risk.

Had EPA mandated that the plants monitor fugitive emissions with real equipment and reduce their emissions to appropriately low levels, some of the plants might well have gone out of business, a result that would have been good for the environment, good for the economy, and a blessing in disguise for the very large companies that continue to nurse them along. The Agency's feckless shirking of its affirmative legal re-

sponsibility to prescribe MACT at such facilities may have been motivated top-down by senior political appointees, or it may have originated
bottom-up from career staff. Whichever theory of EPA's internal machi-
nations one accepts, this episode reveals an Agency so passive in the face
of industry resistance to regulation that it cannot act effectively regardless
of the benefits it could achieve. As long as regulated industry goes along
with its proposals, the Agency conducts only the most perfunctory cost-
benefit analysis and has nothing to fear from its political overseers at the
White House. In an ironic postscript, the rule requiring spot checks of
mercury spills became effective in December 2006, although EPA faces
court action challenging its legality. Meanwhile, grassroots activists led
by the national group, Oceana, pressured company owners to shut down
two plants and convert two others to cleaner technology.

### Trading Poison

In addition to mandating that EPA use a technology-based approach to
reducing hazardous air pollutants, the 1990 Clean Air Act amendments
directed the Agency to perform a study on mercury emissions from power
plants and impose regulatory controls if "necessary and appropriate."[26]
The mercury study was completed and sent to Congress in 1997, three
years after the statutory deadline and three years into the Clinton administration. The Agency continued to dawdle until December 20, 2000,
shortly before Clinton left office, and then issued a regulatory finding
announcing that technology-based mercury controls were in fact both
necessary and appropriate.[27]

For the next three years, EPA staff and a high-level working group
of outside advisors representing the states, environmental groups, and
the utility industry debated the details of how to choose and implement
a requirement that coal-fired plants install MACT. Everyone, including
the industry representatives, assumed that issuance of MACT standards
was a foregone conclusion and that the goal of the working group and
EPA staff was to develop the details of that regulatory regime. EPA had
settled yet another lawsuit with the Natural Resources Defense Council
promising to finalize MACT standards no later than December 2003, and
the group was working against that deadline.[28]

Sometime in the spring of 2003, senior political appointee Jeffrey
Holmstead, the head of EPA's air quality programs, convened a meeting
of the professional staff assigned to the mercury project and dropped a
bombshell: forthwith, EPA would work to develop a "cap and trade" sys-

tem for regulating coal-fired power plants.[29] Holmstead ordered the staff to disband the advisory group without producing additional information on the costs, benefits, and feasibility of MACT controls that the Agency had promised to generate. Career staff were shell-shocked and then paranoid. When I spoke to one of them a few months later to ask an innocuous question about the contents of the Agency's rulemaking record, the staff person implored me to "forget you ever talked to me."

EPA complied with the December 2003 deadline established by its agreement with NRDC, issuing a rulemaking proposal that asked for public comment on two mutually exclusive alternatives: MACT requirements for all new and existing power plants or an emissions trading program that envisioned cleanup by some plants that would then sell their excess allowances to mercury plants that continued to operate without control equipment.[30] The *Los Angeles Times* later revealed that several paragraphs of the text of the trading portion of the proposal were lifted verbatim from materials provided by industry sources, including Latham and Watkins, the law firm where Holmstead practiced before he entered government service.[31]

EPA's final rule, issued in the spring of 2005, rescinded the 2000 finding that mercury was a hazardous air pollutant and embraced a trading scheme.[32] EPA lawyers claim there is no legal impediment to switching horses at the end of the race, so to speak, because the Agency is free to ignore the MACT requirements and use a different part of the Clean Air Act to support its final action. National environmental groups and several northeastern states promptly sued EPA in the federal Court of Appeals for the District of Columbia (D.C.) Circuit, contending that the Agency's change of heart was based on politics and violated the law. Those cases were still pending in late 2006.

Trading systems like the one adopted by EPA impose an overall limit, or cap, on total emissions either nationwide or on a regional basis. The system establishes a "baseline"—e.g., emissions in a given year as reported by all individual power plants—and uses those figures to assign each plant allowances that are akin to mini-permits to emit a certain amount of a pollutant each year. Caps may decline over time, reducing the number of allowances issued on a cumulative and plant-specific basis. If plants do not have enough allowances to cover the emissions they produce in a given year, they must buy additional allowances on the open market, under a privately run auction system.

Conservatives and regulated industries regard trading as far more economically efficient than requiring each plant to install controls, and trading is hailed as the key to reforming the regulatory system. The goal of a trading system is to leverage the fact that newer power plants can install pollution control equipment at significantly lower costs than older plants. Mercury pollution can also be lowered by switching to cleaner coal. If overall caps are low enough and a healthy market for allowances develops, trading encourages the newer plants to install control equipment and recoup their costs by selling excess allowances. If the cap is not low enough, however, the cost of allowances is deflated because none of the dirtier plants really need them to operate.

The final mercury rule imposes caps in two phases: (1) by 2010, covered utilities (primarily coal-fired power plants) must emit no more than 38 TPY; and (2) by 2018, their emissions must decline to 15 TPY. The first important point about these numbers is that the first-phase cap, for 2010, is set at a level that will not compel the dirtiest utilities in eastern and Midwestern states to do anything more than they would already be compelled to do by the Clean Air Interstate Rule (CAIR), which focuses not on mercury but on sulfur dioxide ($SO_2$) and nitrous oxide ($NOx$) emissions.[33] EPA says that while they reduce those unrelated emissions, mercury emissions will also fall, to a level of 38 TPY. The second important point is that the rule allows companies to "bank" allowances from previous years indefinitely. As EPA itself admits, if the utilities bank allowances under the relaxed cap applicable in the first phase and use those banked allowances to cover emissions after 2018, it could take several more years to reach the theoretical 15 TPY limit.

The 15 TPY limit represents a 70 percent reduction from emission levels today, which sounds good if we did not have to wait so many years for it to go into effect. But the limit and its timing are far less ambitious than EPA has estimated could be accomplished by the legally mandated MACT approach. At a meeting on September 18, 2001, EPA career staff told electric utility representatives that one feasible mercury MACT would cut mercury emissions to approximately 5 TPY no later than 2007.[34] The weakest MACT alternative the Agency was then considering, at the behest of the utility industry, was 15 TPY in 2007. Further, in November 2005, disgusted with the laxity of EPA's final standards, two trade associations representing the nation's state and local air pollution control officials announced that they had developed a model rule for possible adoption by as many as twenty states.[35] The model would accomplish 80 percent reductions by 2008. A comparison of the emissions estimated for the various proposals is presented in Table 5.2.[36] As of June 2006, some thirteen states had adopted their own, more stringent requirements for

**Table 5.2. Comparison of Mercury Reductions Under Regulatory Proposals**

| Regulation | 2007 | 2008 | 2010 | 2018–2030 |
|---|---|---|---|---|
| EPA Trading Rule | | | 38 TPY -21% | 15 TPY -70% |
| State Proposal, November 2005* | | 10 TPY -80% | | |
| Strong EPA MACT** | 5 TPY -90% | | | |
| Weak EPA MACT** | 15 TPY -70% | | | |

*STAPPA/ALAPCO 2005 model state rule on mercury emissions
**Estimated results from 2001 advisory committee proposals

mercury control and indicated that they did not intend to opt into the EPA trading program.[37]

Apart from the dramatic differences in pollution control demonstrated by these numbers, trading may well produce side effects that are worse than the status quo in some states. Because trading allows individual utilities to trade at will, it is difficult to predict which plants will simply buy more allowances to cover their high levels of ongoing pollution, with the result that emissions pool around those plants, forming hot spots of toxic pollution.

Mercury is only the third pollutant subject to an EPA-designed national trading program. The other two, $SO_2$ and $NO_x$, are different in one crucial respect: neither is so toxic that pooling of emissions is a problem unless those levels are extraordinarily high. Consequently, although the total amount of $SO_2$ and $NO_x$ emissions needs to be reduced, there is little risk to public health if trading produces hot spots. In contrast, the development of mercury hot spots could prove very dangerous to local populations because the metal is toxic in such small amounts, and even moderate pooling could easily cause significant damage.

A trading system sponsored by the South Coast Air Quality Management District (SCAQMD) in the Los Angeles airshed illustrates the hazards of trading toxins such as mercury.[38] The California program allowed companies emitting volatile organic compounds (VOCs), which are also hazardous air pollutants, to buy and sell allowances, with some of the allowances coming from the retirement of old, dirty cars. The result was that this pollution, which had been spread throughout the metropolitan area, ended up concentrated around four marine terminals in predominantly Hispanic, low-income neighborhoods. Levels of pollution in the ambient air around those terminals ended up several times higher than applicable health-based standards, endangering those populations.

Professor Catherine O'Neill used EPA's own data to conduct an extensive analysis of the potential impact of mercury trading on Native American populations in the upper Great Lakes.[39] The Great Lakes already are heavily contaminated with mercury. In 2020, when trading is in full effect, EPA figures show that reductions in the upper Great Lakes states of Michigan, Minnesota, and Wisconsin will be 26.5 percent as opposed to the promised 70 percent. Emissions are projected to increase at twenty of the forty-four plants, in one case by as much as 68 percent. O'Neill found that women in the Upper Great Lakes who consume fish caught there at the same rate as the general U.S. population already are exposed at the same level as the EPA reference dose. Women who eat fish at the higher rates than are common among populations in the Great Lakes region are exposed at *twice* the reference dose. And Native American women who eat fish as a major component of their diets are exposed at levels *ten times higher* than the reference dose. Far from bringing these women and their children relief, trading could make conditions worse in some locations.

What, you may wonder, is EPA's response? The Agency emphasizes that the new trading regime will mark the first time that mercury has ever been controlled, without mentioning the much stricter alternatives it was considering before Holmstead took office and that many states are considering now. EPA denies that hot spots will be created but says that if they are, it will consider what to do at that time. As for existing problems with contaminated fish, EPA points to the fish advisories provided by the states. These advisories warn fishers and their families not to consume more than a certain level of contaminated species of fish. In other words, the burden is on the women suffering exposure to avoid this risk, just as the burden is on active children to stay inside on Code Red days for ozone pollution.

## The Economics

The third front in the battle over mercury involves a transcending goal of the right wing's deregulatory campaign—cost-benefit analysis as the final hurdle to the issuance of any regulation that is designed to protect public health and the environment. This methodology was first enshrined in an executive order issued by President Reagan and continued by Presidents

Bush, Clinton, and Bush. It requires that whenever the costs of controls outweigh the monetized value of the benefits to be gained by implementing them, regulation should not occur.[40] For background on such analyses and their impact on EPA's ability to fulfill its mission, see Chapter 3, "Battered-Agency Syndrome."

The overriding problem with cost-benefit analysis is its unethical approach to the quantification of devastatingly adverse health effects. EPA's elaborate efforts to monetize the value of the IQ points lost by children exposed to mercury in utero is sufficiently offensive from an ethical perspective that even the Agency's conservative political appointees did their best to hide these sordid details in a morass of paperwork.

A second central problem with cost-benefit analysis is that it involves taking a long string of predictions, assumptions, projections, and wild guesses and reducing them to a set of numbers that lend a false sense of certainty to any agency's justification for its final decision to either issue or not to issue protective rules. Once again, EPA's bizarre fluctuations in estimating both the costs and benefits of the various options it considered to accomplish mercury reductions should make even the most avid fan of such assessments feel queasy. We might as well begin on the more legitimate side of the equation: quantification of compliance costs.

## Compliance Costs

Without a doubt, it makes sense to take costs into account when making an important decision. In the context of regulatory costs, the analysis is relatively straightforward, if prone to error. The government predicts, with the enthusiastic assistance of regulated industries, how much pollution controls will cost to install. Often, such predictions turn out to be overstated, for a variety of reasons.[41] The most significant is that requiring companies to install pollution control technologies creates a market for such equipment, attracting resources to research and development, provoking competition among manufacturers, and, over time, lowering prices.

Congress made a conscious decision to embrace this dynamic and, as discussed above, the 1990 Clean Air Act amendments mandated EPA to address hazardous air pollutants through "technology-forcing" requirements. These mandates by definition involve a leap of faith because it is very difficult to predict at the outset how fast cost-effective technology will emerge. On the other hand, without a certain market for their equipment, inventors might have a difficult time raising capital for new technologies, especially because pollution control equipment produces less obvious and immediate profits than other investments.

In the case of mercury, EPA spent several years working on a technology-forcing result as instructed by Congress. It even developed a tentative cost-benefit analysis for that kind of traditional regulation, concluding that the version of MACT that career staff favored would cost $2 billion annually but would achieve benefits of $15 billion annually, for *net benefits* of $13 billion, a very substantial economic achievement as these things go.[42]

EPA political appointee Jeffrey Holmstead's decision to abruptly reverse course and direct his staff to prepare a trading alternative to technology-based controls caught the Agency's economists off guard. Consequently, the rule proposed in 2003, which offered either the technology-based or the trading option, was missing the regulatory impact analysis that typically accompanies such announcements. EPA was widely ridiculed for these omissions by the majority of non-utility-industry participants in the debate, including the Government Accountability Office (GAO), state regulatory officials, environmental groups, and legal commentators. Temporarily forgoing its role as guardian of rigorous cost-benefit methodology and enforcer of Executive Order 12866, OMB was strangely silent throughout the clamor.

Between the time that the proposed rule was issued in January 2004 and the final rule came out in May 2005, EPA worked frantically to pull together a better justification for its decision to adopt a cap-and-trade system and postpone specific mercury controls until 2018. The result of these efforts was a 570-page document containing nine appendices and hundreds of tables and figures.[43]

That analysis found that annual compliance costs under the trading rule would be between $848 million and 896 million in 2020, two years after the trading system kicked into full gear. Interestingly enough, EPA did not justify trading on the basis that waiting ten years would save close to $1 billion. Rather, the Agency justified its change of heart on the basis of when innovative technologies would become available. It announced in the 2005 preamble to its final rule that activated carbon injection capable of achieving a 90 to 95 percent reduction in mercury emissions would not be available in 2007, as it had predicted in 2003, instead claiming that the technology's future was uncertain and that it would "not be commercially available until 2010 or later."[44]

Given the highly politicized nature of the Agency's reversal, some members of EPA's congressional oversight committees were sufficiently perturbed to ask GAO to conduct an independent review. In May 2005 GAO reported that: the market for technologies would emerge once regulations were in place; the Department of Energy found that technologies were available to achieve reductions of 30 to 95 percent at reasonable costs; and virtually all experts except those representing the utility industry agreed that 50 percent reductions were achievable by 2008, with many agreeing that even 70 percent reductions were achievable in that time frame.[45] In sum, EPA's pessimism regarding technology development was likely unwarranted and certainly evaded its congressional mandate to adopt technology-forcing requirements in this context.

### Human Health Benefits

As convoluted as EPA efforts at cost estimates appear, these difficulties pale in comparison to the challenges the Agency encountered in translating the positive results of regulation into monetary terms. Apart from the threshold question of whether it is possible, necessary, or desirable to place a monetary value on a human life, how much is it worth to save an infant from brain damage? On what basis should such a sum be calculated?

While it covered many subjects, the document focused on only one significant category of benefits: IQ points lost by babies born to American women who eat freshwater fish "recreationally caught" in the eastern half of the country. Two threshold problems are obvious in this analysis: the focus on freshwater fish overlooks the U.S. contribution to the global mercury cycle, which also affects ocean fish. Even more important, the exclusive use of IQ points ignores the other effects on children of mercury exposure, including loss of fine motor skills and cardiovascular problems.

In its published preamble to the final rule, EPA never mentioned the dollar value it assigns to an IQ point. Instead, that number — $8,800 per point — is buried deep in the regulatory impact analysis.[46] EPA assumed that those losses would result in reduced income later in life and then discounted those monetary amounts to reflect how much money a person would have to invest today to come up with that total. At a 3 percent discount rate, said the Agency, a one-point IQ loss is worth $366,021 in *1992* dollars.[47] EPA acknowledged that this figure makes no effort to quantify any effects of lost IQ other than earning capacity and never considers that a substantial loss for a poisoned child could mean the difference between being able to earn a living and being dependent on public support.

But the Agency was not finished. In a particularly hair splitting and cold-blooded turn of analysis, it noted that people with lower IQ generally have less schooling. The average annual expenditure for school per pupil, in an undisclosed year, was $5,500. However, at age nineteen, a person lost $10,925 in income not earned because he or she was enrolled in school. So, the Agency assumed that children who are mercury-poisoned will have less schooling but might earn a few years of additional income because they are not in school. It adjusts the "average present value of net earnings losses per IQ point" to be $8,807 in 1999 dollars.[48] In other words, the good news is that stupider children need less school and earn just a little more money because they are working rather than sitting in a classroom, if one begins with the assumption (questionable enough in itself) that the earnings of everyone in America can be flatlined at $366,021 (in 1992 dollars) per IQ point.

No one but an experienced team of economists with weeks of free time on their hands could possibly hope to evaluate these or any of the other assumptions made in the Regulatory Impact Analysis. Even then, the team would need access to the elaborate computer models as well as all the underlying data that EPA fed into those models to conduct an accurate assessment. Obviously, the judges reviewing EPA's decisions will be hard-pressed to subject these documents to a knowledgeable and thorough review.

Fortunately, though, we do not need to step into this analytical quagmire to make a basic judgment regarding whether the analysis is credible. Here is what EPA had to say about costs and benefits in the preamble to its final rule:

> [T]he social costs of the final rule are estimated to be approximately $848 million in 2020 when assuming a 3 percent discount rate. These costs become $896 million in 2020 if one assumes a 7 percent discount rate. . . .
>
> As is discussed above, the social benefits that EPA was able to monetize in the RIA total $0.4 million to $3.0 million using a 3 percent discount rate and $0.2 million to $2.0 million using a 7 percent discount rate.
>
> Thus, the annual monetized net benefit in 2020 (social benefits minus social costs) of the [final mercury rule] is approximately—[negative] $846 million or—[negative] $895 million (using 3 and 7 percent discount rates, respectively) annually in 2020. Although the final rule is expected

to result in a net cost to society, it achieves a significant reduction in Hg [mercury] emissions by domestic sources. In addition, the cost of reduced earnings borne by U.S. citizens from Hg exposure falls disproportionately on prenatally exposed children of populations who consume larger amounts of recreationally caught freshwater fish than the general population.[49]

Or, in other words, despite a finding by the nation's best scientists that EPA's reference dose for mercury is scientifically justifiable and the further discovery that 6 percent of women of childbearing age and as many as 630,000 babies born annually have blood mercury levels above that number, EPA thinks the annual benefits of reducing mercury run as low as $200,000 and no higher than $3 million annually. Nevertheless, with graciousness and *noblesse oblige*, it will deign to impose almost $1 billion in costs on the utility industry fifteen years from now. Apparently, benefits must exceed costs only if affected industries are actively opposing a rule. For rules that are weakened to the point that they are acceptable to industry, cost-benefit analysis can come to absurd conclusions and still get past the economists.

## Alternative Analyses

In May 2005, faculty from four of the nation's most prestigious medical schools released their own analysis of the benefits of reducing mercury emissions overall and in particular mercury emissions from power plants. Like EPA, they used IQ points and productivity measures, but they reached startlingly different conclusions: the most likely overall benefits of eliminating mercury total $8.7 billion annually, and the benefits of cutting emissions from power plants alone would be $1.3 billion annually.[50] A second analysis, prepared by experts at the Harvard Center for Risk Analysis and issued in February 2005, found potential annual benefits to children in avoiding neurological damage by reducing mercury emissions that would range from $75 million for reductions to 26 TPY and $119 million for reductions to 15 TPY.[51] The second study also attempted to come to grips with mercury's contribution to cardiovascular disease, an emerging area of research that EPA refused to take into account. The authors estimated that if early studies on these health effects proved correct, reducing emissions to 26 or 15 TPY could achieve annual benefits between $3.3 billion and $4.9 billion, respectively.

## Conclusion

For those who have watched the development of environmental policy since the early 1970s, the mercury debate cannot help but provoke a strong sense of déjà vu. Twenty years ago, EPA banned lead in gasoline, rescuing millions of children from irreversible neurological problems. The decision was fought vigorously by regulated industries at the time and came close to derailment, although it is widely regarded as one of the most important successes EPA has yet achieved. In a sense, mercury is lead's evil twin, and efforts to require reductions are on the same journey. At the moment, the national debate is at a stalemate, the government is blocking effective controls but facing a crescendo of public criticism, and a happy ending seems as remote as it must have appeared to those who urged the fledgling EPA to ban lead.

In the distance, however, encouraging signs are beginning to appear. Although it is likely that it will take years to resolve the legal dispute over EPA's trading rule, several states have begun to take matters into their own hands by writing regulations that adopt more stringent, technology-based approaches. Before EPA finalized its rule, William Becker, executive director of the two associations representing state and local air pollution control officials that developed the model rule discussed earlier, warned industry supporters of the EPA trading program to be careful what they wished for:

> What I can predict with almost absolute certainty is that, if this EPA proposal is promulgated close to the original language, you will see an onslaught of actions at the state and local levels to replace or strengthen EPA's program. These programs will vary widely in scope and magnitude, and it will drive industry nuts.[52]

### Mercury Case Study Lessons

*This case study of mercury demonstrates in excruciating detail how EPA career staff and the Agency's traditional mission have been hijacked by special interests. Depending on one's perspective, the battle over how to regulate air toxins was either won or lost when Congress voted in 1990 to chart a different course. Years of work to implement those instructions were dismissed in a matter of months by political appointees who came from the same law firm that represents electric utility firms and contributed large excerpts of EPA's rulemaking proposal. The result is an interminable legal battle in the courts, which once again will delay affirmative action for years to come.*

*This abrupt about-face meant that EPA refused to consider the costs and benefits of the statutorily mandated regulatory approach. The Agency was able to paper over its decision to ignore its statutory mandate only by shoving aside the supposedly sacrosanct conservative precept that monetized benefits must exceed costs. The sheer illogic of this result shows the depth of special interests' influence, exercised opportunistically and without regard to the conservative principle that government should only intervene when the "free" market cannot solve the problem.*

*Adding insult to injury, the chlor-alkali regulations that EPA adopted will perpetuate a situation that makes little sense from the perspective or society as a whole in either cost-benefit or health terms, polluting the commons for the isolated benefit of a few large corporations. As bad, the regulatory tool selected for power plants—unrestricted trading under a high emissions cap over a period as long as three decades—not only fails to address the problem but could make contamination worse in some locations, damaging the future of children whose families cannot afford another source of food.*

*The dive EPA took on mercury will exacerbate the international perspective that the United States does what is best for American industry all the time. This perception will make any effort to arrest the global mercury cycle that much more difficult, in effect rendering the utility industry's argument that other countries must go first both hypocritical and disingenuous.*

*Finally, the mercury situation shows that rather than sponsoring a legitimate campaign on behalf of sound science, those who attack research documenting a public health problem will never be satisfied. Even the blessing of the nation's preeminent scientific academy does not stop this steady drumbeat of criticism, designed to buy as much delay as possible by mercilessly complexifying the scientific consensus.*

## CHAPTER 6

# Perchlorate Case Study

*For most Americans, turning the tap is an Act of Faith. But if our experience is any guide, that Faith is severely shaken. . . . When you play around with drinking water quality you are playing with fire, perhaps the only instance where water can start fires, metaphorically speaking, rather than put them out. A water supply is a long lever, with the weight of the community's health at the other end. Small changes in water treatment are magnified as large movements in health status.*

DR. DAVID OZONOFF, BOSTON UNIVERSITY SCHOOL
OF PUBLIC HEALTH, 1995

## Overview

Perchlorate, sometimes called "powdered oxygen," is the central component of rocket fuel and has been used in this country since the 1940s, when the Navy asked Theodore von Karman, an aeronautics professor at the California Institute of Technology, to develop engines powerful enough to lift planes off aircraft carrier flight decks.[1] Von Karman and his colleagues founded a company called Aerojet to commercialize their discovery: a mixture that produces strong explosive power but can be managed safely on ships. Within a few years, perchlorate became the military's fuel of choice for rockets and other explosive ordnance and was also used in similar private-sector applications such as road flares and fireworks. Other contractors, most prominently the Olin and Kerr-McGee corporations, got into the business of manufacturing hundreds of thousands of tons of perchlorate at large plants in California and Nevada and shipping it to military bases across the country.

Perchlorate is harmful to babies in utero and developing infants because it blocks the uptake of iodide into the thyroid, causing malfunction of the endocrine system that modulates normal neurological development. Iodide deficiency is the most common cause of mental retardation in the world, producing a condition known as cretinism, which can be manifested not only as diminished intellectual capacity but as deaf-mutism, and spasticity, or involuntary twitching of the muscles and irregular gait. The wrong dose of perchlorate at the wrong moment can throw the developing child's delicate thyroid system into upheaval, also causing microcephaly (small brain), paraplegia, quadriplegia, or other movement disorders. According to a National Academies report,

> Newborn infants who have hypothyroidism may have other abnormalities, including lethargy, poor muscle tone, poor feeding, constipation, and persistent jaundice, if not at birth then thereafter. The changes are similar to those which occur in older children and adults, and, in contrast with neurologic abnormalities, they are reversible with adequate [hormone] treatment.[2]

Adults store enough thyroid hormones to cover several weeks of iodide deficiency, allowing them to withstand the periodic shortfalls caused by various dietary changes. But a fetus has no storage capacity, and an infant has only a one-day surplus supply. Ordinarily the fetus would get iodide from the mother and nursing infants from breast milk or formula. But two National Health and Nutrition Examination Surveys (NHANES) indicate that levels of iodide in normal adults are falling steadily, possibly because Americans have decreased the use of iodized table salt or eat iodide-containing foods in smaller quantities. The result is that 14.9 percent of women of childbearing age and 6.7 percent of pregnant women have low urine iodide concentrations, indicating that they suffer from an iodide deficiency and may not be able to supplement their babies' supply.[3] These numbers represent a fourfold increase in iodide deficiency among women of childbearing age and a sevenfold increase in deficiency among pregnant women between two survey periods, 1971–1974 and 1988–1994.

Three characteristics make perchlorate a pervasive environmental contaminant: it is highly soluble in water, it does not degrade into less harmful chemicals once it enters the environment, and it has a short shelf life. Faced with the continual need to install, remove, discard, and repack new fuel, the military took the path of least resistance, washing perchlorate out onto the ground, where it traveled rapidly through the soil and into streams and underground water supplies. Managers of the main Aerojet plant in Azusa, California, even went to the point of connecting floor drains to an industrial sewer line where the contaminated wastewater migrated into the Los Angeles treatment system.

Ammonium and sodium perchlorate continued to seep into ground and surface waters for the next fifty years, especially in the southwestern United States. Spreading from the ground zero of a large Kerr-McGee ammonium perchlorate plant in Henderson, Nevada, millions of gallons of perchlorate wastewater have infiltrated the Las Vegas Wash, the main drain into Lake Mead from Las Vegas and its sprawling suburbs. Lake Mead, the country's largest man-made reservoir, sits astride the Colorado River, which is the primary source of potable water for the Los Angeles metropolitan area.

EPA discovered perchlorate contamination at alarmingly high levels around California military facilities in 1985. In 1997 a new test made it possible to detect perchlorate at levels as low as four parts per billion (ppb) in drinking water. The application of this method to toxic waste sites across the country revealed that perchlorate contamination was even more widespread than first suspected. EPA now estimates that, overall, perchlorate has infiltrated the drinking water supplies of 11 million people. Two public-interest organizations, the Environmental Working Group (EWG) and the Natural Resources Defense Council (NRDC), say this number is significantly higher, totaling 20 million people.

In the spring of 2003 these already high stakes were magnified when EWG announced its discovery of perchlorate in twenty-two samples of lettuce grown in California's Imperial Valley, where fields are irrigated with water containing the chemical and soil also may be contaminated.[4] EWG decided to undertake its own limited testing after the Pentagon refused to pay for comparable government research that would have cost $215,000, a small amount in proportion to what the military spent on perchlorate research.

By 2004, pressure from public health experts and environmentalists had grown to the point that the FDA undertook official but "exploratory" government testing. It found perchlorate in 115 of 127 lettuce samples gathered in five states at levels as high as 71 ppb, with mean numbers ranging from 7.76 to 11.9 ppb.[5] FDA also found perchlorate in 101 of 103 cow's milk samples gathered in thirteen states at levels as high as 11.3 ppb and a mean of 5.76 ppb.[6] And in February 2005, researchers at Texas Tech University announced that they found perchlorate in 81 of 82 samples of breast milk taken in eighteen states at levels as high as 92 ppb and with a mean of 10.5 ppb. These numbers were five times higher than perchlorate contamination in cow's milk samples also tested by the research team;[7] some 64 percent of American babies are breast-fed. Spurred on by these troubling findings, the government is now in the slow process of conducting broader, more definitive testing.

Under pressure from environmental and community groups, EPA slowly prepared to take regulatory action. At that point, an epic battle broke out within the federal government over how to set standards that would limit perchlorate in drinking water and, equally important, would determine how much cleanup the military and its private-sector suppliers would need to accomplish at contaminated sites. The Pentagon insists that cleanup down to levels in the single digits of parts per billion—advocated by EPA staff and preliminarily adopted by California and Massachusetts—would be prohibitively expensive, costing billions better spent on national security.

At some point early in the battle, a fateful decision was made to establish an internal government taskforce—the Interagency Perchlorate Steering Committee (IPSC)—that would supervise scientific research on perchlorate.[8] The task force put EPA, the midsized and embattled agency charged with protecting public health from environmental contamination, on the same footing as the Department of Defense (DOD), the huge, increasingly powerful institution that will be compelled to plead with Congress for the billions of dollars in cleanup funding if a stringent standard is set. The White House has, for the most part, sided with military leaders, further compounding the harmful consequences of this inappropriate and stalemate-prone partnership. At one particularly low moment, senior White House staff went so far as to instruct EPA scientists not to speak publicly about the EWG lettuce study, a move characterized as a gag order by *Wall Street Journal* reporter Peter Waldman in an April 2003 article.[9]

In the two decades since EPA discovered widespread perchlorate contamination, the debate regarding how to respond has not moved beyond the stage of warring over science. The military has spent $60 million either investigating health effects or searching for treatment technologies. Perchlorate manufacturers have spent unknown but most likely large sums. Rather than spur action, however, this research has forestalled it. On the defensive both within the government and outside it, EPA has paused like a doe caught in the bright headlights of an oncoming car. The upshot is that even after the science stalemate is broken, it will take federal and state regulators many years to issue a binding standard, with decades of cleanup left after that.

Once again, the three fronts of the battle against regulation—science, law, and economics—provide the framework for our investigation of this unfortunate situation. If mercury is a case study of government pushing aside relatively clear science and very specific legal mandates on the basis of spurious economic analysis, perchlorate is an example of government paralyzing itself by short-changing scientific research, precluding legal action, and making accurate cost estimates impossible.


## The Science

Unlike virtually all other high-profile pollutants, perchlorate was once used as a medicine to treat hyperthyroidism, or Graves disease. Perchlorate was effective because it blocked the uptake of iodide to the thyroid, preventing the production of hormones that cause the gland to become hyperactive. Pharmaceutical use of perchlorate largely ceased in the late 1960s, when seven patients participating in a clinical trial died.[10] Nevertheless, during the period when it was used as a drug, doctors and pharmacologists were able to develop a good understanding of exactly how perchlorate disrupts normal thyroid functioning in adults. However, perchlorate's effects had never been studied in pregnant women, in infants, or in young children.

This research indicated that the normal adult thyroid produces two hormones—triiodothyronine (T3) and thyroxine (T4).[11] T4 is known as a precursor hormone because it has little or no intrinsic biologic activity and rapidly converts to T3, which is essential to the development of the central nervous system. Iodide is a component of both T3 and T4. Its transfer from the blood to the thyroid, through a protein known as a sodium (NA+) iodide (I-) transporter (NIS), is the precedent condition for the synthesis of the two hormones and, consequently, the formation of T3. As illustrated in Figures 6.1, 6.2, and 6.3, when a person ingests perchlorate, it takes the place of the iodide and is transported to the thyroid, blocking T3 production and causing the thyroid to slow down substantially.

When perchlorate was discovered at low levels in drinking water supplies, scientists became concerned about the impact of such contamination on public health. With the significant advantage of knowing how

The thyroid gland is butterfly-shaped, with two lobes about the size of teaspoons. It is located in the front of the neck, below the Adam's apple.

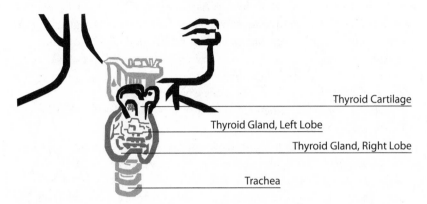

**Figure 6.1.** Structure of the Thyroid Gland. Source: Centers for Disease Control and Prevention.

much of the chemical could disrupt normal thyroid function in adults, they had three remaining issues to tackle: (1) estimating the doses people were receiving from drinking water and food, (2) gauging the effects of those exposures on older children and adults, and (3) determining how to apply their conclusions regarding adults and older children to fetuses and infants. They began a scientific odyssey that has lasted for more than a decade and is far from over.

## Industry-Dominated Science

The Perchlorate Study Group (PSG) is a consortium of the major manufacturers of rocket fuel that includes Aerojet, American Pacific Corporation, Kerr-McGee Chemical, and Lockheed-Martin. The group describes itself as "an alliance of manufacturers and users of perchlorate established in 1993 to fund and perform scientific research" and says its sole interest is in the "accurate, fair and unbiased characterization of potential human health risks" of exposure to perchlorate.[12] PSG uses the science it produces to advocate its members' interests before the federal and state regulatory bodies making decisions on what to do about the chemical.

By 1997 PSG was well on its way toward becoming the preeminent perchlorate health effects research sponsor. As pressure grew to do something about perchlorate contamination, PSG convinced the military to co-sponsor research by a private sector risk assessment consulting firm called Toxicology Excellence in Risk Assessment (TERA). TERA, DOD, and PSG have worked in tandem ever since, effectively managing to control not just the research but the outcome of the federal government's decision making on perchlorate. Of ninety separate pieces of scientific research on perchlorate identified by the GAO, the independent investigative agency for Congress, fifty-six were sponsored by DOD, PSG, or PSG members, while nineteen were sponsored by EPA and fifteen had "unknown" sponsors.[13]

This overwhelming predominance of the scientific research by self-interested parties had two results that in retrospect proved devastating. First, the science itself was myopic. Although millions of dollars were spent, those directing the agenda advertently or inadvertently left gaping

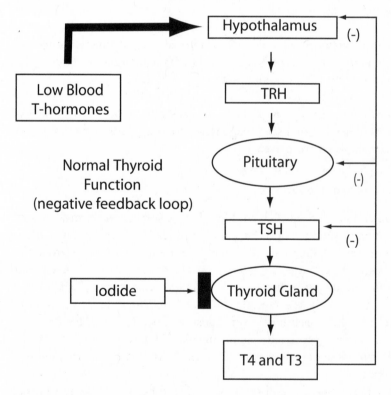

**Figure 6.2.** Normal Thyroid Hormone Production. Source: Drs. Katherine Squibb and Caroline Baier-Anderson, University of Maryland Medical School.

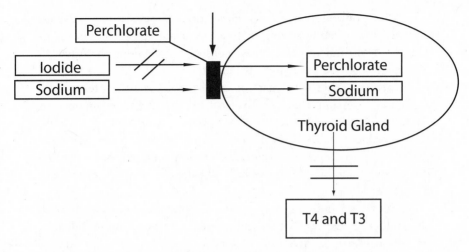

**Figure 6.3.** Effect of Perchlorate on Thyroid Hormone Production. Source: Drs. Katherine Squibb and Caroline Baier-Anderson, University of Maryland Medical School.

holes in the studies they conducted, in the end depriving the peer review panel appointed to analyze the research of the most relevant information needed to develop a reference dose for perchlorate. Second, the credibility of the research was undermined from the start by the perception that it had been rigged to suit the Pentagon's financial interests. This perception was exacerbated as the PSG and its members systematically attacked the methodology used in studies they themselves had designed and implemented when the research so much as hinted that perchlorate exposure in utero hurt babies.

### One Big, Unhappy Family

By 1998, as EPA grew more active, PSG and DOD were ready to take the next step toward cementing their control over any future government action. The IPSC was established, combining representatives from EPA, DOD, DOE, NASA, and FDA into what was to be an all-powerful partnership on perchlorate. The IPSC was co-chaired by Colonel Dan Rogers, a lawyer by training and the Pentagon's point man on perchlorate, and Annie Jarabek, an EPA scientist. Over the next few years, it became clear to any objective observer that EPA had not only lost its autonomy but had been forced to take a backseat in running this enterprise.

EPA's first official sortie was the circulation of a several-hundred page draft risk assessment analyzing the science regarding perchlorate exposures.[14] The document caused great consternation among the Agency's IPSC federal government partners and the private sector partners of those partners. After four years of bickering about its contents, EPA issued a new version, the 2002 External Review Draft, recommending that the RfD for perchlorate be set at 1 ppb (the significance of this number is explained further below).[15] The Agency's federal partners and the private-sector partners of its partners strongly opposed this result and decided that something definitive had to be done to put the Agency back in its place.

On March 19, 2003, to the apparent surprise of EPA's career staff, EPA, DOD, DOE, and NASA sent a referral letter to the president of the National Academy of Sciences asking for a peer review of the "science about the health impacts of perchlorate."[16] The project was assigned to NRC, which convened a panel of experts to review the available science and write a report.

The letter communicating the NRC perchlorate panel's charge, or list of questions the agencies wanted answered, asked that the panel include experts in endocrinology, neurotoxicology, animal toxicology, animal thyroid physiology, animal carcinogenesis, developmental toxicology, physiologically based pharmacokinetic (PBPK) modeling, veterinary pathology, pediatrics or neonatology, pediatric endocrinology, biostatistics, and risk assessment. From March 2003, when the NRC panel was formed, until January 10, 2005, when its final report was released, PSG and DOD partners in IPSC shifted all their attention to lobbying NRC panel members. Whether this extraordinarily bold outside pressure influenced the panel is very difficult to determine. But it unquestionably undermined the panel's credibility and even threatened the National Academies' reputation as the convener of the best scientific minds in the country to undertake an objective search for scientific truth.

## Peer Review Compromised

For long-term observers of such blue ribbon peer review, the intensity of the military's lobbying effort, supported actively by the White House and OMB, were surprising, even shocking. The full extent of those efforts was revealed by materials released to the Natural Resources Defense Council in response to a lawsuit under the Freedom of Information Act and by the panel's public docket containing all the outside submissions it received during its deliberations.[17] The documents show that DOD and the White House were monitoring the NRC selection process long before the panel was announced and had even prepared their own list of candidates for the panel. Nonscientists in OMB edited the charge to the National Academies before it was transmitted. The NRC panel was deluged with submissions during its official public comment period and afterward. Several of these submissions prepared by DOD, PSG, and TERA contained unpublished data from scientific studies that had not themselves been peer-reviewed. No other outside group could possibly keep up with this deluge, much less comment on the merits of such data, in the time that was available.

The composition of the original fifteen-member panel compounded these problems. The list released by the NRC included four scientists with strong industry ties: Drs. Richard Bull, James Lamb, R. Michael McClain, and Gilbert Omenn, with Dr. Omenn designated as its chair. The chair position is particularly important to the outcome of the process because the chair has authority to manage meetings and to play a major role in preparing the final report. Within three weeks after the list was announced, a coalition of public interest groups (NRDC, EWG, and the Center for Science in the Public Interest) wrote to the president of the National Academy of Sciences asking that these members be removed because they appeared to have conflicts of interest and offering the names of four alternative scientists.[18] Drs. Omenn and Bull disappeared, either voluntarily or upon request; Drs. Lamb and McClain remained on the panel until the end; and one person recommended in the public-interest groups' letter was appointed to serve, Dr. Gregory Brent.

The law bars peer review candidates from serving if they have financial conflicts of interest in the subject matter to be considered by the panel. But this requirement can be waived by National Academies representatives.[19] The law also requires that panels be balanced for bias, with "bias" loosely defined as such a strong orientation toward the views of one or another side in the controversy as to make it difficult for the candidate to remain objective. Bias is often judged on the basis of the candidate's professional affiliations because it would be difficult to convince the public that no problem exists simply on the basis of candidates' self-serving answers to a questionnaire. Balancing a panel means making sure that all views are represented in roughly equal proportion. Balance is particularly important to peer review because panels work toward consensus recommendations.

Why, then, would the NRC or any other comparable peer-review body ever risk appointing experts with ties to companies or their customers? One answer is that when members of the industry that make the chemical are the people who have paid for the vast majority of the research regarding its public health effects, it is difficult to find scientists who are both independent of industry influence and knowledgeable about the nuances of the chemical-specific research. Some advocate that more generalized knowledge is preferable to inclusion of potentially biased candidates, as I do in the concluding chapters. Others insist that specific knowledge is too important to set aside. Regardless of one's point of view, the placement of four industry-affiliated scientists on a fifteen-person panel with one industry expert serving as the chair gives the impression that the panel was not balanced, undermining the credibility of the final report and both the NRC and the National Academies as institutions.

This contentious beginning cannot help but have put the members left on the panel feeling defensive, and although their report is written in dry, scientific language, they went out of their way on several occasions to explain how they had embraced a precautionary or conservative approach to gaps in the science, resolving uncertainty in favor of protectiveness. As we shall see in a moment, however, crippling data gaps caused by the conflict-ridden process of having DOD and perchlorate manufacturers control the research agenda made the panel's job difficult, if not impossible, and ultimately undermined the credibility of their best efforts to appear as if they were acting to safeguard public health.

### Politics Versus Science

Before it began its deliberations, the NRC panel met three times in open session to hear presentations from interested parties regarding the charge it had been given and the substance of the scientific work it had to do. Not content to limit its input to the scientific questions confronting the panel, DOD sent Colonel Rogers, its point person and a lawyer by training, to testify:

> We support this review because we very much want to get the science right, because only *credible* science can lead to *credible* decisions. . . . Thousands of men and women in the uniformed services of the United States of America eagerly await the results of your careful and considered and objective deliberations, for what you decide will have a greater impact on their lives than on any others. . . . there is no room for reliance on science *policy* precaution for its own sake. . . . Every layer of science

*policy* precaution inhibits our ability to train . . . [putting] our combat forces and, ultimately, our nation at risk.[20]

In essence, Rogers' testimony amounted to a demand that the panel amplify the scope of its review to include the potential ramifications of its decision on the national security and military readiness of the United States. Rogers told the panel that the uniformed services eagerly awaited the results of its deliberations because if the scientists concluded that perchlorate was dangerous at low doses, it could prevent or circumscribe the use of rockets containing perchlorate, jeopardizing the soldiers' lives as well as national security.

Rogers' apparent premise is right: no satisfactory substitute has yet been found for perchlorate. But he offered the NRC panel a false choice. Managing perchlorate more safely is a good idea no matter what the ultimate result of the panel's deliberations. And concluding that drinking water supplies need to be treated or replaced to eliminate human exposure to the chemical is a decision that need not affect the protection of national security any more than any other decision to spend money on a nonmilitary purpose. The NRC panel was convened to render an honest assessment of the risk to children posed by perchlorate and Rogers' threats amount to one of the most blatant efforts to politicize that science ever recorded.

## What NRC Did

Unlike their colleagues on the NRC methyl mercury panel, the scientists studying perchlorate ultimately decided to exclude all the available animal data from their "weight of the evidence" analysis, and instead focused solely on a two-week study conducted by Dr. Monte Greer (Greer Study) that involved the deliberate dosing of twenty-four healthy men and women.[21] The panel's emphasis on this single human study was controversial, and outside scientists already have begun to question how the panel could rest such an important finding on such a slender reed.[22] Only seven of the twenty-four adults were dosed at the low levels of perchlorate found in drinking water. Twenty-four is scant as these things go and seven is extraordinarily small; these numbers meant that the results of the study cannot be verified by statistical analysis. Furthermore, the subjects were adults, not infants, and the exposures were limited to fourteen days, making it difficult to determine the effects of longer-term exposures.

Outside scientists also question the panel's decision to exclude animal data. The panel said the exclusion was justified because the testing involved rodents that react differently to perchlorate than humans. Critics counter, however, that the panel could have taken these potential weaknesses into account in their weight-of-evidence analysis without throwing out the data. Although the outside scientists are too polite to state the obvious, the panel's judgment on the validity of the rodent data is made more galling by the fact that the military and perchlorate manufacturers controlled this body of research, which was conducted over a period of several years. Either these self-interested sponsors did not recognize the problems with extrapolating rodent data to humans, they fumbled the research deliberately, or the panel's decision is on shaky ground even from the perspective of their conflicted colleagues.

In any event, the fact remains that millions of dollars and close to a decade after they announced their quest for reliable science, neither DOD nor the Perchlorate Study Group had much else to offer. Given the limitations of the data, especially because the panel refused to consider available animal tests, the panel was confronted with a Hobson's choice: it could declare failure because more research was necessary, or it could take the Greer study and improvise from there. Reluctant to risk its reputation as the Solomon-like judge of all scientific controversies, the panel chose the second path.

That improvisation involved adjusting the baseline number of 0.007 milligram/kilogram/day to reflect the scientific uncertainty about perchlorate's potential adverse effects on babies. (A milligram is one one-thousandth of a gram.) Such adjustments involve multiplying the dose shown to be harmful in relevant studies, in this case 0.007 milligram/kilogram/day, by a "safety factor." Safety factors compensate for uncertainty by lowering the dose on the basis of what can only be described as a scientific policy judgment regarding the overall strength of the evidence. Consequently, if the single human study used by the panel is wrong and *underestimates* the risk, at least its results will have been adjusted downward to a safer level of exposure.

The panel issued its final report on January 10, 2005.[23] In the case of perchlorate, it used a safety factor of 10 and ended up with a final number of 0.0007 milligram/kilogram/day. EPA's 2002 External Review Draft risk assessment recommended an RfD of 0.00003 milligram/kilogram/day, about twenty times lower than the NRC recommendation. This change marked a significant correction of EPA's scientific judgment, but press accounts exaggerated its practical implications, giving the misleading impression that the NRC panel had, in effect, given perchlorate a clean bill

of health.[24] Shortly thereafter, EPA updated its Integrated Risk Information System (IRIS), a global database on toxins, to adopt the NRC panel's
RfD for perchlorate, effectively ending the debate over RfD until new,
definitive research emerges proving this number either too large or too
small.

The NRC perchlorate report ended up satisfying no one. Public
health experts and advocates were frustrated that the panel did not use
rodent and other studies to derive an RfD, while DOD and its industry
allies thought the panel had bent too far over backwards to add excessive
safety factors to its analysis. As a practical matter, neither side could do
anything about the decision, so it was time for them to open a new front
in the battle over perchlorate's future.

## New Battlefields

EPA has placed perchlorate on a list of contaminants that it will consider
for regulation under the Safe Drinking Water Act, the law that governs
how clean water must be "at the tap"—that is, when a person turns on the
faucet to get a glassful of water to drink.[25] Once the rulemaking process
begins, it could take as long as a decade to complete.

Meanwhile, on January 26, 2006, for reasons that are unclear, EPA
issued an Assessment Guidance for Perchlorate setting a preliminary remediation goal of 24.5 ppb for the cleanup of sites included on the Superfund National Priorities List.[26] Superfund is the nation's toxic waste
cleanup program, and the list includes approximately 1,250 of the worst
sites in the country, several of which are contaminated by perchlorate.[27]
Susan Bodine, the political appointee who heads the EPA office responsible for setting cleanup policy, wrote in a three-page memorandum to
the Agency's regional office administrators that this number was based
on the NRC reference dose. On March 8, 2006, she received a letter from
the EPA Children's Health Advisory Committee expressing concern that
the new guidance "is not protective of children's health" because a baby's
exposure could be several times higher than 24.5 ppb depending on the
mother's exposure to other sources of perchlorate.[28] The committee
urged the Agency to lower the number immediately. Bodine responded
on May 11, 2006, explaining that the guidance was preliminary and that
final standards will depend on "site-specific goals."[29] In other words, EPA
would pursue military-site perchlorate cleanups on an ad hoc basis where
perchlorate threatens drinking water. It would be left up to individual
citizen groups near the sites to keep an eye on these decisions.

Without much hope for effective action at the federal level, public health advocates turned their attention to the states, particularly those where high levels of contamination had been discovered. California and Massachusetts have taken the first steps toward an enforceable drinking-water standard, while six other states have adopted softer guidance numbers.[30] Naturally, DOD and its industry allies soon joined the crowd trying to influence these proceedings.

The controversy in this phase of the battle is how to extrapolate from the NRC number of 0.0007 milligram/kilogram/day a level of perchlorate in drinking water. Although the NRC panel's RfD was twenty times higher than EPA's RfD, it is likely to result in a regulatory level that is much, much lower than DOD and its contractors had advocated because an RfD is only the first step in determining regulatory levels.

The key limitation of an RfD for regulatory purposes is that it reflects the *total* amount of the chemical a baby can tolerate from all sources. A baby in utero is exposed to perchlorate circulating in her mother's system, and a nursing baby is exposed to perchlorate in breast milk or the water added to formula. The perchlorate in the mother's system may have derived from drinking water, or it may come from contaminated lettuce, some other leafy vegetable, or cow's milk. The difficult task of establishing a drinking-water standard necessarily involves setting a perchlorate limit for water that takes into account all exposures so that the baby's *cumulative* exposure does not exceed the RfD. EPA and state regulators are now struggling with those difficult questions, taking into consideration both public health concerns and the feasibility, from a technical and an economic perspective, of treating water until it reaches the final level they decide is appropriate.

EPA and its state counterparts will probably begin with 24.7 ppb for drinking water, the level of perchlorate in drinking water that would expose a healthy adult at or below the reference dose if the adult weighs seventy kilograms and drinks two liters of water a day. They will then extrapolate from this number to gauge the level of exposure for infants, who weigh substantially less and who in proportion to body weight drink six times more than adults. This extrapolation is complicated by two additional factors: lack of clarity on how perchlorate affects fetuses and babies and the possibility that the babies and their mothers are exposed to perchlorate from other sources such as food or cow's milk.

California's initial goal of 6 ppb in drinking water was attacked from both ends of the interest-group spectrum: industry insisted on 236 ppb, and environmentalists argued for 1 ppb.[31] Industry representatives have urged the panel to remove safety factors they regard as excessive that were built into the NRC's RfD. Environmentalists say that California regulators must take into account recent data showing disturbingly high levels of the chemical in milk, breast milk, and food. The same arguments are likely to be repeated before other state agencies, again delaying a final decision.

In fall 2006, a new study released by researchers at the CDC offered badly needed help to EPA and state scientists struggling to make decisions about controlling perchlorate. The study of 2,299 men and women, by far the largest sample ever scrutinized, found that exposure to perchlorate at the low levels found in drinking water could cause decreased formation of essential thyroid hormones in females age twelve or older who had lower iodine intake than the remainder of the population. The study found no effect in men. The affected population, estimated to comprise approximately *36 percent* of women in the United States, experienced "small-to-moderate size" changes in the formation of thyroid hormones. The study does not document what these changes might mean for babies the women carry, but it does suggest that a concerted effort to discover those implications should be a priority.[32]

## The Law

*Should someone have connected the dots in 1962, 1972, or 1982? Absolutely. But it didn't happen. There isn't one person or one agency that definitively dropped the ball. Everyone did nothing.*
KEVIN MAYER, EPA SCIENTIST, 2002 (IN WALDMAN, "SEEPING THREAT")

It may well have occurred to alert readers that these interminable struggles over a drinking-water standard have little to do with cleaning up contamination that has spiked to thousands and even hundreds of thousands of parts per billion at military and manufacturing sites across the nation. After all, everyone agrees that 2,000 ppb, much less 200,000 ppb is far too much. Why not remove these pockets of contamination as quickly as possible before they spread further into the environment, potentially reaching drinking-water supplies or the human food chain? The answer to that question is almost as convoluted as the scientific debate, revealing the overwhelming leverage the military can exert when it simply sits down in the middle of the road, refusing to take any further action. Such resistance is especially unfortunate given successful cleanups at the Kerr-

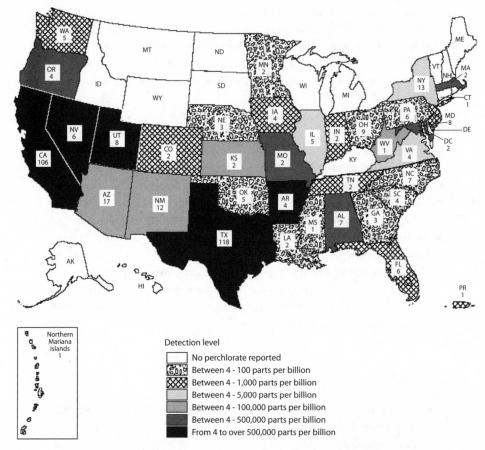

**Figure 6.4.** Maximum Perchlorate Concentrations Reported in Any Media and Number of Sites, January 2005. Source: Environmental Protection Agency, Department of Defense, U.S. Geological Survey, and state environmental agencies.

McGee plant in Henderson, Nevada, and at weapons training and testing sites on Cape Cod, Massachusetts. If the military wanted to move, it could.

## The State of Play in the Field

In May 2005 GAO undertook the first comprehensive analysis of the nature and scope of perchlorate contamination of drinking water, the legal authorities available to EPA and the states to address those problems, and the number of times that federal and state regulators had actually taken action.[33] GAO warned that its numbers might well understate the extent of contamination because there is no systematic, national system for recording the existence of sites where perchlorate was made or used. GAO reported that federal and state agencies have discovered perchlorate contamination in groundwater, surface water, soil, or public drinking water at some 400 locations. One-third of the sites were public drinking-water systems covered by an EPA-mandated testing program.[34] Perchlorate levels ranged from 4 ppb to more than 3.7 *million* ppb (Figure 6.4), although about 70 percent of the sites had levels below 24.7 ppb. It is impossible to determine from the data how many people are threatened at which sites. The 400 sites are located in thirty-five states, the District of Columbia, Puerto Rico, and Guam. More than 200 are located in California and Texas, although this statistic may reflect those states' more aggressive efforts to track the contamination. Arkansas, Nevada, and Utah also are heavily affected.

GAO also researched the activities that resulted in perchlorate pollution at the 400 known sites, and those results are shown in Figure 6.5.

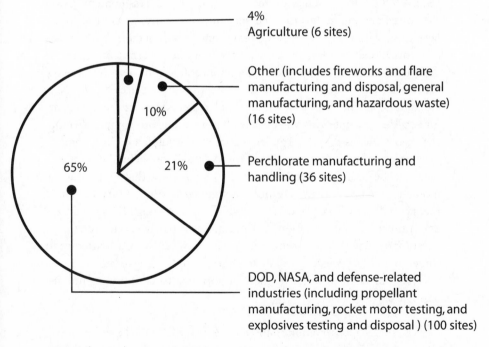

4%
Agriculture (6 sites)

Other (includes fireworks and flare manufacturing and disposal, general manufacturing, and hazardous waste) (16 sites)

Perchlorate manufacturing and handling (36 sites)

DOD, NASA, and defense-related industries (including propellant manufacturing, rocket motor testing, and explosives testing and disposal ) (100 sites)

**Figure 6.5.** Activities Causing Perchlorate Contamination. Source: Environmental Protection Agency, Department of Defense, U.S. Geological Survey, and state environmental agencies.

Military manufacturing and weapons testing lead the pack at 65 percent, while general perchlorate manufacturing comes in at 21 percent.

GAO's bottom-line recommendation was that EPA should develop a "formal structure to centrally track and monitor perchlorate detections and the status of cleanup efforts across the federal government and state agencies."[35] Both EPA and DOD rejected this recommendation in the comments they submitted to GAO before it issued its final report.

As for what has been done in response to these discoveries, GAO reported that EPA and state regulators have initiated or planned cleanup at 51 of the 400 sites. The regulators told GAO that the military has stalled those efforts on the grounds that cleanup should wait for a drinking-water standard. Clearly, the regulators are hesitant to pick a fight, given DOD's intransigence, despite their strong legal authority to take action.

### Legal Avenues Become Dead Ends

Four federal statutes give federal and state regulators the authority to require DOD and perchlorate manufacturers to address contamination that threatens public health. The substantive requirements of all these laws apply with equal force to the public and private sectors, but the federal government has long had the policy that one government agency or department cannot sue another. This limitation is known as the "unitary executive theory" because for judicial purposes it conceives of the agencies and departments as a single unit under the control of the president. Since EPA may not bring the military before a judge to compel cleanup, the theory means that the Agency is forced to cajole DOD into compliance unless it has the full support of the White House behind it, in which case browbeating is also possible. EPA does not enjoy that support at the moment. State regulators are not constrained by the unitary executive theory, and many have played a leadership role in forcing DOD to address environmental contamination in the past. Their passivity with respect to perchlorate may reflect resource shortfalls, however, since any attempt to force the military's hand would likely mean lengthy litigation.

The four laws, in order of their importance to cleanups at military bases, are:

- Resource Conservation and Recovery Act (RCRA): The statute provides authority to impose requirements on the management of "hazardous wastes," from "cradle to grave." Wastes are products that have been discarded. In addition to mandating that hazardous wastes be managed in secure facilities onsite, RCRA authorizes the Agency to require cleanup of leaks into the environment.[36]

- Comprehensive Environmental Response, Compensation, and Liability Act (CERCLA, or Superfund): The statute allows EPA to order the cleanup of abandoned rather than active dump sites of hazardous substances, a somewhat larger universe of toxic chemicals than hazardous wastes. In 1986 Congress amended the statute to require that DOD evaluate such sites. It ordered EPA to supervise these efforts and, if a site was causing sufficiently serious environmental contamination, to place it on the National Priorities List. The list includes approximately 1,250 sites, 171 of which are military facilities.[37]

- Clean Water Act (CWA): This law precludes the discharge of wastewater containing pollutants into surface waters, such as rivers, lakes, and streams, without a government permit specifying limits on the amount and content of discharge. Military bases typically have several such permits, issued under the National Pollutant Discharge Elimination System (NPDES), EPA's name for the program that enables implementation of these requirements.[38]

- Safe Drinking Water Act: The act is the source of EPA's and the states' authority to ensure that drinking water is safe at the tap. The statute's primary targets are publicly and privately owned drinking-water systems. Regulators may seek civil and even criminal penalties against owners and operators who do not maintain a clean water supply. As indicated by the perchlorate situation, EPA goes through an elaborate process to identify contaminants covered by these requirements and to specify maximum levels of the chemicals in the finished water. The Act gives regulators the power to seek emergency orders against any source of a contaminant that is posing an "imminent and substantial endangerment" to public health.[39]

A handful of military bases and privately owned facilities have become Superfund sites where perchlorate is among the contaminants subject to cleanup.[40] A few have NPDES permits that control discharges of perchlorate.[41] But further progress on all these fronts ground to a halt under the Bush administration.

In September 2003 the Pentagon decided that it would refuse to take water or soil samples of perchlorate contamination at sites except in three circumstances: the samples are legally required by a final EPA standard; the military has a reasonable basis for concluding that perchlorate has been released; and the perchlorate is likely to reach drinking-water supplies.[42] This policy means that when EPA manages to issue such a standard, there will be no inventory of the actual condition of sites under the military's control, further delaying cleanup until one can be prepared. Moreover, contamination will have spread, making cleanup more expensive and more difficult. The Pentagon's resistance to any further movement on the issue was on full display in Aberdeen, Maryland, where a remarkably independent group of EPA career employees decided to address a small problem in a small way, only to find themselves thwarted at the highest levels of government.

### The Aberdeen Incident

Aberdeen Proving Ground (APG) is a 79,000-acre facility in northern Maryland used primarily for weapons testing over the past seven decades.[43] APG is ranked as the third most expensive base cleanup in the country, with cleanup projected to cost $751 million. Like several other communities spread over three counties, the town of Aberdeen, population 13,000, adjoins the base. In 2002 perchlorate was found at a level of 4 ppb in one well. In a rare moment of candor, APG spokesman George Mercer told the *Baltimore Sun*, "We no longer have breathing room" and added, "I don't think anyone expected it [the perchlorate] to move that fast."[44]

Soon after this discovery, the Aberdeen Proving Ground Superfund Citizens' Coalition, a community group organized to monitor the Army's efforts to clean up massive amounts of contamination at the base, sought help from EPA regional office that covers Maryland as well as the Maryland Department of the Environment. The citizens met with Thomas Voltaggio, the deputy administrator of the office and a twenty-five-year Agency veteran, and EPA staff. Well aware of the intensity of the battle over perchlorate at the national level, Voltaggio nevertheless decided to wade into the controversy. Experts estimated that installing treatment equipment to remove perchlorate would cost $500,000. Voltaggio reasoned that this expense was modest and that the future threat to public health was significant. He directed his staff to draw up an order requiring the Army to take immediate action to provide treatment for the town's wells under the Safe Drinking Water Act.

Ordinarily, enforcement actions like this one would be handled by the regional office, perhaps with some input from headquarters experts in federal facility compliance cases. But this was no ordinary case in no ordinary time. Voltaggio's small cleanup ballooned into a consultation between EPA's No. 2 political appointee, a seasoned lawyer named Linda Fisher, and her DOD counterpart, Raymond Fatz, the deputy assistant secretary for defense in charge of environmental matters.

Fisher's mission was to persuade Fatz that DOD should accept the order requiring treatment of the Aberdeen drinking-water wells. He turned her down flat, but not before further sampling at APG turned up contamination at levels between 930 and 15,000 ppb at a distance of 600 feet from the nearest well. A Maryland Department of the Environment (MDE) official estimated that groundwater in the area moves at a pace that covers 100 to 200 feet per year, although pumping to meet the town's daily requirement of 1.7 million gallons could accelerate that pace. All further action has been suspended, although the Army continues to test for perchlorate in the water the town delivers to its residents. If and when perchlorate will infiltrate the Aberdeen drinking water wells at dangerous levels is anyone's guess.

## A Free Pass from Congress?

In the spring of 2003, a few months before DOD stopped sampling soil and water at perchlorate sites, the *Wall Street Journal* reported that the Bush administration had requested amendments to legislation under active consideration by Congress that would shield DOD from state or private lawsuits seeking cleanup at its "operational ranges."[45] The measure failed, largely because of opposition by the states. DOD was back before Congress in 2004, however, requesting broad waivers of requirements covering the 28 million acres of land it uses across the country for combat exercises and weapons testing.[46]

With those requests still pending, then–DOD Deputy Secretary Paul Wolfowitz sent a memorandum to the secretaries of the Army, Navy, and Air Force urging them to redouble their efforts to press EPA and the states for waivers under existing environmental laws. Wolfowitz wrote that his memorandum was "not intended to signal a diminished commitment" to environmental programs but that "first and foremost" these lands were "entrusted to our care" in order to ensure that "our Armed Forces are the best-trained and best-equipped in the world."[47] In an eerie echo of the comments by Colonel Rogers before the NRC perchlorate panel, Wolfowitz concluded that "we owe it to our young men and women to request an appropriate exemption."

## The Economics

DOD and its contractors are years away from having to prepare an official cost-benefit estimate for perchlorate, but—as we have seen—this convenient fact has not stopped them from warning that overly stringent public health protections will break the bank. In a period when deficits are spiraling out of control, the war in Iraq may continue indefinitely, and the worst natural disaster in the country's history—Hurricane Katrina— could cost $200 billion, these claims have fallen on very receptive ears in the executive and legislative branches.

But wait, you may think. How can the Pentagon possibly know how much it will cost to clean up perchlorate when it does not know how many bases are contaminated, the extent of that contamination, or the cost of the technologies that will prove effective in cleaning it up? As GAO pointed out in another critical report, the answer is that it cannot possibly know; its cleanup cost estimates are unreliable, and the military should stop projecting costs until it compiles a complete site inventory and knows the scope and magnitude of the problem.[48]

## Conclusion

The long story of perchlorate, which began with its discovery at California military bases in 1985 and will not end for many more years, stands for at least one discouraging proposition: without changing the law or otherwise admitting the implications, the Pentagon has withstood wave after wave of negative press simply by either ignoring or attacking EPA behind the scenes. No match for the combined force of the military and its industry allies in the Age of Terrorism, EPA is in retreat, and the states may follow its example. And yet there are glimmers of light on the horizon. It is difficult to see how the Pentagon could continue to resist taking action in the face of continued reports of perchlorate in the food supply. And scientists may develop a safer alternative explosive. One thing is certain, however. To achieve long-term remedies for this problem, we need to resurrect EPA to a position where it can carry out its core missions with autonomy and respect.

## Perchlorate Case Study Lessons

*The military has largely escaped the conservative attack on government. It has proved a formidable adversary not just to its enemies abroad but to institutions that attempt to influence its direction at home, especially when the nation is pre-occupied with military action abroad. Few are willing to risk the accusation that they are undermining the troops by questioning the Pentagon. These dynamics make it even more important for the military to remain at arm's length when other units of government are rendering judgments on its behavior.*

*Given the Pentagon's blatant conflict of interest as the party responsible for creating the perchlorate problem, there is no good reason for the powerful position it has assumed in determining the federal government's response to perchlorate threats.*

*In this context, EPA has been not so much captured as it has been vanquished, without the power to do more than go along for a very rocky ride. The decision to convene an Interagency Perchlorate Steering Committee putting EPA and the military on the same footing suggests that EPA's statutory mission to protect the environment is no more important than the Pentagon's reluctance to pay for cleanup. Nothing could be more devastating to EPA's authority in other contexts, its credibility with the public, and its own self-respect.*

*As in the mercury situation, controversies manufactured by "sound" science proponents have had the effect of delaying action to control pollution without advancing an understanding of the public health issues at the core of these disputes. The cost of the tests necessary to resolve the effect of perchlorate on fetuses and infants is significantly less than the millions of dollars that the military and manufacturers have already spent spinning their wheels.*

*The law fares no better. As it turns out, all the legal authority in the world is worth very little if the agency assigned to enforce the law lacks the will and the resources to carry out its responsibilities and the potential defendant openly scoffs at the law's requirements.*

*And then there are the economics. Without the benefit of any substantive backup data, the military has claimed that if perchlorate is in fact a problem at the levels suggested by the NRC panel, letting EPA loose will cost uncounted billions of dollars. Those expenditures will in turn compromise national security. That these figures lack a factual basis is troubling enough. But if they are true, how much more will we end up spending because DOD dawdled while the perchlorate moved through groundwater?*

## CHAPTER 7

# Ozone Case Study

*National primary ambient air quality standards . . . shall be standards the attainment and maintenance of which in the judgment of the Administrator, based on such criteria and allowing an adequate margin of safety, are requisite to protect the public health.*

CLEAN AIR ACT

## Overview

Few people noticed the announcement in September 2004 that EPA had designated 474 counties as "non-attainment" for ground-level ozone, more commonly known as smog.[1] EPA labels areas non-attainment when they have failed to lower ozone to levels that do not threaten public health. The primary group affected by ozone non-attainment is what participants in the epic struggle to contain the pollutant have euphemistically labeled "the outdoor child"—a child who is physically active during the summer months in one of the nation's major cities.[2] Elevated ground-level ozone in metropolitan areas exacerbates children's asthma and other respiratory diseases because they breathe much faster than adults, taking in more of the pollutant, which is a lung irritant.

Childhood asthma rates have skyrocketed since 1980. The CDC estimates that self-reported asthma cases increased by 75 percent from 1980 to 1994 and that the largest increases in prevalence occurred in children. Forty percent of asthma sufferers are children under eighteen, although children comprise only 25 percent of the population. CDC experts estimate that 9 million American children have been diagnosed with asthma.[3] Almost 4 million had asthma attacks in the twelve months prior to the

CDC survey. Boys suffer more than girls, children in poor families suffer more than those with resources, and children in fair or poor health overall are more than six times more likely to have asthma attacks.

Ozone forms when two precursor pollutants, VOCs and NOx, combine in the presence of sunlight. NOx emissions come primarily from transportation (56 percent) and power plants (38 percent), and VOCs are emitted by manufacturing plants (44 percent) and transportation (42 percent). In blunter language, major contributors to both categories of precursor chemicals are trucks, trains, planes, and the American love affair with the automobile.

EPA regulates ozone under the provision of the Clean Air Act that mandates the setting of National Ambient Air Quality Standards (NAAQS, pronounced "nacks") when scientific research shows that levels of pollution in outdoor (as opposed to indoor) air threaten public health.[4] A "primary NAAQS" is set to protect public health, and a "secondary NAAQS" addresses the damage pollution causes to the environment itself, including natural resources such as forests and diverse species.

To write a primary NAAQS, EPA must determine the maximum acceptable level of pollution to be tolerated in the ambient air, generally expressed as parts per million (ppm). This level must protect public health with an adequate margin of safety, and EPA is prohibited from taking the costs of reducing the pollutant into account. Ambient air that meets the standard may or may not cause problems for especially vulnerable populations, including children, because the air often contains a wide range of other pollutants; for better or worse, the system is designed to address problems on a pollutant-by-pollutant basis. EPA is obliged to review each NAAQS every five years to ensure that the standard is still adequately protective. However, the Agency often ignores these mandates; it missed deadlines for reviewing the ozone NAAQS in 1984 and 1989 and began a review in 1994 only after it had been sued by the American Lung Association.

To be sure, EPA has made impressive progress in improving air quality since the enactment of the CAA in 1963; the most common types of air pollution were cut by 48 percent, even though the country's population increased by 38 percent and Gross Domestic Product (GDP) increased by 164 percent.[5] But according to the EPA inspector general, the Agency's internal, independent watchdog, progress has been slowest for ozone, and levels have shown little improvement in 80 percent of the most polluted areas (Figure 7.1).[6] The American Lung Association estimates that 52 percent of the U.S. population, some 157 million people, live in areas

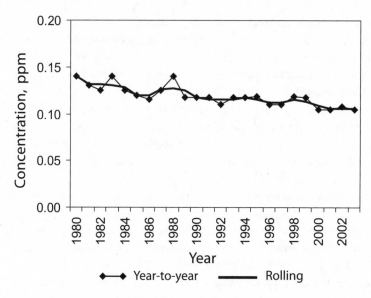

**Figure 7.1.** National Eight-Hour Ozone Trends, 1980–2003. Source: U.S. Environmental Protection Agency.

where ozone levels are unhealthy some of the time.[7] EPA is more upbeat in the rhetoric it uses to characterize these trends, but it does not dispute their magnitude or direction.[8]

Despite high stakes for public health, the promulgation of a new NAAQS has such significant economic implications that in the three decades since EPA was created, it has only managed to set such standards for six of the most ubiquitous and harmful air pollutants. These "criteria pollutants" are NOx, carbon monoxide, lead, sulfur dioxide, ozone, and two sizes of particulate matter typically contained in soot or smoke. With billions of dollars at stake, the development of the NAAQS and the initiation of each NAAQS review have triggered ferocious battles between EPA and the powerful outside constituencies affected by a final decision.

Although Congress was keenly aware of these controversies and the Agency's Herculean struggles to proceed, it decided to expand the statute's scope dramatically in the 1990 CAA amendments, putting many more challenging mandates on the Agency's agenda. The legislation was very popular politically and had strong support from President George H. W. Bush, and it passed both houses by wide margins. However, behind the scenes during long sessions spent crafting legislative language, Congress was unable to resolve a set of many contentious issues. So, as it has with other environmental laws, Congress wrote statutory language that gives the most powerful interest groups an opportunity to re-fight these disputes as EPA writes rules to implement these mandates. Rulemakings are lengthy and arduous, with tens of thousands of public comments filed and years of EPA deliberation.

Since 1977 the statute has explicitly instructed EPA *not to consider economic costs* in setting primary NAAQS. The prohibition on considering costs is unusual among environmental statutes, most of which require that costs be considered at some point in EPA's formulation or implementation of a standard. This "health-based" approach was most recently upheld by the U.S. Supreme Court, which made clear in its unanimous opinion that the only way to change this mandate was to persuade Congress to amend the statute.[9] That alternative is not considered likely by anyone involved in the debate, at least in the short term, because legislation to reform the act has faced a stalemate in Congress since the draining battle to enact the 1990 amendments. More than any other environmental issue except perhaps visibly polluted rivers or abandoned toxic waste dumps, air quality is a third rail in electoral politics, feared by both parties not least because opponents are invariably quick to thrust the rail into the careless politician's hands. Most recently, President George W. Bush asked Congress to pass legislation overhauling the act, shrewdly naming the proposal "Clear Skies."[10] But the bill's progress ground to a halt in the Senate Environment and Public Works Committee, where members could not overcome a likely tie vote.

Despite the Agency's agonizing, the promulgation of final rules does not end the controversy. Not surprisingly, EPA's efforts have been mired in the mud produced by its warring constituencies until a more powerful institution—Congress, the courts, the public during election season—pulls the Agency out, only to have it travel a few yards and sink in up to its hubcaps once again. Multiple lawsuits brought by environmentalists, a broad range of regulated industries, and the states have become a routine component of EPA's efforts to create and revise NAAQS, especially those with a high price tag. Litigation is far less expensive than the cost of compliance and buys regulated industries years of delay.

In 1997 EPA decided that despite all the controversy that was likely to ensue, it had to both lower and toughen the ozone NAAQS to better protect children as well as the elderly and those of any age with respiratory ailments. It began a battle that is still far from over. The large industry coalition that formed to oppose EPA's proposal did not concede any significant point regarding the science, the law, and the economics that underlie those decisions. As with the arguments of any heavily invested stakeholder group, the quality and credibility of their positions varies. This chapter does not attempt to refute all the arguments they have raised but rather focuses on the most prominent. Further, while regulated industries continue to dispute the intrinsic merits of the government's health evidence, those concerns are not at the heart of their opposition to the new standard. Instead, the gist of their opposition is a profound disagreement with public health experts and environmentalists over whether those health protections are worth their high cost. As done in the case studies of mercury and perchlorate, this chapter considers first the science, then the law, and finally the economics of EPA's decision making.

## The Science

### Built-in Science

In the case of mercury, EPA was vindicated by the NRC's findings, but regulated industries simply stepped around this inconvenient reality and continued to strafe the science supporting action to protect babies in utero. In the case of perchlorate, EPA found itself embedded in an interagency committee that included its major adversary, the Department of Defense, an implacable opponent of any effort to reduce perchlorate in children's drinking water. In the case of ozone, EPA had one of the few strokes of good fortune associated with its efforts to implement the Clean Air Act. Congress had the foresight to provide a built-in framework for scientific peer review of NAAQS revisions, creating the Clean Air Scientific Advisory Committee (CASAC) in 1977 amendments to the statute.[11] CASAC is organized and funded by EPA but prides itself on its scientific candor and independence. The statute mandates that the NAAQS process depends upon close collaboration between CASAC scientists and EPA staff. The EPA administrator initiates a five-step process when a NAAQS revision is necessary:

1. EPA staff prepares a "criteria document" summarizing the scientific research available on the pollutant and submits it to a CASAC panel for review. Staff and CASAC members then debate the contents of the draft until they develop a revised document that reflects their consensus interpretation of the research.

2. On the basis of the revised criteria document, EPA prepares a "staff paper" summarizing both the science and the policy options for the administrator and submits it to CASAC for review, triggering a new round of collaboration and negotiation.

3. CASAC sends a "letter of closure" advising the administrator on the scientific soundness of the staff documents and offering any advice it chooses on available policy options.

4. The administrator proposes a new NAAQS and puts the proposal out for comment.

5. The administrator considers all of the above information, including public comments received by the Agency, and determines the final standard.

### Science Versus Policy

The statutory language states clearly that the final NAAQS shall be the number that *"in the judgment* of the Administrator" protects public health, making it clear that the person appointed by the president and confirmed by the Senate has full authority to make a final decision. As Professors Wendy Wagner and Sheila Jasanoff have explained, there is a fine but distinguishable line between CASAC advice on scientific issues and whatever advice the panel offers on the administrator's policy options.[12] CASAC has more legitimacy when it confines itself to the first category, but the temptation to weigh in on policy judgments is strong.

Unfortunately, however, the conservative campaign to ensure that EPA uses "sound science" has created a poisonous dynamic for CASAC-EPA staff consultations. If a decision can be portrayed as based on "pure" and therefore "objective" science, the short-term thinking goes, it will be impervious to attack. The claim that "the science made me do it" can appear irresistible to an embattled EPA administrator. Yet attempting to justify a controversial decision by arguing that it is based solely on science requires a quixotic quest for a broad group of scientists who will remain committed to one number, without deviation, despite the substantial uncertainty that is inevitable in this area.

As it embarked on its consideration of a new ozone standard, CASAC was unanimous on one point: EPA needed to switch from the existing "one-hour standard" designed to address short-term ozone spikes and immediate health effects to an "eight-hour standard" designed to protect against long-term adverse health effects. Under the one-hour standard, levels were recorded for one-hour increments; if an area had levels that exceeded the standard more than three times over the course of a year, it was labeled non-attainment. Under the new, eight-hour standard, EPA and the states would measure levels over a period of eight hours, or eight times as long, presenting more opportunities for exceedences to occur and therefore requiring pollution sources to more tightly control their emissions.

While CASAC endorsed the eight-hour metric, the panel differed on what number of parts per million (ppm) of ozone in ambient (outdoor) air should be tolerated; members argued in favor of numbers from 0.08 to 0.12 ppm. After some heated debates, the panel issued the required letter of closure certifying the quality of the staff paper's scientific analysis and allowing EPA Administrator Carol Browner to make a final decision on a new and more stringent NAAQS. She chose 0.08 ppm of ozone measured over eight hours and averaged over three years.[13]

Browner clearly had the legal authority to make this judgment and the scientific analysis to back it up. But she made one serious mistake as she crossed the finish line, still under unrelenting fire from political opponents on and off Capitol Hill. She succumbed to the temptation to justify her decision as the sole product of "the" science, as opposed to policy informed by the best available science. George Wolff, a scientist with General Motors and the chair of the CASAC panel, went out of his way to contradict her, telling a Senate committee that "there is no bright line which distinguishes any of the proposed standards" and that EPA's decision was driven solely by policy, not science.[14] His fellow panelist Dr. Morton Lippmann, a scientist at the Institute of Environmental Medicine at New York University, tried to defend Browner, applauding her decision as a "prudent call,"[15] but the damage had been done. Not only did Browner appear self-serving in her characterization of the available science, she missed an opportunity to educate the public, judges, and members of Congress about the true nature of the NAAQS process. Most troubling of all, her approach unintentionally strengthened the central argument of the right-wing campaign against regulation: that we should wait for conclusive science before acting to protect children's health.

### The Conservative Case Against Regulation

There is little controversy that levels of ozone exposure in the 0.08 ppm to 0.12 ppm range exacerbate respiratory distress in susceptible populations—children, the elderly, and people of any age with pulmonary disease. EPA's many critics raise three underlying questions: whether 0.08 ppm rather than 0.09 or 0.12 ppm is the right number; whether an asthma attack or other respiratory symptom that is "reversible" justifies expensive control measures; and whether it is better for society as a whole to simply ask vulnerable people to stay inside.[16]

As for the first argument, conservative commentators argue that the science supporting a 0.08 ppm standard is unsound. They note that asthma rates are higher in "clean" countries than the "dirty" developing world, suggesting that the disease is rooted in factors other than air quality. They assert that the same trend has occurred even within the United States—despite improving air quality, asthma continues unabated, suggesting that the disease is primarily the result of household exposures to irritants such as dust or cockroach excrement, genetic predilection, or poor health care, making expensive pollution controls pointless.

There are three problems with this line of reasoning. First, the issue fairly stated is whether ozone exposure *exacerbates* asthma, not whether it causes new cases. EPA scientists would be the first to agree that other factors both cause and exacerbate the disease, although they would also say that an opportunity to lessen the severity of the attacks is well worth the effort. Second, there are many possible explanations for why asthma rates are higher in developed countries. The most prominent reason is that poor health care systems in the developing world are not nearly as efficient in diagnosing and reporting the problem. Third, the argument that ozone does not exacerbate asthma because the incidence of the disease is rising despite air quality improvement depends on a misleading oversimplification of the problem. Air quality in general has improved, but ozone levels have not shown a marked change in the past decade, especially in the nation's largest cities.

Experts will continue to debate the relationship between asthma and ozone for many years, although there are early signs that scientific research will move in the same direction as most pollution issues—that is, it will demonstrate that the problem is even worse than we thought. On September 2, 2005, in the context of its 2002 review of the ozone NAAQS, EPA released a revised criteria document.[17] The document says that the science showing a link between ozone exposure and mortality is strengthening, as is research showing that ozone exposure increases the incidence of cardiovascular disease and stroke. As further confirmation, a 2005 report by the National Academies' National Research Council stated with unusual forcefulness that "there is little doubt that public health is measurably affected at [ozone] exposure levels that exist in many areas in the United States."[18]

## The Law

### The Constitutionality of EPA's Power

EPA's 1997 decisions to tighten the ozone NAAQS, along with its decision to expand the particulate matter NAAQS to cover significantly smaller particles, were immediately appealed to the federal Court of Appeals for the District of Columbia Circuit. The case was brought by the broadest possible coalition of companies and trade associations, presented below, to give the reader some sense of the ferocity of this battle. The states of Michigan, Ohio, and West Virginia sided with the industry petitioners, while Massachusetts and New Jersey sided with EPA. Nine additional states supported EPA by filing amicus (advisory) briefs: California, Connecticut, Maine, Maryland, New Hampshire, New York, Pennsylvania, Rhode Island, and Vermont.

---

## CORPORATE PETITIONERS IN AMERICAN TRUCKING

*American Forest and Paper Association; American Iron and Steel Institute; American Petroleum Association; American Portland Cement Alliance; American Public Power Association; American Trucking Associations, Inc.; Appalachian Power Company; Baltimore Gas and Electric Company; Burns Motor Freight, Inc.; Carolina Power & Light Company; Centerior Energy Corporation; Central and South West Services, Inc.; Central Hudson Gas & Electric Corporation; Central Illinois Light Company; Central Illinois Public Service Company; Central Power & Light Company; Chamber of Commerce of the United States of America; Chemical Manufacturers Association; Cinergy Corporation; Citizens for Balanced Transportation; Cleveland Electric Company; Columbus Southern Power Company; ComEd Company; Consumers Energy Company; Dayton Power & Light Company; Delmarva Power & Light Company; Detroit Edison Company; Duke Energy Company; Duquesne Light Company; Edison Electric Institute; Equipment Manufacturers Institute; FirstEnergy Corporation; Florida Power Corporation; Garner Trucking, Inc.; Genie Trucking Line, Inc.; Gloucester Company, Inc.; Michael Gregory; Idaho*

*Mining Association; Illinois Power Company; Indiana Michigan Power Company; Indianapolis Power & Light Company; Jacksonville Electric Authority; Judy's Bakery, Inc.; Kansas City Power & Light Company; Kennecott Energy and Coal Company; Kennecott Holdings Corporation; Kennecott Services Company; Kentucky Power Company; Kentucky Utilities Company; Louisville Gas and Electric Company; Madison Gas and Electric Company; Meridian Gold Company; Midwest Ozone Group; Minnesota Power; Monongahela Power Company; National Association of Manufacturers; National Association of Home Builders; National Automobile Dealers Association; National Coalition of Petroleum Retailers; National Indian Business Association; National Mining Association; National Paint and Coatings Association; National Petrochemical & Refiners Association; National Rural Electric Cooperative Association; National Stone Association; National Small Business United; Nevada Mining Association; Newmont Gold Company; Non-Ferrous Founders Society; Northern Indiana Public Service Company; Oglethorpe Power Corporation; Ohio Edison Company; Ohio Power Company; Ohio Valley Electric Corporation; Oklahoma Gas & Electric Company; PacifiCorp; Phoenix Cement Company; Plains Electric Generation & Transmission Cooperative, Inc.; The Potomac Edison Company; Potomac Electric Power Company; PP&L Resources; Public Service Company of New Mexico; Salt River Project Agricultural Improvement & Power District; Small Business Survival Committee; South Carolina Electric & Gas Company; Southern Company; Tampa Electric Company; Toledo Edison Company; Union Electric Company; United Mine Workers of America; AFL-CIO; Virginia Power; Western Fuels Association; West Penn Power Company; West Virginia Chamber of Commerce; Wisconsin Electric Power Company.*

Source: Carol M. Browner, Administrator of the EPA, et al., Petitioners v. American Trucking Associations, Inc., et al., Petition for Writ of Certiorari, filed January 27, 2000.

---

One step down from the Supreme Court, the judges who sit on federal appellate courts across the country are at the apex of the judicial elite. Few question their intellectual ability, although many are troubled by their steady drift to the right. The D.C. Circuit Court's decision on ozone typified this trend.[19] Written by Judges Douglas Ginsburg and Stephen Williams, with a dissent by Judge David Tatel, the court decided for the first time since the 1930s that Congress had given a federal agency too much authority to decide too many important issues.

The majority reasoned that the Constitution provides for a division of power among the judicial, legislative, and executive branches. The legislative branch is empowered to write the laws, which it then hands off to the executive branch for implementation. This "strict construction" interpretation of the Constitution is known as the "non-delegation doctrine." Strict constructionists argue that the Constitution does not permit the legislative branch to re-delegate its lawmaking authority to any other branch of government. Browner's decision to adopt an eight-hour, 0.08 ppm standard was not explicitly mandated by Congress and therefore amounted to an unconstitutional abrogation of the power granted exclusively to the legislative branch. Or, in other words, Browner, a political appointee of President Clinton to head a non-cabinet agency, did not have the power to make a decision that had such profound effects on the economy; only Congress could make such far-reaching decisions.

In the nearly two years between the Court of Appeals decision and the Supreme Court's unanimous opinion overturning it, the excitement among conservatives was palpable. Could it be that their long years of wandering in the desert, decrying the expansion of the administrative state, had come to an end? That deeply desired outcome was not to be. In a wry opinion authored by Justice Antonin Scalia, one of the Supreme Court's most conservative members, the Court held that the only quid pro quo for a constitutional delegation was that Congress articulate an "intelligible principle" to guide administrators in implementing the law. The Court rejected the far more demanding approach urged by industry, that Congress must specify a "determinate criterion" that would spell out exactly how much of a harm was unacceptable rather than leaving such weighty issues to agencies to resolve. The revival of the non-delegation doctrine was stifled before it got off the ground, sparing the federal appellate courts and the Supreme Court years of draining and contentious litigation that would have attempted to apply the doctrine in thousands of contexts as agencies offended constituencies with the wherewithal to mount litigation.

Although this particular story ended well for EPA, it is vital to keep in mind that as the lengthy list of participants indicates, tens of thousands of hours were spent on this ultimately fruitless battle, at times flooding government attorneys in a tidal wave of paper. Win or lose, the threat of litigation alone has an enormous potential to influence—or, as a practical matter, deter the Agency's regulatory decision making. And, as we discover in the next section, even this troubling scenario is only one of the many problems plaguing EPA's efforts to implement the act's NAAQS provisions.

## A Bold Experiment in Cooperative Federalism?

Like most major environmental programs, NAAQS are written by the federal government and implemented by the states. States that wish to participate—and most of them do—apply to EPA for a delegation of authority.[20] Assuming that their applications demonstrate adequate capacity to undertake permit writing and enforcement, EPA grants the delegation and often provides financial contributions to help states run federally designed programs. A participating state is then obligated to prepare a state implementation plan (SIP) for each of the six NAAQS criteria pollutants.[21] EPA periodically reviews SIPs to make sure states stay on target in reducing emissions. If a state opts out of this system, EPA writes the SIP and implements the program in that jurisdiction. This chapter focuses on SIPs for areas that are *non*-attainment for the ozone NAAQS and therefore subject to the most stringent requirements.

The law compels states that have non-attainment areas for ozone or any other NAAQS to require pollution controls that will put all sources of emissions on a gradual downward trajectory toward acceptably clean air. The first step is the creation of an inventory of all emissions sources that produce the pollutant addressed by the SIP or, in the case of ozone, that produce the precursor chemicals NOx and VOCs, which combine to form the pollutant. Because the Clean Air Act broadly defines sources to include large and small businesses and public operations like schoolbus fleets or sewage treatment plants, compiling an inventory is no simple task. Once covered sources are identified, the states or EPA must estimate the amount of different pollutants they emit. Since many sources do not have continuous emissions monitors, regulators use complex formulas to estimate their output.

As arduous as it is to compile an inventory and predict emissions, the next step is even more difficult. States must develop a plan for reducing total emissions to a level that returns the area's air quality to attainment. States have flexibility to decide which categories of sources to regulate most stringently. The participating state must then estimate how much emissions can be reduced by installing certain kinds of pollution control equipment such as smokestack scrubbers or adopting cleaner practices like switching to low-sulfur coal. The calculations employ complex mathematical models that are difficult to design and to run. If the estimated levels are still too high, the state must find additional ways to reduce emissions to meet the standard. EPA is vital to this process in two ways: the Agency reviews and approves all SIPs and SIP revisions; and it issues regulations and guidance documents that specify how to construct inventories, estimate emissions, and impose requirements for sources to clean up their emissions.[22] The Agency issues requirements explaining how categories of sources should reduce their pollution, and the states then have an opportunity to adopt them.

States with areas in non-attainment must periodically demonstrate that they are on track to reach attainment by the statutory deadline. The methodology used to make such demonstrations involves calculating how much pollution will be reduced once EPA rules are adopted. If those numbers indicate that reductions will bring areas into attainment, the state passes the test. While states officially are allowed to pick from various federal regulatory programs, in areas that are badly polluted they must apply nearly all of the EPA options to prove that they are on track. Finally, it is worth noting that the states cannot simply pull EPA rules off the shelf and pronounce them as the law in their jurisdictions. Rather, they must obtain statutory authority from their legislatures to promulgate such regulations and then conduct full rulemakings, with opportunities for public notice and comment, before their adoption of federal rules becomes final.

### Process Over Substance

The SIP process has been heavily criticized for its burdensome complexity.[23] States cannot combine their SIPs into one comprehensive document, even if the NAAQS pollutants at issue come from the same sources. A state must have separate SIPs for ozone and NOx, even though the utility industry and transportation are at the root of both problems and are therefore covered by separate sets of requirements. Individual sources within an industry may also be covered by additional regulations formulated outside the SIP process, such as controls on hazardous air pollutants. Consequently, the operators of power plants, truck fleets, or manufacturing facilities may be covered by multiple plans and regulations with overlapping demands. Compounding this inordinate complexity is the reality that many states do not coordinate with each other, imposing disparate requirements on plants operated by the same company.

In a report it issued in May 2000, GAO informed Congress that "large industrial complexes operated by the petrochemical and refinery, chemical manufacturing, and electric power industries are prime examples of sources that are regulated under multiple programs of the [Clean Air] act."[24] As needlessly difficult as regulated industries find the system, it is probably even more frustrating for the federal and state officials who must work together to implement it with declining resources. According to GAO, one expert familiar with state programs estimated that states then faced a $140 million shortfall in funds for CAA implementation.[25]

According to an interdisciplinary panel of experts convened by the NRC, federal and state regulators have become inordinately preoccupied with these regulatory complexities, which can take years to resolve.[26] As they become more entwined in their dealings with each other and regulatory funding declines, their working relationships are put under considerable pressure, with multiple unwanted results. A running joke among cognoscenti of the act is that EPA staff hold SIPs at arm's length, squinting hard to read into them an acceptable demonstration that the promises made in the documents will lead to attainment. The areas designated non-attainment for ozone decades ago still have not corrected the problem, suggesting the possibility that bad SIPs are approved as EPA struggles to keep the process moving along.

### A Tangle of Missed Deadlines, Budget Shortfalls, and Failure of Will

A major impediment to the implementation of NAAQS is that EPA often misses its statutory deadlines for the tasks it is assigned under the Act, throwing an already burdensome process into upheaval at the state level. The 1970 amendments to the original 1967 CAA required state SIPs to demonstrate that NAAQS would be attained throughout the country by 1977 at the latest. When this outcome did not happen, Congress passed an amendment in 1977 that extended the deadline to 1987 and authorized EPA to impose sanctions on states that did not submit adequate plans or that missed their attainment deadlines.[27] The law also instructed EPA to step in and write federal implementation plans (FIPs) in tough cases.[28] EPA staff was extremely reluctant either to impose these penalties or to write its own plans. So in 1990, with many areas still far from attainment, Congress got serious, or so it thought.

The 1990 amendments extended these deadlines once again, giving areas in the worst shape the longest time to achieve attainment and labeling them "marginal," "moderate," "serious," "severe," or "extreme."[29] Congress also strengthened the sanctions available in such cases. The first is withholding federal highway funding, and the second is prohibiting construction of new air emission sources until the area returns to attainment. In egregious cases, these sanctions are supposed to be imposed automatically. Congress instructed EPA to bump up into the next highest level any area that failed to meet its interim goals. And it required that, in all but marginal areas, states periodically demonstrate "reasonable further progress." The 1990 amendments are widely perceived as by far the most ambitious (and, depending on your point of view, unreasonable) federal environmental laws on the books. Congress imposed 171 mandates related to the implementation of NAAQS and 237 mandates related to the control of hazardous air pollutants. Many of these tasks involved difficult and time-consuming technical analysis as well as extensive consultation and negotiation with EPA's state counterparts.

The congressional authorizing committees that wrote these requirements have very little to do with the appropriations committees that determine the level of the Agency's actual funding from year to year. The disconnect between authorizing and appropriations committees has proved extremely destructive to EPA, which is subject to citizens' suits if it misses a statutory deadline.[30] As explained in Chapter 3, "Battered-Agency Syndrome," the situation has deteriorated to the point that EPA commonly waits until a "deadline suit" is filed to implement a rule. Congress imposes mandates on the Agency, often despite its protests that those goals are unrealistic. EPA leadership then pleads with OMB for the money it needs to implement the mandates. The EPA administrator typically fights a bitter battle behind the scenes but falls into lockstep in support of the president's budget once it is sent to Congress. In fact, in the Agency's three-decade history, no administrator has even come close to telling Congress what every outside observer already recognizes: that the gap between funding and mandates is huge and getting worse.

Given the disproportion between its statutory mandates and its funding, it is not surprising that EPA was habitually late on all of its mandates, including those with a specific statutory deadline and those that were mandated with no specific deadlines set. Table 7.1 shows the aggregate number of deadlines EPA missed, and Table 7.2 shows the time it took EPA to produce a final work product.

The further EPA fell behind, the more often it overlooked problems with the states' performance in meeting NAAQS. The Agency struggled mightily to avoid imposing sanctions, particularly for failures to demonstrate reasonable progress. By 2005, many areas had not yet met their attainment deadlines. Rather than go back to Congress and request another extension, the Bush administration's EPA decided instead to simply revoke the one-hour standard for ozone at the same time that it began to implement the eight-hour standard, automatically extending the deadlines to 2007 and beyond. That decision has also been challenged in court. In

**Table 7.1. EPA Deadline Performance**

| Type of Requirement | Title I (NAAQS) | Title III (Hazardous Air Pollutants) |
|---|---|---|
| Requirements with statutory deadlines | | |
| Met on time | 16 | 13 |
| Met late | 45 | 195 |
| Unmet as of April 2005 | 22 | 21 |
| SUBTOTAL | 83 | 229 |
| Requirements without statutory deadlines | | |
| Completed | 85 | 8 |
| Not completed | 3 | 0 |
| SUBTOTAL | 88 | 8 |
| TOTAL | 171 | 237 |

Source: Government Accountability Office

an article on the 1990 amendments that he wrote shortly after their enactment, Professor Howard Latin accurately predicted this outcome:

> When statutory mandates require administrators to make decisions they would find threatening, inconvenient, or distasteful, it is vital for legislatures to ensure that regulatory responsibilities are clear and certain. The diffuse structure of the SIP process achieves just the opposite effect, creating ambiguous responsibilities that all agencies may seek to evade.
>
> The SIP process is permeated by politics, and *politics usually prevail over technocratic requirements.* Indeed, the principal reason Congress chose the decentralized SIP mechanism was to maintain state and local political control over many social policy choices.[31]

## The Economics

### Monetizing Costs and Benefits

As explained in Chapter 3, "Battered-Agency Syndrome," Circular A-4 issued by OMB in September 2003 may be the most important single deregulatory initiative accomplished by the Bush administration.[32] The document is the forty-eight-page explanation of how agencies are to comply with Executive Order 12866, issued by President Clinton and requiring cost-benefit analysis for all major rules.[33] Weighing regulatory

**Table 7.2. EPA Delays in Completing Work Product**

| Length of Delays | Title I | Title III |
|---|---|---|
| Up to 12 months | 24 | 41 |
| 13–24 months | 9 | 75 |
| 25–36 months | 4 | 50 |
| More than 36 months | 8 | 29 |
| TOTAL | 45 | 195 |

Note in GAO-05-613, Clean Air Act: EPA completed most actions required by the 1990 amendments, but many were completed late (May 2005).
Source: Government Accountability Office

costs and benefits under the Bush administration begins with monetization of the value of human life and nonfatal diseases, discounts those amounts if ill effects will be delayed for several years, and refuses to adjust these numbers on behalf of our children or their children. One of the most important problems caused by this kind of number crunching gone amok is the veneer of precision—and therefore credibility—it lends to decisions that in fact grapple with both scientific and technological uncertainty. The ozone problem provides a disturbing portrait of cost-benefit analysis in practice.

The Clean Air Act required EPA to produce its first cost-benefit report on the implementation of its mandates in November 1991, but the Agency did not get its act together until October 1997, when it issued a retrospective report covering the period between 1970 and 1990. The report concluded that compliance cost regulated industries a *total of* $523 billion—or $26 billion annually.[34] The *total twenty-year* monetized benefits of the law are between $5.9 *trillion* and $49.4 *trillion*, with a "central estimate," or mean, of $22.2 trillion. Subtracting costs from benefits, EPA joyfully announced that the statute's net benefits, or benefits minus costs, were in the range of $5.1 trillion and $48.9 trillion, with $21.7 trillion the central estimate for the act's first two decades, when amazing progress was made in controlling visible and destructive pollution.

How did the Agency arrive at such an astoundingly large, remarkably wide range of numerical estimates? It used the following assumptions to tally how much money the prevention of disease or death is worth and then multiplied these amounts—prices, really—by the number of incidents of disease or death that it expected to occur in the absence of any Clean Air regulation. The five assumptions were:

1. The value of one human life saved was assumed to be $4.8 million.
2. The value of a single lost IQ point (due to lead exposure) was assumed to be worth $3,000 per individual. (Remember that this amount had risen to $8,800 by the time EPA quantified it for the purposes of assessing mercury contamination in 2005.)
3. Chronic obstructive pulmonary disease, caused by ozone, was assumed to be worth $8,100 per case.
4. Acute asthma was assigned a value of $32 per incident.
5. "Mild restricted activity days" were valued at $38 per day.

In November 1999 EPA compiled an estimate of the costs and benefits of the act for the period from 1990 to 2010, after the 1990 amendments went into effect.[35] Estimating costs for 1990 to 2010, EPA predicted that regulated industries would pay compliance costs of $19 billion annually by 2000 and that those costs would increase to $27 billion annually by 2010. The assumptions used in this second report to calculate the benefits changed only modestly. Because requirements—and the benefits they produce—are phased in over a period of several years, the Agency decided to use 2010 as its reference year. Its range of direct benefits in that reference year is $26 billion to $270 billion *annually*, with a central estimate (again, the mean) of $110 billion. The EPA estimate for net benefits (benefits minus costs) over the twenty-year period is $510 billion. Monetized health benefit numbers from the 1990 to 2010 report were as follows:

1. A human life was still worth $4.8 million.
2. A hospital emergency room visit for asthma was worth $194.
3. A full-fledged hospital admission for all respiratory problems was worth $6,900, and admissions for cardiovascular problems were worth $9,500 per case.
4. Acute respiratory symptoms were worth $18 per case, although an "asthma attack on Moderate or Worse Asthma Day" was worth $32 per case.

To its credit, EPA, then headed by Carol Browner, peppered both cost-benefit reports with warnings that some benefits cannot be monetized. It also acknowledged that personal and social values addressed by the act cannot be reduced to dollars. Those wise caveats on what otherwise seems like a strange, misleading, and even unethical process would never be included in reports prepared today. Rather, cost-benefit analysis in all its glory has become the most important tool for judging and restricting regulatory proposals.

## Does the Clean Air Act Kill People?

This discussion of the costs and benefits of clean air would not be complete without a visit to the far right end of the spectrum, where some argue that implementation of the law actually kills people.[36] The theory behind this remarkable claim is that the costs of regulation are passed directly on to the consumer in the form of higher electricity prices and more expensive consumer goods. These costs must be absorbed by families and will have an especially devastating impact on people with low incomes because the money lost will not be available to pay for essentials that make people healthier. The researchers never specify what those essentials might be, but we can imagine that they mean medical care, safer housing, and nutritious food. The researchers say these "economically transmitted impacts" of the new ozone and particulate matter NAAQS could kill between 2,201 people (for $10 billion in annual regulatory costs) and 22,589 people (for $100 billion in annual costs). Families with incomes below $15,000 in 1994 dollars will pay by far the highest price, accounting for some 40 percent of lives lost at all levels of cost. In a particularly harsh twist, the researchers estimate that 25 percent of the fatalities will occur in African-American households.

A string of questionable assumptions underlies these claims. They include the notions that all costs are passed through to consumers, rather than being deducted from stockholder dividends and that these amounts will mean enough worsening of poverty to result in death. But by far the most important—and questionable—premise is that the cost of environmental regulation is the only factor to be weighed against survival needs in determining the fate of these imagined people, as opposed to unequal education, a low minimum wage, the withdrawal of government benefits, and such outsized expenditures as the defense budget and the war in Iraq.

## Conclusion

The Clean Air Act does not allow EPA to even consider the alternative of telling people to stay inside when air quality is bad. Instead, the solution of putting the burden on the victim to avoid the risk has become the default reality as a direct result of the powerful combination of a dysfunctional legal framework and hollow government. For the many parents who live in cities afflicted by Code Red days and who bring their children's asthma inhalers every time they venture from home, all of these elaborate, convoluted calculations, research projections, and public policy quarrels may seem bizarre. To be sure, we drive cars, we depend on a stable supply of electricity, and we value the vast variety of products that are available to American consumers. But would we really choose to impose smog on our and other people's children so that some of us have the option of buying the largest SUV on the market? Is it fair to expect the youngest among us to shoulder so much of the burden of allowing pollution to rise to levels that cause clear health problems, even if the economists tell us that such incidents are only worth a few dollars? We expect government to mediate such profound conflicts in values, but some among us appear to be intent on ensuring that government is not allowed to meet those expectations.

Clearly, we cannot afford to pay any conceivable amount of money to bring air quality back to what it was at Jamestown, when the colonists first saw the New World. But the domination of the policy debate by those who are almost always hostile to pollution control means that it is extraordinarily difficult for the American people or their elected representatives to ever get to the bottom of these questions. What would be a better system? That subject is the focus of the remainder of this book.

### Ozone Case Study Lessons

*Ozone is a more mature problem than mercury or perchlorate in the sense that we have been working on solving it for close to three decades. While this relatively extensive experience enriches the lessons we can learn, our failures to achieve health-based goals are also a more ominous indication of how much the existing system needs reform.*

*The good news is that the new eight-hour ozone standard and all other Clean Air Act rules survived cost-benefit analysis as administered in the Bush administration to the point that the White House actually bragged about these beneficial interventions on the free market. The bad news is that litigation stalemated such a good regulatory bargain, and the implementation of the new ozone standard remains entangled in the courts.*

*The fact that the Clean Air Act passes cost-benefit analysis with such flying colors should be profoundly embarrassing for the conservatives who have spent years condemning environmental regulations as a massive waste of money. Yet these critics have not acknowledged these great benefits, indicating that they are not really after objective analytical results, but prefer number crunching that either stops protective action or goes on forever.*

*The details of cost-benefit analysis and the implications of its application are the ultimate example of decision making buried so far in the bowels of the bureaucracy that the American people cannot possibly realize what is going on. Assertions by the proponents of such number crunching that their calculations reflect "what the people want" or "the people's willingness to pay" are groundless because the studies of the public's preferences are methodologically flawed and fragmented to the point of being nonsensical. Nevertheless, in what amounts to a quintessentially anti-democratic exercise, the combined power of monetization and discounting derail public health protections, leaving cost-benefit practitioners in the luxurious position of debating with themselves about how to make their calculations without ever subjecting themselves to backlash if people were given an opportunity to respond.*

*Meanwhile, back in America's inner cities, state officials approach with dread the formidable challenges of squeezing non-attainment areas into compliance with the eight-hour ozone NAAQS. Major changes in everyday life will be required, from lower-emission cars to limits on the volatile organic compounds in paint to the retirement, preferably sooner than later, of outmoded and excessively dirty power plants in the Midwest. No one should be surprised if state officials ask for another extension.*

*Implementation of the NAAQS provisions of the Clean Air Act has become so convoluted and requires so much wheel spinning at all levels of government that it is past time to face the underlying problem: the sheer unreasonableness of the CAA's demands on the Agency. Many participants in the process are convinced that we are so far from compromise on environmental issues that it is best to preserve this discouragingly inefficient tangle of mandates. After all, if given half a chance, conservatives in Congress might well repeal large swaths of the CAA, shutting down even flawed efforts to implement it.*

*But refusing to entertain the possibilities of fundamental reform, as compelling as this position appears in the heat of daily skirmishes between the right and the left, is a strategic and not a principled position. While I would be the first to acknowledge its wisdom as a practical matter, progressives cannot afford to remain in a defensive crouch, living with a deeply flawed system because we fear that matters will only get worse. Instead, we must believe that if the trade-offs were presented to people honestly and comprehensively, their choices would be better for both public health and the strength of democratic institutions than the status quo.*

**PART III**

# CURES

# Introduction to Part III

The ink was barely dry on the Nixon administration's executive order creating EPA when its many critics, not to mention its numerous friends, started compiling proposals to improve it. Such critiques have intensified in the past decade as a series of bipartisan institutes, multi-stakeholder groups, academics, and investigative committees have issued thousands of pages making hundreds of recommendations for reform. These suggestions fall somewhere along a continuum from modest changes designed to accomplish a gentle redirection of the existing system to radical overhaul that would rebuild it from the ground up.

The enormous popularity of environmental protection among the public gives commentators favoring deregulation a strong incentive to characterize even their most extreme ideas for EPA reform as modest. Conversely, people favoring fundamental reform to strengthen government's role soon learn to soften their proposals or risk ridicule by ever-vigilant representatives of regulated industries. Although there was a period in the mid-1990s when the two groups actually sat down and talked to one another on occasion, even reaching consensus on controversial issues, politics have become sufficiently polarized in recent years that honest exchanges, much less compromises, are few and far between. Inevitably, crises like global warming and, as EPA's first administrator, Bill Ruckelshaus, described it, the inevitable swing of the environmental pendulum back toward the left will drive the warring sides back to the negotiating table. The challenge, then, is to prepare for that day by proposing far-reaching reforms that will provoke honest responses from the opposition when the time is right.

The two chapters that follow do not soft-pedal the reforms that are necessary to revive the existing, dysfunctional system. Chapter Eight, "A

Question of Values," explores why the conservative campaign to deregulate has been so successful, given the popularity of stronger environmental protection and anxiety about what the future holds in store for our children. It tackles the essential job of eliminating the political cognitive dissonance that allows government to operate in one way when people say they want it to operate in a 180-degree opposite manner.

Chapter Nine, "New Government," proposes revisions to each of the assumptions that pervade the existing system with such devastating effects: from the premise that costs and benefits can be quantified down to the last dollar to the rule that science must trace causes and effects with great certainty before government can act. I advocate restoring confidence in EPA by removing the numerous constraints on its freedom—from excessively harsh judicial review to contentious congressional oversight to petitions for affirmative action from public-interest groups.

As I hope this book has communicated adequately, the polarization that dominates politics has stymied even incremental reforms. Some observers expect that it will take a catastrophe on the scale of the Exxon oil spill off the Alaskan coast or the fatal Bhopal chemical-plant explosion to break the gridlock on environmental policy. Such tragedies have acted as catalysts for productive changes before. But they are unlikely to have similarly powerful effects this time. *Nothing*—not even modest reforms of EPA's authority, methodologies, or structure—will be possible until the polarization shifts and voters elect leaders who are both capable of and willing to chart a different course for the federal government.

## CHAPTER 8

# A Question of Values

## Overview

In the winter and spring of 2004, I did a series of talk radio interviews about *A New Progressive Agenda for Public Health and the Environment*, a book that I wrote with my colleagues at the Center for Progressive Reform.[1] There I was, saying similar things to what I have said in these pages, confronted by right-wing hosts and listeners who quickly lost patience with me. One listener was so enraged by what he heard that he took the time to tell me off by e-mail:

> Your logic makes me sick to my stomach. We should, you say, want to make the world safer and healthier for our children. Did our parents do this for us? Even if they did, they created challenges for us and we answered them. . . . The fact is that I do not want to go out of my way to make the world a safer and healthier place for my children if it interferes with my lifestyle. I am one of those people who you derided, who has more cars than drivers. I have five vehicles. And you know what, I earned them. They are all paid for by my hard work and sweat. And no one is going to tell me I cannot have them or should not have them because of the environment.
>
> The fact is that if my children are faced with problems that may very well be good for them. It will enable them to work them out and become better people, just as I have become a better person by working on problems and solving them. When I fell off my bike when I was a kid, without a helmet, by the way, which I am sure you safety people would demand now, I got up, cried if I was hurt and got back on the bike and rode. It is called life.

I am sick and tired of people like you who are trying to make the world such a safe place that there is no room for a hangnail. Get a life and grow up.

I offer the message here not in an effort to shock the reader (although I was pretty surprised on first reading), but rather because I think it expresses a nontechnocratic, mercifully blunt view that is the exact opposite of mine. My correspondent does not beg the question of whether a problem exists, nor does he apologize for his lifestyle. He assumes that his ownership of five cars will cause environmental problems for his children, but he puts his needs first. Most important, he refuses to take cover behind quibbling about the details of which problems might be serious, whether we need more science to evaluate these problems, what it would cost to address them, and so forth. Instead, he stands at the opposite end of the rhetorical battlefield: I say things are bad and we are betraying our ethical obligations to our children, and he says there may be problems but each generation should use technology to fend for itself.

The public debate rarely frames the issues so clearly. Instead, it spins out in seemingly endless spirals of vague generalities about the importance of a clean environment, whether or not we have made adequate progress in achieving that goal, government missteps in protecting natural resources, and, in its most distasteful incarnation, how excessive regulation will hurt the disadvantaged among us by compelling them to choose between reasonably priced electricity and smog-free summer days. Or the debate evolves into intricate, invariably tedious discussions of why, where, when, and how we should decide to spend large sums for indefinite benefits, leaving the average person in the dust and causing even expert participants to lose track of the real issues.

This chapter considers three related aspects of this stark divergence of views. The first is who is right about what the American people say they want. Are most people in favor of protecting children from environmental pollution but do not realize that the government has turned its back on those aspirations? Or do people know very well that environmental conditions are worsening but do not care to modify their behavior to take the next generation into account? At least so far as public opinion polling is concerned, this examination shows that I have the better part of the argument, although a small but identifiable segment of the population agrees with my correspondent. The second aspect is how mainstream American values should inform where we go from here. Opinion may change, after all, and to close my case more convincingly, I explore how environmental threats to children fit into a broader conception of what national values should be. The third aspect is whether we have the luxury of a real choice among options any more. Can my correspondent and others who share his views realistically expect that the next generation can invent its way out of deep trouble? Or has that argument become fantastic, given the pressure the human race is already putting on the planet's natural resources?

## What People Think

### About Environmental Protection

As discussed in Chapter 2, "The Rise of Special Interest Conservatism," the best conservative political strategists urge their clients to discuss environmental issues only in positive and euphemistic terms. Frank Luntz, the fabled creator of the 1994 Republican Contract with America, advises politicians to talk in soothing language about their concern for the environment, emphasizing the need to use common sense in finding solutions to the risks posed by industrial pollution:

> Your plan must be put in terms of the future, not the past or present.
> We are carrying forward a legacy, yes, but we are trying to make things
> even better for the future. The environment is an area in which people
> expect progress, and when they do not see progress being made, they get
> frustrated.[2]

Luntz tells politicians to avoid using the phrases "sound science," "cost-benefit analysis," and "risk assessment" because "your constituents don't know what those terms mean, and they will then assume that you are pro-business."[3] Luntz makes these recommendations because he thoroughly understands the results of public-opinion polling.

In its comprehensive report *Trends 2005*, the Pew Research Center found that a whopping 78 percent of Americans believe that "this country should do whatever it takes to protect the environment."[4] These numbers have held steady within a point or two since Pew began asking these questions in five-year polling cycles beginning in 1994. The large majority of Americans believe the environment is in danger and will only deteriorate with time. A poll conducted in spring 2006 by ABC News, *Time*, and Stanford University found that 76 percent of respondents believed that the condition of the environment was fair, poor, or very poor; 60 percent of those respondents believed that the environment was worse than it was ten years earlier; and more than half the respondents believed that the environment would be worse ten years later.[5] Similarly, the Gallup Organization reported in April 2005 that "two-thirds of Americans [were] distressed about the environment."[6] These numbers break down as 35 percent who worry "a great deal" and 31 percent who worry "a fair amount." Gallup also found that young people worry more than older people (40 percent for the eighteen to twenty-nine age group versus 26 percent for people sixty-five and older) and that nonwhites worry more than whites (43 percent versus 31 percent).

Polls show that concern about environmental issues also breaks down along party lines. The *Trends 2005* report shows that although "large and unchanging majorities of the public endorse environmentalism," 83 percent of liberal Democrats said stricter laws were worth the cost, compared to 49 percent of conservative Republicans.[7] As a whole, 60 percent responded that stricter regulations were worth the cost.

A mandate of 60 percent is significant as far as it goes, given the narrow margins in the past two U.S. presidential elections. But the message from the middle is more ambiguous than the messages from the right and left. This phenomenon means that environmental issues are sometimes eclipsed in battles for so-called "swing" voters. Except during primary season or in decidedly partisan districts, politicians address undecided voters more than any other group. Because polling suggests that a candidate's position on environmental questions would not be enough to change swing voters' minds, politicians perceive little advantage in stirring up the antipathy of either end of the spectrum, or so the popular wisdom goes.

One final poll offers interesting evidence on how people conceptualize environmental problems and what to do about them. In the fall of 2005, Public Opinion Strategies and Peter D. Hart Research Associates released an unusually comprehensive study on environmental attitudes conducted for Duke University's Nicholas Institute for Environmental Policy Solutions.[8] The pollsters focused on why people express such broad support for environmental protection and yet rank it low on their list of priorities, including issues that inspire them to vote the way they do. The pollsters concluded that this disconnect exists for five reasons:

1.  People do not think there is any crisis in environmental protection. This contradicts recent findings that 75 percent of people believe the environment is in danger, although without access to the polling

questions, it is hard to evaluate whether methodologies or attitudes account for these differences.

2. Environmental problems have long-term effects that seem remote.

3. Most respondents (87 percent) said better protection would mean higher taxes, and many (56 percent) said it would hurt the economy and cause job loss.

4. "The environment" encompasses a broad range of issues, which divides people's attention. Some worry about global warming, others about clean water, and so on.

5. People do not see the environment as a clear-cut issue. Unlike abortion, gun control, or other social issues that also occupy the second tier, one is not simply "for" or "against" the environment.

The Duke pollsters sorted their respondents into groups that they labeled with vivid, even humorous names. Some 34 percent of voters belong in The Empathizers group, who are most likely to embrace "altruistic messages" such as "leaving a legacy for future generations, protecting people's health, or [knowing] that special places and wildlife are preserved."[9] The next third of the electorate is divided evenly at 18 percent each between The Compromisers and The Narcissists. Compromisers want to chart a middle ground, taking into account the views of "sportsmen, farmers, scientists and conservationists" so that we simultaneously protect the environment and meet human needs.[10] Narcissists, on the other hand, are completely preoccupied with how such policies affect their jobs, their health, and their personal finances.[11] My correspondent quoted at the outset of this chapter probably belongs in this group, although the Duke pollsters did not say whether or not Narcissists share his degree of hostility to those like me who preach more environmental protection and less consumerism.

Regulators and Capitalists comprise a quarter of the electorate, breaking down almost evenly at 12 and 11 percent, respectively. Regulators are the "most liberal, most likely to hold post-graduate degrees, highest income, most secular, and most likely to view the environment as the top problem facing the country."[12] As their label implies, Regulators are also most likely to embrace government rules as the best methodology for improving environmental quality. The Capitalists are situated to the right of the middle, and as their name implies, they are more concerned about "a policy's impact on jobs and the economy" and are more likely to identify themselves as Republicans.[13]

Lastly, 7 percent of respondents are Contrarians, so named because they are the least likely to support affirmative government action. But even here, 66 percent favor stronger protection of the environment and only 26 percent oppose it.[14] Contrarians tend to be older, religious, and somewhat more concerned about "being good stewards of God's creation."[15] Religious beliefs like these are just beginning to emerge as potentially influential factors in the environmental arena, with evangelical Christians tying concern about global warming directly to the story in Genesis 2:15 about God putting Adam in the Garden of Eden "to work it and take care of it."[16] These numbers indicate that a significant number of survey respondents reacted well to the idea of preserving the planet for our children, but the polls did not provide definitive evidence regarding whether people thought that this legacy is threatened or would be willing to do much about it.

### About "Jobs Versus Environment"

As the Duke poll suggests, support for environmental protection is often tempered by anxiety about the economic impact of controlling pollution. According to the Gallup poll, despite growing concern for the environment, the percentage of respondents who believe it is worth the risk of curbing economic growth to strengthen environmental protection has dropped; 67 percent of respondents in 2000 said protection is worth the risk, but in 2006 only 52 percent said the trade-off was worth it.[17] In contrast, the percentage of respondents who believed that economic growth should be given priority even if the environment suffers to some extent rose from 28 percent in 2000 to 37 percent in 2006.[18]

On the other hand, a poll conducted in April 2004 for the Nature Conservancy and the Trust for Public Lands found that 66 percent would be willing to pay $10 more per year to fund environmental programs; 60 percent would pay $25 more per year; and 56 percent would pay $50 more per year.[19] The pollsters did not raise the figures any higher, nor did they explain how the money might be used. The U.S. population in 2005 totaled 186.2 million working-age adults eighteen to sixty-four years old.[20] If 60 percent each contributed $10, the total raised would be more than $1 trillion. We have no real idea of how this offhand commitment would play in practice because the government has never come close to asking people to actually make such a contribution. The real point is that for surprisingly small amounts of money per household, resources could be raised that would be well-spent on more efficient and effective government cleanup and prevention efforts.

To briefly follow one relevant tangent, it is worth noting that, given the obvious anxiety many people harbor with respect to the trade-off between economic prosperity and environmental protection, scores of economists have studied the nature and extent of this dynamic. However, they have not been able to develop much convincing evidence that this trade-off actually exists. In his book *The Trade-Off Myth: Fact and Fiction About Jobs and the Environment*, economist Eban Goodstein provides convincing evidence that "employment gains or losses from environmental protection are small, gradual, and tend to balance each other out."[21] Goodstein explains that environmental regulation has resulted in localized job loss—timber workers caught up in efforts to save the spotted owl in the Northwest and high-sulfur coal miners in the Southeast who lost jobs when acid rain provisions led utilities to shift to low-sulfur coal. But these effects pale in comparison to other causes, especially the availability of low-cost labor in other countries.

Rather than stripping jobs from the domestic economy, new pollution control requirements create jobs, especially in the construction industry. Between 1977 and 1991, the last year that EPA undertook these calculations, jobs created by spending on environmental cleanup climbed from 1,267,000 to 1,965,000, making this area one of the most successful and dynamic growth sectors nationwide. Loss of a job is traumatic to the person who experiences it. But those in search of the causes of such economic upheaval must look beyond environmental regulations for accurate answers.

In any event, the polling data on people's attitudes toward environmental protection are far from systematic and, especially in the area of people's perceptions of the trade-off between economic disruption and enhanced environmental protection, raise more questions than they answer. As the Duke pollsters pointed out, concern for the environment is not an either/or, one-dimensional reaction; people may be more or less concerned about various categories of problems depending on their perceptions of a problem's severity and how much it affects them. The polls give us, at best, only inklings of how people would respond if they were convinced that unsolved environmental problems would harm their children. Emerging opinions on the threats posed by global warming are likely to offer greater insight into the legacy question and bear watching over the next several years.

Yet at the risk of oversimplifying, the upshot of available data seems to be that a large majority of people are concerned about the environment but not as concerned as they are about other, seemingly more immediate problems. People are willing to make a greater investment in environmental quality, but how much greater an investment they are willing to make is unclear. They are not willing to risk significant economic disruption on the basis of what they know now. Barring a specific local problem, environmental issues are unlikely to determine election results because the voters at either end of the spectrum who most vehemently support or oppose stronger protection are the least likely to switch their votes. Finally, people are open to the idea that we need to think about our environmental legacy to our children but do not yet see that legacy as being under threat.

However one interprets these results, only a small handful of the most conservative pundits would ever argue that the public's support for environmental protection is soft to the point that we can afford to officially dismantle the elaborate regulatory system we have built to cope with the job of preserving environmental quality. Everyone wants the system to work better. Until it does, rational and cost-effective decisions concerning whether and how to address major problems cannot be made. The effort to chart a better course is further complicated by people's ambiguous attitudes toward the government.

## About the Government

Polls consistently show that at least half of Americans are cynical to the point of hostility about the government. Public trust in government stood at 76 percent in the early 1960s, before Vietnam, Watergate, Enron, the Iraq War, Hurricane Katrina, and a variety of other troubling events took their toll on public perceptions. Attitudes have followed a downward trend ever since, with the only break point a short-lived surge of support for government in the wake of the traumatic events of September 11, 2001.[22]

According to a 1995 *New York Times*–CBS News poll, only 18 percent of Americans answered that they could trust the government "always" or "most of the time."[23] This number "rebounded to a patriotic 55 percent" after September 11 and then sank again to 36 percent in the summer of 2003.[24] The Pew Research Center's *Trends 2005* offers somewhat more optimistic numbers, pegging the public as about equally divided, with 45 percent of Americans stating that the government "does a better job than it gets credit for" and 47 percent saying that "government is almost always wasteful and inefficient."[25] A national poll conducted for the nonpartisan Partnership for Public Service found that less than half of surhe space shuttle up and performs about 12,000 other necessary and vital functions. Yet calling someone "a Washington bureaucrat" remains an insult.[30]

## Political Dissonance Revisited

Parts I and II of this book argue that government efforts to protect children from pollution have not only stalled but begun to fall backward. They explain how the dysfunction of government institutions is at the root of such problems. Previous chapters hypothesized that people would not sanction this state of affairs if they knew of its existence. And the immediately preceding analysis of public opinion polls verifies that argument. Taken together, the evidence assembled up to this point suggests that the canyon between what people say they want and what the government actually does is the product of several converging trends.

The nation is preoccupied by international conflicts, leaving little room for progress on our most important and difficult domestic problems. Politics in America are polarized, and debates over public policy are strident. People see environmental problems as important and they are concerned about the future, but they do not know what to do. The popularity of environmental protection makes it necessary for politicians who are hostile to regulation and government to dissemble in public, adding further confusion to issues that are already complex. Even when decision makers manage to discuss the issues honestly, protecting environmental quality is portrayed as revolving around intricate economic and technical questions, as opposed to widely shared ethical values. This complexification drags the resolution of these issues back into the realm of confusing double-talk, quickly alienating all but the most self-interested parties who have a financial or professional stake in the outcomes.

Unraveling this mess requires new beginnings on two planes: a recommitment to central values widely shared throughout American culture, the subject of the next section, and a series of essential reforms to change the way government works, the topic of the book's closing chapter.

## Shared Ideals

The ethical and religious foundations of American society include the conviction that all people are created equal and that no life is worth more

vey respondents said they would consider a jo
percent said excessive bureaucracy "explained t
cent could not answer when they were asked wi
excluding the military, does especially well.[26]

Historical hindsight should inform our interpr
An important part of America's historical tradit
Boston Tea Party, a rebellion against autocracy t
republic, and this tradition of rebelliousness remai
of the culture today. On the other hand, public opi
stood highest after the New Deal and Great Society
ernment was playing a badly needed but intrusive rol
More recently, conservative presidents beginning wit
have demeaned government's competence and importa
delivered on their numerous promises to cut government

Finally, in evaluating how seriously to take this asp
opinion polls, there is the time-honored question "Comp
Do people see alternatives to government, especially wi
solving environmental issues? In a November 2002 CBS–Ne
poll, 62 percent of respondents said that the federal governm
do more to regulate the environmental practices of business."
surveyed for *Trends 2005*, 76 percent said "too much power
trated in the hands of a few large companies."[28] In a similar v
asked by the Harris Poll in August 2005 whether various intere
"doing their share" to "help reduce environmental problems," 71
said large corporations were doing less than their share.[29] The
does not have a private-sector alternative in mind to achieve goa
most people say are very important.

All of these disparities suggest that as a society we are perfectly cap
of railing against government authority at the same time that we er
the benefits it can provide. Or, as *Washington Post* columnist Paul Fa
put it,

> It's our birthright to criticize government, of course. We started the
> country on a fundamental suspicion of those in power, and armies of
> journalists, commentators, inspectors general and late-night comedians
> are employed to keep them honest. But let's get some perspective. Many
> people like big government, no matter how much they complain about
> it or posture about it for political effect. Big government builds roads,
> fights disease, directs air traffic, fights wars, inspects food, takes the cen-
> sus, doles out food stamps, Medicare and Social Security checks, sends

than another. Everyone has the right to equal opportunity and equal protection under the rule of law. After equal opportunity is secured, though,
people are on their own. Government provides an increasingly tattered,
shrinking safety net to prevent extreme hardship and, as a practical matter, to keep the desperately poor off the streets. But we believe that able-
bodied adults who do not work hard deserve what they get so long as
they begin life with equal opportunity. While harsh, these outcomes are
the price of the freedom and individual autonomy that American society
treasures at least as intensely, as *The Economist* has observed:

> More than any other country, America defines itself by a collective
> dream, the dream of economic opportunity and upward mobility. Its
> proudest boast is that it offers a chance of the good life to everybody
> who is willing to work hard and play by the rules.[31]

This finely calibrated mixture of egalitarianism and hard-nosed "prosperity for the fittest" has served the country very well, along with our
extraordinary access to some of the planet's richest natural resources and
the oceans that lie between us and many of the worst wars between fac-
tions of the human race.

The best translation of these values as applied in an environmental
context is the blunt question I have heard on two memorable occasions
in my thirty years of practicing law. Both instances involved working-
class neighborhoods beleaguered by pollution to an absolutely unacceptable extreme. In each case, I was serving as a lawyer representing the
community and was sitting with a mixed group of corporate executives,
government officials, environmental activists, and neighborhood residents, listening to first-person accounts of how people were affected by
these problems. As the sessions broke up and people walked away in small
groups shaking their heads, first an oil company executive and second a
high-ranking municipal fire department official asked me in exasperated
tones: "Why don't they just move?"

I had no ready answer. I could have said "because they are not middle
class and don't have enough money, unlike you and me." Or I could have
replied "because there is no familiar or accessible place for them to go." I
could have accepted the assumption embedded in the question and said,
"many did get in this situation because they did not work hard enough,
but that does not mean that a compassionate society should leave them
there." Or I could have said what I really believed: "People stay because
they have lost track of how bad it is in the course of getting from day to

difficult day, and they justifiably feel trapped." Any or all of these answers might have continued the conversation in a productive direction, although we might not have gotten very far in our mutual understanding of root causes and the appropriate social response.

Instead of giving any of these answers, however, I took what seemed to me to be the easiest way out of these polite but loaded confrontations. Like a good advocate, I did not challenge my interlocutors' view of race, class, social mobility, work ethic, corporate power, or municipal zoning. Instead I said, "There are dozens of kids living there—regardless of what their parents do, should they be left behind?" The conversations stopped dead in their tracks.

I have no real idea what these two people thought as they walked away. On some level, both men undoubtedly found the entire situation, up to and including my answer, infuriating. Comfortable in their personal lives and optimistic about what lies ahead for their children, they reacted with hostility to these very troubling, demonstrably true stories about suffering that should not be possible within the borders of the richest country on earth. They were clear that they would never stay in such circumstances, especially with a family, and they could not fathom why any other able-bodied adults, especially with families, would remain behind. Like an impatient pedestrian walking past a panhandler, they perceived the two communities as intruding on their personal space. "I gave at the office," both thought. "What do you expect me to do about all this?"

If I had them both in front of me today and had a second chance to give a more effective answer, I am not sure exactly what I would say, but it would be some variation of the appeals made throughout this volume. "In the end," I might respond, "Garrett Hardin was right about the tragedy of the commons. No one has a personal airspace and everyone lives downstream from someone else. We cannot afford to indulge in compassion fatigue and turn our backs on other people's environmental misery because, as the song goes, 'There but for fortune go you and I.'[32] If we do not change, there will come a time when much of the commons disappear, and we will be left hoping we do not live long in such a day."

Then, if I could keep my wits about me as I continued to attract baleful glances, I might say, "We can preserve liberty and individual autonomy without tolerating the destruction of the commons, and those who argue otherwise have their own—and not society's—overall interests in mind. If we want to ensure that all children have equal opportunity to have a good life and we want our children's children to have the same opportunities, we must change the way we make decisions, beginning with the way the government conceives of its role in these kinds of situations. Blaming the victims and leaving them to fend for themselves, outmatched by the overwhelming power of the free market, is not the way to go."

"OK," I imagine my questioner retorting—and now I have really departed from anything that has ever happened to me, "I see your point. But what would environmental policy look like if you were in charge. And how would it differ from the way it looks today?"

## Competing Visions of the Future

### The Conservative Vision

Traditional conservatives and the wide range of industry-based special interest groups that are introduced in these pages believe that the cornerstone of America's astounding success as a nation is the capitalist, or free-market, system. Not only do they cherish the great value of the free market, they fear it is fragile and easily perturbed by ham-fisted government intervention. Because capitalism must be free to function and, if it is, will provide the best possible quality of life for the most people, conservatives impose a heavy presumption against regulation.

This presumption not only is very difficult to overcome, it can only be overcome in *economic* terms. Conservatives acknowledge that there are intangible values that are crucial to American society, including equal opportunity, but they believe that regulation is the wrong way to preserve those intangibles and that the free market is a far preferable route. Proponents of regulation must demonstrate "market failure" before government intervention is allowed and, even then, it should be as minimal as possible. Conservatives think that market failure is very rare and is caused by disparity in information and unequal bargaining power among parties. Those intermittent problems are easily resolved with relatively modest requirements that missing information be disclosed. The fact that one party gets a bad deal is not proof of failure and could just as easily mean that the market is working properly.

As applied in the environmental arena, conservatives insist that the only way to overcome the presumption against regulation is to show that a situation in the market produces significantly more costs than benefits for society as a whole and that this situation will not self-correct. To make adequately careful and fine-tuned decisions, conservatives believe that it is essential to quantify the costs and benefits of the market versus the intervention in monetary terms. This practice invariably has the effect of sacrificing the needs—or "rights"—of a minority to the over-all well-being of the collective whole because even a great yet expensive benefit to a small number of people would fail the cost-benefit test. In response, conservatives would probably say that they are interested in freedom from interference, not the freedom provided by government protection, but the tension between the right-wing's militancy with re-spect to individual autonomy and its willingness to sacrifice that value to the economic advantage of the majority is worth considering.

Conservatives acknowledge that it is sometimes controversial and dif-ficult to monetize lives lost and the suffering caused by disease, but they categorically reject the idea of shirking this challenge. They are willing to commit very significant resources to the pursuit of such calculations. They assume that people voluntarily place themselves in the path of risks large and small every day, making implicit economic decisions about how much they are willing to pay to avoid potential harm. Conservatives do not believe that the children of such workers should be considered separately from their parents. Nor do they accept the argument that we owe any debt to future generations because they will almost certainly be richer than we are.

## The Progressive Vision

Progressives also accept capitalism and the free market as the central orga-nizing structure of the American economy and, ultimately, our society. In our youth, some of us embraced other ideas, but we have long since recognized that as applied, they left something to be desired. However, progressives reject the notion that the market in this country is "free" in any objective sense of the word. Government-sanctioned monopolies, tax preferences and loopholes, agricultural subsidies, below-market sale of grazing, mineral, and water rights, and similar add-ons have compro-mised the market's freedom at least as much as regulation.

Progressives do not assume that the market will correct itself if left alone. Rather than starting with market failure as the quid pro quo for action, progressives focus on the occurrence of harm to children as a result of the activities of corporate or other public and private sector entities. Progressives would consider regulation any time it appears that the public health is placed at risk by pollution that could be avoided. Pollution should be the factor presumed invalid, not interference with the marketplace. By putting the burden on the source of the risk to jus-tify why it cannot cease the harmful behavior, progressives would stack the deck in favor of mandatory controls, although—we would argue—no more than conservatives stack the deck against it.

Progressives believe that government exists for the purpose of helping people who are harmed by the unfettered operation of the market to have a better life. Our most important goal is moderating the capitalist free-for-all to ameliorate racial inequities, disparities in educational opportunities, the demoralizing impact of poverty and disease, and the growing gulf between the rich and the poor, and—above all—to fulfill the imperative of giving all children equal opportunity regardless of their status at birth. All children deserve equal opportunity, regardless of race, class, ethnicity, and even their parents' deficiencies.

Rather than struggling to find market failure and prove that the benefits of action outstrip the costs, government's threshold presumption should be that children deserve protection from industrial pollution. The people's agents—in Congress, on the bench, and in government agencies—are responsible for ensuring that this presumption is overridden only in carefully defined circumstances when we have no reasonably available technology to protect people or when the activity is sufficiently valuable to society as a whole that it would be wrong to help the few at the expense of the many. Overcoming this presumption should be the responsibility of the entity that causes the harm, and the burden of proof should be heavy. Government should categorically reject arguments that it would be better to spend money on bicycle helmets or vaccinations, as if there is an invisible and very limited budget for safeguarding children's welfare.

## Poor Children

Progressives believe that the urgency of a fundamental change in America's approach to environmental policy is underscored by the effects of poverty on American children. According to the U.S. Census Bureau, 37 million people, or 12.7 percent of the U.S. population, were poor in 2004, up from 31.6 million and 11.3 percent in 2000 (Figure 8.1).[33] Roughly 33 percent were children under eighteen, representing a poverty rate in that age group of 17.8 percent, compared to a rate of 11.3 percent for people aged eighteen to sixty-four and 9.8 percent of people over sixty-five (Figure 8.2).

Even these staggering numbers understate the problem by a significant and discouraging margin. Professor David Wood notes that the U.S. gov-

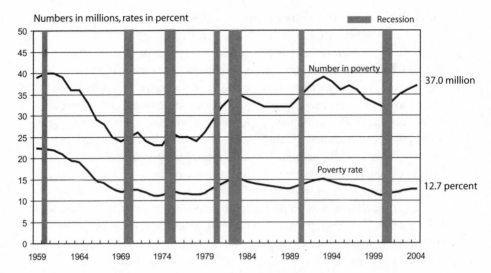

Note: The data points are placed at the midpoints of the respective years.

**Figure 8.1.** Number of Americans in Poverty and Poverty Rate, 1959–2004. Source: U.S. Census Bureau, Current Population Survey, 1960 to 2005 Annual Social and Economic Supplements.

ernment uses a "poverty line"—meaning "an economic state that does not allow for the provision of basic family and child needs, such as adequate food, clothing, and housing"—that was set in 1965 at a rate three times the cost of the basic food basket for a family.[34] It has never been adjusted for the disproportionate increases in housing, transportation, medicine, and other nonfood essentials. Expenses such as child care are left out of the mix entirely. In 2006 the federal poverty guidelines set $20,000 as the level defining destitution for a family of four.[35] The government allots $3,400 for each additional person added to a family.

Wood notes that child poverty has increased in the past thirty-five years for three reasons: decreased real value of wages; decreased government safety-net payments; and growing numbers of families headed by single women. He explains that of the money allocated to government income-support programs, including Medicaid, Medicare, and Social Security, 20 percent goes to poor families and 80 percent goes to the elderly.[36]

The implications of these discouraging statistics are obvious. Poor children suffer a significantly higher incidence of chronic health conditions and serious physical disabilities. They also suffer more from inadequate nutrition and deteriorating housing. About 11.2 percent of all children have no health insurance coverage; this rate climbs to 18.9 percent for children living in poverty, again under the very conservative definition of the poverty line used by the Census Bureau. These data indicate that poor children get ill at rates significantly higher than the general population but often lack access to medical care to make them well.

Remarkably little scholarly writing analyzes the destructive interaction between childhood poverty and environmental exposures. One recent exception is a study by Professors Janean Dilworth-Bart and Colleen Moore, for the March/April 2006 issue of the journal *Child Development*.[37] The authors analyze the relationship between environmental exposures and poverty, using as their primary—and well-chosen—examples lead paint contamination of inner-city rental housing populated by poor children and the exposure of migrant worker children to pesticides. They conclude that these children, disproportionately African American and Hispanic, bear a double burden when the disadvantages of poverty are exacerbated by toxins that diminish mental capacity and further damage overall health.

No one should argue, and I am most definitely not arguing, that childhood exposures to pollution are any more acceptable when they harm rich children than when they harm poor ones. Rather, my point is that

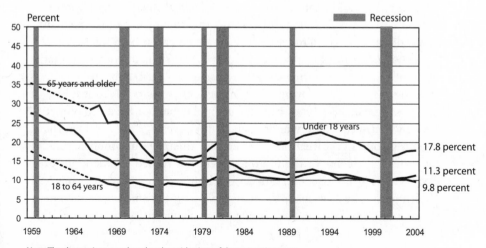

Note: The data points are placed at the midpoints of the respective years.
Data for people 18 to 64 and 65 and older are not available from 1960 to 1965.

**Figure 8.2.** Poverty Rates by Age, 1959–2004. Source: U.S. Census Bureau, Current Population Survey, 1960 to 2005 Annual Social and Economic Supplements.

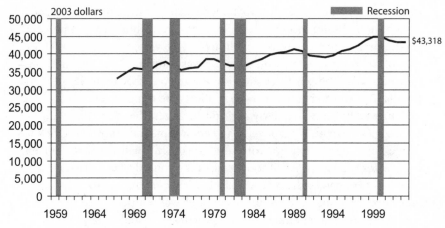

Note: The data points are placed at the midpoints of the respective years. Median household income data are not available before 1967.

**Figure 8.3.** Real Median Household Money Income, 1967–2003. Source: U.S. Census Bureau, Current Population Survey, 1960 to 2005 Annual Social and Economic Supplements.

poor children exposed to crippling pollution suffer a knock-out blow given the other problems they must surmount to have a chance at a better life.

As for the notion that a rising tide will lift all boats, this notion is also refuted by the data. Figure 8.3 shows that the income of the median family doubled between 1947 and 1973, but the increase between 1973 and 2003 was 22 percent. Princeton economist Paul Krugman points out that much of the increase during the latter period was attributable to women entering the workforce or people working longer hours.[38] "All it takes," writes Krugman, "is a bit of bad luck in employment or health to plunge a family that seems solidly middle-class into poverty."[39] In contrast, the average income of the wealthiest 1 percent of Americans has doubled since 1973, and the income of the top 0.1 percent has tripled. These kinds of observations infuriate conservatives. The right wing argues that stronger government intervention in the marketplace would amount to income redistribution and would "undermine economic incentives and reduce all of us to shared misery,"[40] presumably in the same way that environmental overregulation of American business has had such devastating effects on the economy and, not to be overlooked, the poor. Whatever one thinks about the importance of equal opportunity as a value in society, as opposed to the free market, unrestrained consumption, competition, or the myth of Horatio Alger, societies with large extremes between wealth and poverty are less stable and less democratic than ones where "most people can reasonably be considered middle class."[41]


## The Luxury of the Present

This volume is focused on domestic environmental problems and American children, although the mercury case study gives an insight into the need to think about such threats from a global perspective. If it is not clear to us now, it will be clear in a matter of just a few years that the degradation of the global environment is the greatest challenge to life as we know it, more so even than the jeopardy posed by the use of nuclear weapons.

Garret Hardin, the biologist who explained the tragedy of the commons, followed in the footsteps of Thomas Robert Malthus, an ordained minister of the Church of England who published "An Essay on Population" in 1798.[42] According to Malthus, "Population, when unchecked, increases in a geometrical ratio, and subsistence for man in an arithmetical ratio."[43] The overall sustainability of the earth's ecology is possible only because of phenomena like famine and disease and affirmative human choices like the postponement of marriage or conscious population control. Now, however, there are signs that the human race may not have time for such natural or voluntary corrections to restore ecological balance. Instead, we may confront nonlinear changes that overwhelm the planet's ecology, producing disaster and suffering on an almost unimaginable scale.

As of late 2006, the global grain harvest was projected to fall short of consumption by 61 million tons, marking the sixth time in seven consecutive years that production did not equal demand.[44] Global climate change scientists predict temperature increases that will melt polar ice caps, raising sea levels and driving hundreds of millions of people inland to live.[45] The Millennium Ecosystem Assessment Board, a project initiated by then–United Nations Secretary General Kofi Annan, among others, has involved the work of 1,360 experts worldwide and is co-chaired by Robert Watson, the chief scientist of the World Bank. The board issued this statement in 2005:

> Humans have made unprecedented changes in ecosystems in recent decades to meet growing demands for food, fresh water, fiber, and energy.

These changes have helped to improve the lives of billions, but at the same time they weakened nature's ability to deliver other key services such as purification of air and water, protection from disasters, and the provision of medicines. Among the outstanding problems identified by [our] assessment are the dire state of many of the world's fish stocks; the intense vulnerability of the [2] billion people living in dry regions to the loss of ecosystem services, including water supply; and the growing threat to ecosystems from climate change and nutrient pollution. . . . At the heart of this assessment is a stark warning. Human activity is putting such strain on the natural functions of the Earth that the ability of the planet's ecosystems to sustain future generations can no longer be taken for granted.[46]

In this amount of space, with other subjects to address, I cannot offer much more than a brief mention of such scenarios. Yet there is little question that these predictions are far more credible and prominent than they were in Malthus' day.

## Conclusion

As of this writing, there are emerging signs that the stridency of conservatives is wearing thin and that the nation cannot sustain this degree of polarization over the long haul. If you look, you can discern preliminary signs that change is afoot. Some Fortune 100 corporations are articulating their concern about global warming publicly. The states with the worst ozone, mercury, and perchlorate problems are exploring what they can do in the absence of federal action. Schoolchildren express disgust about the environment, trained from the cradle to be aware of the health of the earth in ways we never imagined. Even if these signs of change take a long time to build, it is worth considering what we should do when we are ready to reform government. And it is to that subject that we now turn.

## CHAPTER 9

# New Government

*When you've lost an election by that much, it isn't the case of whether you made the wrong speech or wore the wrong necktie. It was just the wrong time.*

*Extremism in the defense of liberty is no vice. . . . Moderation in the pursuit of justice is no virtue.*
BARRY GOLDWATER

## Overview

With the full backing of the White House, single-minded focus, and a thick skin, an EPA administrator could accomplish far-reaching, meaningful, and effective reforms. With the participation of a critical mass of the Agency's key constituencies and skillful negotiating, many of those reforms could happen within a relatively short time—say, two to four years. If Congress was able to participate in the dawning of this new day, the changes could be even more profound and wide-ranging, although they might take longer to accomplish. And once reforms take hold, changing the way EPA conducts business, the Agency might renew its appeal to the best and the brightest of committed scientists, lawyers, and economists, gradually winning back its self-respect and the deference it should receive from the courts and congressional oversight committees.

All of these outcomes seem elusive at the moment. EPA administrators have never had the full backing of any president and for much of the Agency's history have looked more like dogs on a very, very short leash than independent leaders trying to accomplish the Agency's well-articulated mission. A critical mass of special interest groups will be un-likely to assemble for negotiations until they believe either that they have no other choice but to try and work something out with their sworn ene-mies or they have something significant to gain from the process. Con-gress does not look like it can agree on anything, much less waste politi-cal capital on a set of issues that appear low priority to the president and second-tier to the public. The polarization of American politics, which is the condition precedent for all this paralysis, does not seem likely to end soon, despite broad public support for stronger environmental protection.

At times like these, I often think of Barry Goldwater's landslide defeat in the presidential election of 1964, which, more than any other event, catalyzed the development of the modern version of conservatism that has become so dominant in American politics. Lyndon Johnson's rout of Goldwater and his followers was so thorough that only a special breed of politicians and ideologues, one more strong-minded and persistent than any other in recent memory, would have been able to chart a phoenix-like ascension from a landscape filled with ashes as far as anyone could see. Given the obvious tilt of this book in the exact opposite ideological direction, it may seem both odd and a tad too cute for me to say that the odyssey of Goldwater and his allies is my inspiration. But it should be true, not just for me but for most professionals. His example shows that there is very little point in nibbling around the edges of the environmen-tal policy changes that are necessary to get protection of children back on track. A bold agenda, pursued indefatigably, has a far better chance of making a real difference.

This chapter proposes eight reforms, listed below in the order in which they will be discussed over the following pages.[1] Explanations of the re-forms touch briefly on how hard they will be to achieve, but in the best Goldwater tradition, none were censored on the basis that their viability appears far-fetched at the moment. These reforms remain on the plane of broad generalities to keep them accessible to a reader not steeped in all the nuances of the issues that would need to be resolved if people sat down in good faith to design their implementation.

- Federal police power to protect public health. The executive and legislative branches' constitutional authority to establish EPA and give it work to do, which is based on the broad provisions of the Commerce Clause, should be reconceived as authority to protect public health through the exercise of federal police power rather than

a one-dimensional effort to ensure the free flow of business trans-
actions interstate.

- Independent priority-setting. EPA should be given expansive authority to set priorities among the pollution problems that Congress
  has assigned it to address, placing at the top of the list the threats that
  pollution (especially persistent toxics) pose to the very young.
- More money. The budget for government environmental protection
  programs should be enlarged significantly.
- Clean science. Public funding for basic research on environmental
  hazards should be increased. The scientific process must be reformed
  to increase transparency, guarantee independence, and avoid conflicts
  of interest.
- Precaution. Risk assessments should be based on protective—or precautionary—assumptions because the central goal of environmental
  laws is to prevent harm rather than compensate the injured. Remedies
  that involve instructing the victims of pollution to avoid the risk—for
  example, the exhortation that children should be kept inside on Code
  Red days—should never be adopted on a permanent basis and instead should be used only as an interim measure until the risk can be
  controlled.
- Best available solutions. Remedies that involve selecting the best available pollution control technology should be used whenever possible.
- Monetization of costs, not benefits. The value of human life should
  never be monetized. Costs should be analyzed carefully before, during, and after protective rules go into effect.
- Judicial deference. The courts should defer to EPA's scientific judgment and policy decisions in all but egregious cases where the Agency
  has clearly ignored an explicit statutory mandate or done a demonstrably poor job of gathering information to support its decision.

Before wading into the content of these reforms, the reader deserves an
explicit statement of the broad—and unquestionably controversial—
theme that connects them.

## Free EPA

### Institutional Autonomy

The core premise of all eight proposals is that EPA must be given more
money, more authority, and more autonomy and then be allowed to do its

job. Everyone from the most conservative ideologue to the most liberal pundit, from diehard environmentalists to vehement corporate representatives, from agitated members of Congress to overly confident federal appellate court judges, must back off and wait for a long time—a matter or years, not months—to see how a self-directed bureaucracy handles its many missions. For a long honeymoon period, courts should defer to final Agency judgments; Congress should defer to EPA's interim decisions and priority-setting efforts; friends and enemies should holster their weapons in the running battles that afflict every controversy that lands in EPA's lap; think tanks should stop issuing exposés; and politically opportunistic investigations of malfeasance should be suspended. Not until EPA has amassed an adequate track record in an area—for example, childhood exposures to toxins through drinking water or chronic air pollution that exacerbates childhood respiratory disease—should its performance be examined from a harshly critical point of view.

Thousands of pages have been written in the past fifteen years explaining to government how it can do a better job. Very few have called for government to be left alone to bungle some things and get others right. Why should anyone on the left, on the right, or in the middle consider such a drastic step now?

The simplest answer is that professional experts, working full-time in the public sector and remaining focused on specific issues for years at a time are unquestionably the best choice to lead us out of the mess we have created. The bureaucracy has several advantages over any other institution that might be considered as an alternative. The vast majority of bureaucrats are career civil servants. In EPA's case they include professionals in a range of disciplines, including scientists, engineers, economists, communications specialists, lawyers, and other technical experts. They were hired because they have the right training to analyze the complex challenges that stand between them and effective solutions. These professionals are paid to find the best solution from the public's point of view, and they are capable of shouldering the responsibility for developing better solutions to chronic, apparently intractable environmental problems.

This book began by targeting complexification as among the major shortcomings of the current system. As the narrative unfolded, no easy solutions to this most enervating of problems emerged. We live in a free country, after all, where everyone is allowed to speak their mind. It is inconceivable that we could simply order affected interest groups to stop adding their views to an open debate. If you pursue this dilemma a bit further, though, it becomes obvious that a major cause of complexifica-tion is the catastrophic erosion of EPA's authority. Aggrieved parties can challenge EPA's decisions by pleading their cases to a dozen legal or sci-entific institutions, getting them to second-guess virtually every decision its career staff makes.

The most prominent of those entities—the National Academy of Sci-ences, the National Research Council, the federal appellate courts, or any one of several congressional committees—increasingly do not give EPA's administrative decisions any benefit of the doubt. The result is that each decision is revisited again and again and again, serving the interests of those who oppose action and injuring the interests of those who need it to happen.

Forum shopping and endless appeals are not the exclusive bailiwick of regulated industries; environmentalists and other guardians of the pub-lic interest also pursue them. On the losing end more often than not in recent years, the left has enormous difficulty seeing why it should relin-quish a tool that its opposition wields with great force.

These recommendations do not mean that EPA will be left free to run amok. The Agency will still be compelled to exist in a political fishbowl, sustaining media and public scrutiny, coping with vigorous advocacy in every rulemaking, and answering to focused congressional oversight. What will be different is that decisions will be made and we will have an opportunity to see if they work, as opposed to spending all our resources on fights designed to derail decision making and implementation.

If these other institutions retreat, deferring to EPA as they would to any other group of highly trained professionals, there will be far fewer opportunities to reinvent the science, expand the scope of the debate, confuse the issues, and distract participants from the business at hand. Complexification will continue, but on a smaller scale. Most important, the public will know that the government will make timely decisions. The merits of those conclusions—and not endless arguing over the technical nuances that underlie them—will become the appropriate focus of the public's attention.

Advocates across the political spectrum will not cease their efforts to pressure government easily. Environmentalists will never believe that business will withdraw, and business will never walk off the field of play while environmentalists are still on it. All players will fear losing every advantage if they are foolish enough to disarm before the other side. Yet we should not underestimate the power of a turn in public opinion and strong leadership by the president to accomplish a détente that could give civil servants the breathing space they need to begin to act independently on the basis of their best judgments on the merits of an issue as opposed to their anxiety about political backlash.

## Workforce Competence and Morale

People aghast at the prospect of elevating the bureaucracy to a position of real power are likely to raise three distinct objections. First, they will argue that the most important priority is to deregulate the private sector, lifting the heavy weight of misguided government rules off the shoulders of American businesses as they struggle to remain competitive in a global economy. The bureaucrats who constructed this wasteful system should be the last ones we trust to remain objective and creative enough to reform it. Even if you are willing to acknowledge the importance of regulatory rollbacks to make environmental protection more palatable and efficient, real reform will be far easier to accomplish in a less polarized atmosphere. Revitalizing government is one indispensable way to restore the stability that will make it possible to reach that state of affairs. Moreover, as I have argued through this volume, many would not identify rollbacks as the top priority at the moment. Rather, the demonstrable and crucial need to address a host of neglected environmental problems justifies a strong and competent cadre of regulators.

Second, opponents of strengthening EPA's authority will argue that the private sector can be trusted to act in the public's interest and that we must keep the bureaucracy at bay so that business can undertake those more cost-effective initiatives. As discussed in Chapter 4, providing ample opportunity for corporate ingenuity to develop technological solutions to seemingly intractable pollution problems is an overriding goal, but this objective is different from abolishing government mandates that everyone implement these solutions once they are available. Businesses that are genuinely ready to take voluntary steps should applaud government intervention because it will prevent their less willing competitors to meet the same goals.

The third, and arguably most telling, objection to giving the bureaucracy more power targets the competence and even the ethics of those in the civil service. A few pointed accusations characterize these attacks. The most prominent is that EPA career employees are not very smart or well-trained, especially in comparison to their counterparts in the private sector. Another charge is that the bureaucracy has run amok, exercising its power arbitrarily and without reason and blocking innovations that are tremendously valuable to society as a whole.

Both allegations are grounded in reality and becoming more widespread, as anyone who has dealt with EPA staff for any substantial period can testify. Overworked and overextended people often appear stupid and incompetent. They can even seem arbitrarily power-hungry and are rarely held directly accountable for delays. Even if we can agree that the EPA bureaucracy is nonresponsive, disorganized, and extremely slow, we must ask, "Compared to what?" If we are not willing to walk away from environmental protection on a large scale and we do not trust the private sector to achieve these goals unsupervised, there are no feasible alternatives in the public sector. Congress has a sizeable professional staff, but these essentially political operatives do not have the ability to manage an agency of this size from afar. The courts also have legal professionals who assist the judges, but their number is tiny in comparison to the resources it would take to chart a different direction for government policy, and the courts are further hampered by a dearth of technical expertise. Therefore, the real question is whether keeping the bureaucracy in its harassed, maligned, and resource-starved state is a responsible solution to these difficult circumstances or will only serve to make matters much worse.

Are EPA professionals (engineers, scientists, attorneys, economists) significantly less competent than their counterparts in the private sector? Without a doubt, government employees are paid much less, largely because the demand for this expertise dramatically exceeds supply. Narrowing this salary gap must be a priority, although real solutions are not likely to occur any time soon. The American tradition is to implement such reforms government-wide, a seemingly never-ending and far more difficult prospect than adjusting pay scales for a single agency.

Fortunately, people who enter government service are motivated by a great deal more than money. Idealism has always played a substantial role in EPA staffing. These motivations are reinforced by the generic advantages of government service: more flexible and forgiving human resource policies than highly competitive private practice. In recent years, the Agency's repeated humiliation by deregulators has eroded idealism as a motivation for new recruits, and its workforce as a whole is increasingly demoralized.

In sum, although the civil service assigned to protect the environment has seemed quite susceptible to losing track of that mission when confronted with overwhelming pressure by outside parties, the solution to that dilemma is not to add more voices to the cacophony at later stages of the process. We have tried that already, using the courts, the media, Congress, and the White House, and it has not worked. Rather, the solution is to support and reinforce the bureaucracy so that it is capable of standing up to such pressure, restoring its dignity and self-confidence at the same time.

## Eight Reforms

### Federal Police Power to Protect Public Health

Professor Richard Andrews has documented the historical genesis of EPA's mission to reduce industrial pollution in the sanitation movement of the 1850s, which launched a heroic, unprecedented, and publicly funded effort to clean up urban pollution. A noxious combination of animal waste, industrial chemicals, and untreated sewage caused contamination of drinking water, the ground, and the air that caused epidemics of yellow fever, typhoid, smallpox, diphtheria, and tuberculosis.[2] With infectious and toxic waste literally running in the street, an American's life expectancy was less than fifty years, and infant mortality rates skyrocketed—in New York City, for example, baby deaths were 65 percent higher in 1870 than in 1810.

The movement had its roots in the eighteenth-century Enlightenment movement in Europe led by Voltaire, Jeremy Bentham, Adam Smith, and John Locke, who espoused the importance of science and human rationality in improving living conditions. By the time the movement reached America, it combined a determination to improve public health with an understanding of the urgent need for government-sponsored infrastructure for wastewater management, clean water supplies, and garbage disposal. By the early nineteenth century, all of these activities had become public services, with bureaucracies established to both construct and enforce such protections.

The success of the sanitation movement was of critical significance to the development of modern environmentalism because, Professor Andrews explains, it signaled "a rising belief in the efficacy of government services [including] a call for public management of environmental conditions for the benefit of the general population in place of the previous laissez-faire ideology of private management for the benefit of those who could afford it."[3] This consensus on the need for a strong government role in protecting public health begs the question of which level of government should be preeminent. Supreme Court decisions in 1824 and 1905 suggested that these efforts should be assigned to state—and not national—governments, and the states took the lead on public-health initiatives throughout the nineteenth century.[4]

With the publication of *The Jungle*, Upton Sinclair's hair-raising exposé of the meat-packing industry, and the consequent passage of the Pure Food and Drug Act in 1906, the national government moved onto the battlefield.[5] The federal role has expanded ever since, and the national government is now responsible for funding health care, ensuring the safety of drugs and the food supply, setting the pace and content of environmental protection programs, and providing billions of dollars in funding for local wastewater treatment projects. In fact, it is no small irony that as late as 1956, President Dwight Eisenhower vetoed legislation that would provide federal funding for the construction of sewage-treatment plants, arguing that the establishment of such programs would make the federal government both too large and too powerful.[6] Those views quickly became an anachronism.

Contemporary federal and state public health programs have their conceptual roots in the activities of the early sanitarians who policed public spaces to eliminate activities that caused epidemics of disease. Then and now, government has assumed responsibility for controlling crime in the streets in order to protect law-abiding citizens. Similarly, government then and now has a responsibility to compel cleanup of comparably dangerous environmental conditions.

The key attribute of police-power analysis is that it emphasizes the degree of risk confronting the public, as opposed to whatever economic justifications individual polluters might offer for their conduct. So, for example, the question of whether to invoke the police power to combat air pollution would hinge on the nature and scope of the threat and the feasibility of eliminating it, as opposed to the economic benefits to society as a whole contributed by the factories that produced those emissions.

Over time, all three branches of the federal government lost track of this police-power reasoning. Instead, advocates of expanded federal power focused on economic legislation needed to keep commerce moving freely across state lines. Professor Wendy Parmet notes that throughout the New Deal and into the Great Society, the Supreme Court upheld government activism without reference to the government's role in protecting "the security of the social order."[7] She argues that the disassociation of public health and constitutional theory deprives health and safety regulation of the legitimacy that only a constitutional foundation can provide:

> [S]ince the New Deal, public health has been both enlarged and enfeebled. Today the health of the public means everything and nothing at all. Our constitutional law has gained much from this transformation, but it has also lost much. So has our health. . . .
>
> In some ways the transformation has empowered and enlarged public health. Freed from the necessity of fitting the police power into tight categories, governments since the New Deal had been able to enact a vast array of regulations and programs. . . . In this sense, public health authority, though less clearly focused, is far broader and more powerful than it was a hundred years ago.
>
> At the same time, public health has also been diminished. The abandonment of classical police power jurisprudence has meant that governmental actions are legitimated primarily on the basis of majoritarian action.[8]

Commerce Clause jurisprudence is so well developed that it will be difficult for the courts and Congress to shift gears. Yet there is no question that Parmet is onto something profound and important. For example, when Congress passed the Safe Drinking Water Act, it noted that it was taking federal action so travelers who engaged in interstate commerce should not be burdened by the risk of encountering unsafe drinking water. In 2003, taking this reasoning to an outlandish and jarring conclusion, the state of Nebraska argued that the Act could not constitutionally be applied within its borders because the state receives very few visitors. The needs of Nebraska citizens, the state implied, are not the business of Congress, the executive branch, or the federal courts. The Eighth Circuit Court of Appeals swiftly rejected this challenge on procedural grounds.[9] But Nebraska's approach provides an apt illustration of how strained the Commerce Clause rationale has become.

As a consequence of purely economic Commerce Clause reasoning, EPA is a public health agency forced to masquerade as an occasional intervener in the free market. For at least a decade and a half, whenever the Agency has taken action, it has justified what it is doing on the basis of a failure, or "externality," in the free market that warrants federal intervention if the benefits of regulation outweigh the costs. The implicit assumption is that in addition to evaluating the public health, EPA will be held accountable for any and all economic dislocations it produces. These dual roles are enough to make any institution schizophrenic.

## Independent Priority Setting

As described in some detail in Chapter 3, "Battered-Agency Syndrome," EPA has far too much to do. The Agency does not have nearly enough resources, but it would have great difficulty managing its existing mandates even if Congress and the president gave it as much money as it could spend wisely in the near term.[10] The result is an agency so dysfunctional that it has lost its sense of how to tackle the worst problems first and has not spent much time in the past two decades figuring out what the worst problems might be.[11] The Agency desperately needs to get traction on a few major tasks in order to rebuild its institutional credibility, and setting priorities is the condition precedent for that effort.

The only solution to this debilitating state of affairs is to give EPA the freedom it needs to evaluate its agenda and establish priorities that can be accomplished with its available budget, whatever that amount turns out to be. The Agency's political leadership could seize the initiative, but it would be far better for this grant of freedom to be ratified by Congress through passage of a freestanding law or by the president through issuance of a presidential executive order. Either alternative should establish general criteria for making these choices, and those criteria should elevate problems that harm or threaten children to the top of the list.

Enforcement of existing law is the one clear exception to the proposal that EPA should have discretion to choose the priorities it can feasibly address with its current level of resources. For the most part, EPA operates on a "deterrence-based" enforcement system that depends on finding a few chronic violators, prosecuting them, and holding them up as examples to others in an industry who might be tempted to stray. Enforcement costs relatively small amounts of money. As important, any implication that the Agency is abandoning enforcement in an area will likely cause widespread reversion to noncompliance, causing harm that dwarfs the costs of the program.[12]

A firestorm of opposition will erupt at the very idea of allowing the government to do officially what it already does in a more haphazard, less accountable, and less transparent manner. The cacophony of voices pleading for their own pet programs will be deafening, and whoever leads the effort on behalf of the Agency will need a strong stomach and powerful will. The most serious argument against this idea is that setting priorities will tempt Congress to further defund environmental programs. Once priorities are set, other important initiatives that do not make the list will be put on the back burner, and money for their implementation will disappear forever. No honest observer of the existing system can possibly argue, however, that doing a totally inadequate job on a larger universe of issues is a clearly better alternative. Making choices explicit also has the advantage of forcing the hand of politicians and others who support neglected programs to get them the resources they need rather than merely claiming credit for their existence.

### More Money

EPA and the states need massive supplements to their annual budgets just to stay even with existing mandates, much less forge ahead. The size of the federal deficit and inescapable commitments abroad make it seem as if we could not possibly afford significant increases in any kind of domestic spending. The steady drumbeat of criticism regarding the government's overall performance and EPA's performance specifically make it easy to rationalize this neglect. The strongest response to this rhetoric is that one way or another, society ends up shouldering the costs of pollution left unaddressed.

Consider the social costs of depriving EPA of the resources it needs to enforce the ozone NAAQS. Only one of many results of this neglect is the expenditure of an estimated $3.2 billion annually to treat asthma in people younger than eighteen.[13] Children afflicted by asthma miss an estimated 14 million days of school; adults miss 14.5 million workdays.[14] Overall, the U.S. spends $11.5 billion annually, more than 150 percent of the EPA budget, on health care costs for those who have the disease. Not all asthma is attributable to air pollution, and pollution that exacerbates asthma is only one relatively small part of EPA's workload. The fact is that the costs of medical care do not vaporize because conservative economists wish they would but rather are distributed back through the economy. The money it would take to make EPA effective in this specific area should look like a great bargain.

One alternative to supporting environmental programs through general taxpayer revenues is to impose costs directly on polluting industries, either through the assessment of permit fees or targeted taxes. The equities of asking specific industries to pay for regulation must be evaluated, especially in the case of small business, but as the best right-wing economists would point out in other contexts, compelling the industries that nature of environmental laws and policies; for example, as described in Chapter 7, "Ozone Case Study," the claim by opponents of EPA's more stringent Clean Air Act regulations that the choice of a single number for tolerable levels of ozone in the ambient air was not based on "sound" scientific determinations but instead was an arbitrary policy choice by EPA Administrator Carol Browner.

4. Rejection of the long scientific tradition of making aggregate judgments regarding risk on the basis of judgments regarding the overall weight of the evidence, as opposed to nit-picking attacks on individual pieces of research or the rejection of certain types of evidence out of hand; for example, arguments that animal studies on mercury and perchlorate should be ignored in favor of equally flawed but nevertheless informative epidemiological research.

These issues are further analyzed in two recent books—*The Republican War on Science* by journalist Chris Mooney and *Rescuing Science from Politics: Regulation and the Distortion of Scientific Research*, a collection of essays by experts in the interaction of law and science that Professor Wendy Wagner and I edited.[16] *Rescuing Science* recommends the adoption of a series of neutral principles against which intrusions on science should be judged, with enforcement mechanisms available both to scientists who are the target of such attacks and to members of the general public:

*Independence*—Scientists must be able to conduct research without unjustified restrictions, including undue influence by research sponsors.

*Transparency*—The data and results of research must be communicated honestly and expeditiously to the research community and broader public. Researchers and those using their research must be careful to represent the findings accurately, including the limitations of that research.

*A public infrastructure for science*—Government support of independent research is essential to produce discoveries that benefit the public good. In appropriate circumstances, peer review may serve an important role in assisting the government's decision making regarding the use and funding of science, but peer review must never be used to censor research.[17]

Increasing public funding for basic research is among the most important reforms that could be adopted to protect children from environmental threats because those threats lie at the cutting edge of available science. Disruption of normal neurological development before and after birth

caused the problems to internalize the costs of ameliorating the
just fair, but economically efficient. This tradition has weakened in
years, another casualty in the battle to deregulate. In this regard, a s
set of numbers is worth noting.

The corporate taxes that support Superfund cleanups of the app
mately 1,250 worst abandoned toxic waste sites in the country ra
about $1.5 billion annually but were allowed to expire in 1995 and h
never been reinstated, largely because of industry opposition to the pr
gram.[15] The number of cleanups accomplished annually fell by half sind
2000 as the federal fund slowly ran out of money. Much of the mone
lost when the tax expired came from the oil and petrochemical chemical
industries, which have enjoyed record profits and bloated executive compensation packages in recent years. In fact, Superfund taxes could have
been replenished by just 2 *percent* of the 2006 *profits* of six companies:
Exxon Mobil, Chevron, Conoco Phillips, Valero Energy, Marathon Oil,
and Sunoco. The chief executive officer salaries for the six companies
were enough to replace the lost taxes for one month.

## Clean Science

The erosion of scientific independence, transparency, and integrity
began with government efforts to limit tobacco use, when a well-funded
and shrewd defense mounted by the tobacco industry set up a virtual field
of land mines for research regarding health hazards. These troubling developments include the following:

1. Misrepresentation of research and peer review results; for example,
   as described in Chapter 5, "Mercury Case Study," as happened in
   the electric utility industry's systematic omission of the results of
   the National Resource Council's peer review of available health data
   on children's exposure to mercury, as typified by the U.S. Senate
   testimony of Dr. Gary Myers, lead investigator on the only one of
   four epidemiological studies that found no detriment to cognitive
   development.
2. Blatant conflicts of interest in setting the scientific research agenda;
   for example, as described in Chapter 6, "Perchlorate Case Study," the
   Department of Defense and the perchlorate industry's tacit sabotage
   of research on the effects of perchlorate on the unborn.
3. Overall insistence that scientific support for action be airtight and
   open-and-shut, an approach that effectively nullifies the preventive

is a relatively underdeveloped field, especially in the environmental context, because of the difficulties we have encountered in identifying, much less measuring, the contaminants that cause such effects. Unless they are under great public pressure to produce research, as manufacturers of perchlorate were after the chemical was detected in so many drinking water sources, searching for the subtle negative effects of a new product is rarely at the top of the list. As explained by Professor John Applegate, basic—or mechanistic—research into the reasons certain exposures have adverse effects within the body must have government support or remain largely undone.[18]

Although more public funding would help expand the knowledge we need to protect children better, the cumulative toll exacted by the deconstruction of science by special-interest groups is reaching crisis proportions, especially in fields like toxicology and climatology where what scientists say has multibillion-dollar implications. Affirmative action by mainstream scientists is critical to get these destructive trends back under control. For their part, environmental policy makers could contribute to these efforts by reaffirming the central premise of all environmental-protection statutes, which have as their overriding goal *preventing* harm rather than compensating the injured after the fact.

### Precaution

Our willingness to address environmental threats will always be proportional to our understanding of what will happen if the risk evolves into reality. We cannot afford to chase every phantom of risk. Nor can we afford to ignore risks until we have definitive proof the harm has occurred. Any environmental scientist will tell you that uncertainty plagues environmental research more than many other areas of empirical study. Environmental toxicology—the study of poisons in the air, water, and soil—has existed as a research field for only three decades or so. We simply have not had the time or the technology to discover all the things we must know. Adding to these challenges is a central characteristic of the culture of science: great hesitation to draw conclusions until hypotheses have been proven true.

As explained in Chapter 3, "Battered-Agency Syndrome," Richard Nixon's decision to create EPA was consistent with a profound shift in public attitudes during the 1960s and 1970s. No longer was it acceptable for the government to wait until consumers had been bilked, people had been injured by unsafe products, or pollution had caused chronic disease.

While the country had a well-developed system for compensating the victims of such unfortunate events, a powerful social movement wanted harm averted by stronger rules for the industrial activities that posed such risks.

These days, it is fashionable in liberal circles to talk in glowing terms about the "precautionary principle" that increasingly animates the European Union's efforts to protect the environment.[19] But we do not need to look to Belgium or France to discover the roots of the same tradition in American law, as far buried as those roots have become by the deceptively appealing demand that we base decisions on "sound"—or definitive science.

The precautionary principle is applied in two distinct phases: deciding when to take action and determining which levels of exposure are acceptable. Mercury and perchlorate are examples of problems at both stages. The decision of whether to do anything about mercury took fifteen years to resolve; a large chunk of this time was consumed by arguments over what the reference dose for determining the stringency of regulation should be. In the case of perchlorate, we have not yet decided whether to take action. However, in determining the acceptable reference dose, the NRC panel applied "uncertainty factors" that had the effect of lowering maximum levels to account for scientific uncertainty.

As explained in Chapter 1, "Predicates," and illustrated throughout this volume, it is difficult to identify any significant instance when emerging hazards were revealed as less alarming upon further research. Or, in other words, in hindsight we have a virtually perfect batting average in identifying problems that justify action. As we learned more about the toxics we have regulated, we became more convinced that we were right in the first place. In the vast majority of cases, more research indicated that reference doses and levels of exposure should be lowered. The strength of the science supporting pollution controls is always an important consideration. But the wrong-headed idea that the definitiveness of science must be the ultimate test determining if, when, and how we take action can only result in worse problems and more expensive solutions.

## Best Available Solutions

EPA's most successful programs require sources to install the best available pollution control equipment. This technology-based regulatory approach has proven more effective than health-based regulatory programs that depend on the assessment of risks posed by toxic exposures. To prescribe technology-based controls, EPA must undertake three straightforward and manageable tasks. First, it must find technologies that are feasible to use—not too expensive, not too complicated, tested and proven in the field. Second, it must determine the amount of emissions the equipment can eliminate in order to determine the level of emissions that would be left if the equipment was installed. Third, it must require regulated parties to meet that level of performance, giving them the choice of either installing the technology identified by EPA or finding another, equally effective technology capable of producing the same results. This relative ease of administration is the primary reason Congress shifted EPA's efforts to combat hazardous air pollutants to a technology-based approach in the first instance, as explained in Chapter 5, "Mercury Case Study."

Technology-based controls should be the first option considered under every statute that permits such an approach, and Congress should consider amending specific provisions of the law to authorize this approach. If equipment, work practices, and other technologies are available to prevent, neutralize, or reduce pollution, they should be implemented. The law should do its best to inspire the development of such technology, pushing scientists and engineers to seek it by creating markets through regulation. We should press the envelope of innovation, asking for improvements even before we are absolutely sure they are feasible, and canceling these requests at the last possible moment.

## Monetization of Costs, Not Benefits

Since the first humans began to barter among themselves for bits of food, a particularly good rock, or a burning ember, all cultures have organized life around commerce and the monetization of valuable items. Paradoxically, all religions sanctify the value of human life and would never suggest that a human being's existence can be bought and sold. This deep-seated ambivalence creates a yawning gap in popular culture, although religious values almost always prevail when the bartering comes too close to the sanctity of life.

Slave-owners violated every precept of fundamental morality, buying and selling human beings at will, but they did not go so far as to slaughter their slaves for profit. Slavery in the United States is a shameful memory. No one can pay any amount for the privilege of killing someone else. And no live person is allowed to auction their or anyone else's body parts, much less their children, to the highest bidder.

In more modern times, lawyers began monetizing lives as a way to recover damages for their clients, and the modern life insurance industry developed as a close corollary to this application. Modern economists took this practice one fatal step further, and began to estimate how much money a life will be worth in the *future* and, if the amount is not enough, to write the life off with impunity. To pretend that it is possible to assign market value to such "commodities" as illness or the very existence of life conflicts with our most fundamental values, which are essential not only to our constitutional democracy but to the coherence and integrity of American culture.

Refusing to monetize life does not mean ignoring how many lives are changed by exposure to pollution and how these lives could be improved if pollution was prevented. To gather the best available evidence regarding the number of people who might become ill is critical not only to deciding if regulation is necessary or affordable, but to targeting remedies in the best way possible. Counting in this way makes as much sense as bartering the value of lives does not.

Costs are a different matter. They will always be a central consideration in regulatory decisions, and proposals that they be ignored or given lower priority are both fruitless and inappropriate. We can make them more accurate, however, beginning with a commitment to conduct retrospective studies that measure the difference between what industries estimate they will have to spend before rules go into effect and their actual costs once markets develop for pollution control technologies and competition drives the price of compliance down. Existing data indicate because of these market forces, costs are significantly overestimated at the outset. In some cases, such overestimates block rules that would bring great benefits to the public.

### Judicial Deference

Although the courts profess to give significant deference to decisions made by administrative agencies like EPA, a handful of harsh opinions have sent shock waves through the general counsel's offices that advise the regulators, turning already insecure officials into extraordinarily cautious decision makers. Frustrated by the slow pace that results from excessive efforts to shield EPA rules from reversal by the courts, environmentalists and other public interest groups routinely lobby for strict statutory mandates and do not hesitate to drag the Agency before the same judicial overseers when they drag their feet.

The most egregious example is the *Corrosion Proof Fittings* case discussed in Chapter 3, "Battered-Agency Syndrome." Readers may remember that EPA had attempted to prohibit the use of asbestos in consumer products. The judges hearing the case overturned the decision, chiding the Agency for not having investigated all conceivable alternatives to a complete ban. The result was that EPA abandoned efforts to control the use of asbestos in consumer products. As bad, it has never tried again to tackle any problem posed by the use of toxic materials in consumer products under the Toxic Substances Control Act, the statute at issue in the case.

Rather than assume the responsibility for micromanaging the way EPA builds a record in support of rulemaking to this extreme, the courts should restrict decisions overturning a final decision to instances in which the Agency either ignored clear statutory mandates, or was so cavalier in building a record that it deserves to be found "arbitrary" and "capricious" in the true sense of those words.

## Conclusion

Despite unprecedented affluence, the World Wide Web and other technological breakthroughs, the elimination of diseases that ravaged earlier populations, and progress on dozens of other fronts that make life more convenient and interesting, it is hard to envy the next generation of American children. They face challenges that would make their most intrepid forefathers blanch, not the least of which is coping with an environment increasingly overwhelmed by the unforeseen ramifications of human consumption. When I teach environmental law, I often see my students' faces change from expectant to dismayed. "It will be up to your generation to solve this problem," I say brightly, and I am relieved when they do not tune me out completely.

Of course, this is the easy way out, as tempting as it seems to those of us who have been immersed in environmental controversies for too many years. As the generations that are still in power, we cannot shirk our own responsibility to work our way out of these dilemmas. People we know and those yet to come will thank us or curse us. In the final analysis, which one they do is up to us.

# Notes

## Prologue

1. Donald T. Wigle, *Child Health and the Environment* (New York: Oxford University Press, 2003); Colleen F. Moore, *Silent Scourge: Children, Pollution, and Why Scientists Disagree* (New York: Oxford University Press, 2003); Sandra Steingraber, *Having Faith: An Ecologist's Journey to Motherhood* (New York: Berkley Books, 2001); Theo Colborn, Dianne Dumanoski, and John Peterson Myers, *Our Stolen Future* (New York: Plume, 1997); John Wargo, *Our Children's Toxic Legacy* (New Haven: Yale University Press, 1996).

2. F. A. Hayek, *The Road to Serfdom*, 50th anniv. ed. (Chicago: University of Chicago Press, 1994); Milton Friedman, *Capitalism and Freedom*, 40th anniv. ed. (Chicago: University of Chicago Press, 2002).

## Chapter 1

1. The article reporting these results and containing an insightful analysis of the problem is Catherine A. O'Neill, "Mercury, Risk, and Justice," *Environmental Law Reporter* 34 (2004): 11070–11071.

2. U.S. Environmental Protection Agency (EPA), *National Emission Standards for Hazardous Air Pollutants: Mercury Emissions from Mercury Cell Chlor-Alkali Plants*, Federal Register 68, no. 244 (December 19, 2003): 70904, 70920. http://www.epa.gov/ttn/atw/hgcellcl/fr19de03.pdf (to be codified at 40 CFR pt. 63). Three plants have now converted to cleaner technologies.

3. EPA, *Standards for Performance for New and Existing Stationary Sources: Electric Utility Steam Generating Units*. Federal Register 70, no. 95 (May 18, 2005): 28606. http://a257.g.akamaitech.net/7/257/2422/01jan20051800/edocket.access.gpo.gov/2005/pdf/05-8447.pdf (to be codified at 40 CFR pts. 60, 72, and 75).

4. Peter Waldman, "EPA Bans Staff from Discussing Issue of Perchlorate Pollution," *Wall Street Journal*, April 28, 2003.

5. National Research Council (NRC), *Health Implications of Perchlorate Ingestion* (Washington, DC: National Academy Press, 2005).

6. In comparison, adults suffer at a rate of 60 per 1,000. American Lung Association, Epidemiology and Statistics Unit, Research and Program Services, *Trends in Asthma Morbidity and Mortality*, May 2005, 1–2. http://www.lungusa .org/atf/cf/{7A8D42C2-FCCA-4604-8ADE-7F5D5E762256}/ASTHMA1 .PDF.

7. *Clean Air Act, U.S. Code* 42 (2000), §§ 7401–7671q. The provisions mentioned here are at §§ 7401–7431 and 7501–7515.

8. The provisions instructing EPA to provide designations and review state implementation plans (SIPs) for non-attainment areas appear at *Clear Air Act*, § 7502.

9. Stephen J. Read and Lynn Carol Miller, "Dissonance and Balance in Belief Systems: The Promise of Parallel Constraint Satisfaction Processes and Connectionist Modeling Approaches." In *Beliefs, Reasoning, and Decision Making: Psycho-Logic in Honor of Bob Abelson*, edited by Roger C. Schank and Ellen Langer (Hillsdale, NJ: Lawrence Erlbaum Associates, 1994), 209–235, 211–213.

10. For more information on the survey see Marianne Lavelle, "Environmental Vise: Law, Compliance," *National Law Journal*, August 30, 1993, S1.

11. *Federal Water Pollution Control Act, U.S. Code* 33 (2000), § 1251(a)(1).

12. Michael Schudson, *The Good Citizen: A History of American Civic Life* (Cambridge, MA: Harvard University Press, 1998), 310–311.

13. Richard J. Lazarus, "The Tragedy of Distrust in the Implementation of Federal Environmental Law," *Law and Contemporary Problems* 54 (1991): 311.

14. P. J. O'Rourke, *All the Trouble in the World: The Lighter Side of Overpopulation, Famine, Ecological Disaster, Ethnic Hatred, Plague, and Poverty* (Boston: Atlantic Monthly Press, 1994), 201.

### Chapter 2

The quote in the chapter epigraph is from Mara Liasson, "Conservative Advocate," *Morning Edition*, National Public Radio, May 25, 2001. http://www.npr.org/ templates/story/story.php?storyId=1123439.

1. I recognize that "liberal" ideology has distinctly different historic meanings. For example, Milton Friedman, the archetypal conservative discussed later in this chapter, described himself as a "classic liberal" in his famous book, *Capitalism and Freedom*.

2. William Jefferson Clinton, *State of the Union Address as Delivered*, January 23, 1996. http://clinton4.nara.gov/WH/New/other/sotu.html.

3. Alexander Hamilton, James Madison, and John Jay, *The Federalist Papers*, edited by Clinton Rossiter (New York: New American Library, 1961), viii–xxii. First published 1788.

4. Ibid., 77–78.

5. Ibid., 78.

6. Ibid., 81. "Either the existence of the same passion or interest in a majority at the same time must be prevented, or the majority, having such coexistent passion or interest, must be rendered by their number and local situation, unable to concert and carry into effect schemes of oppression."

7. Ibid., 292–293.

8. Alex Kozinski and Steven A. Engel, "Recapturing Madison's Constitution: Federalism without the Blank Check." In *James Madison and the Future of Limited Government*, edited by John Samples (Washington, DC: Cato Institute, 2002), 238.

9. Friedman, *Capitalism and Freedom*.

10. Ibid, 2–3.

11. Ibid., 35.

12. Ibid., 132.

13. Ibid., 38. Specifically, Friedman targeted the Federal Reserve System as the culprit in this historic tragedy, asserting that by mishandling monetary policy, it pushed a "moderate contraction into a major catastrophe."

14. Ibid., vii–x. Friedman explained that Reagan was unable to "curb the Leviathan" of government but that the collapse of the Soviet Union provided hope that the developing world would eschew experiments with any form of communist system.

15. Ibid., 15.

16. Ibid., 38.

17. Ibid., 199.

18. Ibid., 30.

19. Garrett Hardin, "The Tragedy of the Commons," *Science* 162, no. 3859 (1968): 1243–1248.

20. Hayek, *Road to Serfdom*. The forward to the fiftieth-anniversary edition of Hayek's work was written by Professor Friedman, who described it as a "true classic" that was "timeless" and "even more relevant to the United States today than it was when it created a sensation on its original publication."

21. Ibid., 43.

22. Edward H. Crane, "The Republican Congress in Historical Context." In *The Republican Revolution 10 Years Later: Smaller Government or Business as Usual?*, edited by Chris Edwards and John Samples (Washington, DC: Cato Institute, 2005), 19–20. At this writing, Mr. Crane is president of the Cato Institute.

23. Ronald Reagan, "A New Republican Party." Address to the Fourth Annual Conservative Political Action Conference (CPAC) Convention, February 6, 1977. http://www.presidentreagan.info/speeches/new_republican_party .cfm.

24. Ibid.

25. Ronald Reagan, "To Restore America," speech, March 31, 1976 (emphasis added). http://www.reaganlegacy.org/speeches/reagan.torestore.3.31.76.htm.

26. Ronald Reagan, acceptance of the Republican nomination for president, July 17, 1980. http://www.4president.org/speeches/reagan1980convention.htm.

27. Susan J. Tolchin and Martin Tolchin, *Dismantling America: The Rush to Deregulate* (Boston: Houghton Mifflin, 1983). Executive Order 12291, February 17, 1981, *Federal Register* 46 FR 13193, 3 CFR, 1981 Comp., p. 127, http://www.archives .gov/federal-register/codification/executive-order/12291.html.

28. Reagan, "New Republican Party." Two notable exceptions are his comment that environmentalists "won't be satisfied until they turn the White House into a bird's nest," and his assertion that trees cause as much pollution as people.

United Press International (UPI), "Environmentalists: Reagan Is Soiling the Nest," March 11, 1983.

29. Richard N. L. Andrews, *Managing the Environment, Managing Ourselves: A History of American Environmental Policy* (New Haven: Yale University Press, 1999), 240.

30. I write these words with difficulty, as a participant and not an onlooker in the events I now criticize. From 1983 to 1988, I was staff counsel to the U.S. House of Representatives Committee on Energy and Commerce, working directly for the subcommittee chaired by James Florio, D-NJ, on the second-generation Superfund statute. In our defense, we were aware that our efforts to micromanage EPA were not the ideal role for Congress to play, but we could see no other way to forestall the radical changes sought by the right wing.

31. Ed Gillespie and Bob Schellhas, editors, *Contract with America: The Bold Plan by Rep. Newt Gingrich, Rep. Dick Armey, and the House Republicans to Change the Nation* (Washington, DC: Republican National Committee, 1994).

32. Luntz Research Companies, "The Environment: A Cleaner, Safer, Healthier America," National Environmental Trust, 2004. http://www.luntzspeak .com/graphics/LuntzResearch.Memo.pdf.

33. For a thorough discussion of these views see Chris Edwards and John Samples, editors, *The Republican Revolution 10 Years Later: Smaller Government or Business as Usual?* (Washington, DC: Cato Institute, 2005).

34. For an incisive analysis of President George W. Bush's big-government conservatism see two articles in *The Economist* of October 1, 2005: "The Conservative Movement, A Hammer Blow" (27–29) and "The Fiscal Mess, or Is It an Opportunity?" (29–32).


**Chapter 3**

The first chapter epigraph is from *Ethyl Corporation v. EPA*, 541 F.2d 1, 6 (D.C. Cir. 1976). The second is from William D. Ruckelshaus, "Stopping the Pendulum," *Environmental Forum* 12, no. 6 (November/December 1995): 25. The third is from Bruce Burkhard, "Year in Review, Congress vs. Environment: Environmental Laws Suffer under GOP-Controlled Congress," Cable News Network, December 29, 1995. An audio recording of Congressman DeLay's comments is available through the online version of this article, http://www .cnn.com/EARTH/9512/congress_enviro/. The remarks were widely reported in the press and have been repeated in the media numerous times.

1. For a more detailed description of these health effects see Centers for Disease Control and Prevention (CDC), National Center for Environmental Health, "Background," In *Preventing Lead Poisoning in Young Children*, CDC. http://www.cdc.gov/nceh/lead/publications/books/plpyc/contents.htm.

2. Rachel Carson, *Silent Spring*, 40th anniv. ed. (Boston: Mariner Books, 2002).

3. For an excellent summary of these events see Andrews, *Managing the Environment*, 228–232. Professor Andrews explains the role played by President

Richard Nixon in creating EPA and its downsides at pages 201–226. His book is the most authoritative, comprehensive, and insightful of any of the histories written about environmental protection in America.

4. Ibid., 230.

5. For an interesting account of these developments see Andrew J. Hoffman, *From Heresy to Dogma: An Institutional History of Corporate Environmentalism* (Stanford, CA: Stanford University Press, 2001), 64–86.

6. Ruckelshaus, "Stopping the Pendulum," 25.

7. Andrews, *Managing the Environment*, 261.

8. Food Quality Protection Act, Law 104-70, *U.S. Statutes at Large* 110 (1996): 1489 et seq.

9. Monthly average Consumer Price Index (CPI) information from the Bureau of Labor Statistics was used to adjust for inflation. U.S. Department of Labor, Bureau of Labor Statistics, Consumer Price Index, ftp://ftp.bls.gov/pub/special.requests/cpi/cpiai.txt. CPI numbers from October through September were averaged to obtain an average CPI for each fiscal year from 1970 through 2005. The real budget (or outlay) for any given fiscal year was obtained by multiplying the nominal budget (or outlays) from EPA by the ratio of the FY 2005 CPI to the CPI for the given year. For example: (Real 1970 budget) = (Nominal 1970 budget) x (Avg. CPI for FY 2005)/(Avg. CPI for 1970). EPA budget information through FY 2003 was obtained from http://www.epa.gov/history/org/resources/budget.htm. EPA budget information for FY 2004–2005 was obtained from EPA *Budget in Brief*, http://www.epa.gov/adminweb/budget-goals.htm.
Nominal outlays were obtained from the OMB, *Budget of the United States Government, Fiscal Year 2005*, http://www.whitehouse.gov/omb/budget/fy2005/sheets/outlays.xls.

10. J. Clarence Davies and Jan Mazurek, *Pollution Control in the United States: Evaluating the System* (Washington, DC: Resources for the Future, 1998), 12. In order of the dates they were enacted and using their original names, those statutes are: the Federal Insecticide, Fungicide, and Rodenticide Act (1947); the Water Pollution Control (or "Clean Water") Act (1948); the Air Pollution Control (or "Clean Air") Act (1955); the National Environmental Policy Act (1970); the Safe Drinking Water Act (1974); the Resource Conservation and Recovery Act (1976); the Toxic Substances Control Act (1976); the Comprehensive Environmental Response, Compensation and Liability Act ("Superfund") (1980); and the Pollution Prevention Act (1990).

11. In chronological order from earliest to latest, those reauthorizations include: *Hazardous and Solid Waste Amendments of 1984*, Public Law 98-616, *U.S. Statutes at Large* 98 (1984): 3221; *Safe Drinking Water Act Amendments of 1985*, Public Law 99-339, *U.S. Statutes at Large* 100 (1985): 642; *Water Quality Act of 1987*, Public Law 100-4, *U.S. Statutes at Large* 101 (1987): 7; *Federal Insecticide, Fungicide and Rodenticide Act Amendments of 1988*, Public Law 100-532, *U.S. Statutes at Large* 102 (1988): 2654; *Clean Air Act Amendments of 1990*, Public Law 101-549, *U.S. Statutes at Large* 104 (1990): 2399; *Safe Drinking Water Act Amendments of 1996*, Public Law 104-182, *U.S. Statutes at Large* 110 (1996): 1613; *Food Quality Protection Act*, Public Law 104-170, *U.S. Statutes at Large* 110 (1996): 1489 et seq.

12. For a good overview of changes made by the 1987 Clean Water Act amendments see *Section-by-Section Analysis of Water Quality Act of 1987*, 133 Cong. Rec. H131 (1987), reprint 1987 USCCAN 5, 19.

13. For a good overview of changes made by the 1990 Clean Air Act amendments see U.S. Congress, House of Representatives, *H.R. Conf. Rep. on Clean Air Act Amendments of 1990*, H.R. Conf. Rep. No. 101-952, reprint 1990 USCCAN 3385, 3874–3876.

14. For an explanation of how this reauthorization legislation expanded the law see U.S. Congress, House of Representatives, *H.R. Conf. Rep. on Hazardous and Solid Waste Amendments of 1984*, H.R. Conf. Rep. No. 98-1113, reprint 1984 USCCAN 5576, 5673–5675.

15. U.S. Congress, House of Representatives, *H.R. Conf. Rep. on Safe Drinking Water Act Amendments of 1986*, H.R. Rep. No. 99-575, *reprinted in* 1986 USCCAN 1566, 1595.

16. This second set of amendments is summarized in U.S. Congress, House of Representatives, *H.R. Conf. Rep. on Safe Drinking Water Act Amendments of 1996*, H.R. Conf. Rep. No. 104-741 at 6-9 (1996).

17. Federal Insecticide, Fungicide, and Rodenticide Act Amendments of 1988, Public Law 100-532, § 102, *U.S. Statutes at Large* 102 (1988): 2654, 2655–2667.

18. A leading administrative law treatise defines "agency capture" as follows: "An agency is captured when it favors the concerns of the industry it regulates, which is well-represented by its trade groups and lawyers, over the interests of the general public, which is often unrepresented." Richard J. Pierce Jr., Sydney A. Shapiro, and Paul R. Verkuil, *Administrative Law and Process*, 2d ed. (Westbury, NY: Foundation Press, 1992), § 1.7.2.

19. *Natural Resources Defense Council v. U.S. EPA*, 422 F. Supp. 2d 105 (D.D.C. 2006).

20. Davies and Mazurek, *Pollution Control*, 18.

21. For more information on the man born Theophrastus Philippus Aureolus Bombastus von Hohenheim but self-named Paracelsus see John G. Simmons, *Doctors and Discoveries: Lives that Created Today's Medicine* (Boston: Houghton Mifflin, 2002).

22. For basic background on toxic risk assessment see Joseph V. Rodricks, *Calculated Risks* (New York: Cambridge University Press, 1992), and Vincent T. Covello and Miley W. Merkhofer, *Risk Assessment Methods* (New York: Plenum Press, 1993).

23. Environmental Defense Fund, *Toxic Ignorance: The Continuing Absence of Basic Health Testing for Top-Selling Chemicals in the United States* (New York: Environmental Defense Fund, 1997), 15. For a general analysis of data gaps and their implications see Wendy E. Wagner, "Commons Ignorance: The Failure of Environmental Law to Produce Needed Information on Health and the Environment," *Duke Law Journal* 53, no. 6 (1997): 1628–1630. The cited text reviews the literature on missing toxicity data.

24. EPA, Office of Pollution Prevention and Toxics, "What Do We Really Know About the Safety of High Production Volume Chemicals?" *Chemical Regulation Reporter* (BNA) 22 (May 1, 1998): 261.

25. Bureau of National Affairs Inc. (BNA), "CMA More Optimistic Than

EDF on Lack of Data for 100 Chemicals," *Daily Environment Report* 230 (December 1, 1997): A-4.

26. Adam Smith, *The Wealth of Nations* (New York: Modern Library, 1937).

27. OMB, *Circular A-4*, September 17, 2003, http://www.whitehouse.gov/omb/circulars/a004/a-4.pdf.

28. Executive Order 12291.

29. Executive Order 12866, Regulatory Planning and Review, September 30, 1993, *Federal Register* 58, no. 190 (October 4, 1993): 51735–51744, http://www.whitehouse.gov/omb/inforeg/eo12866.pdf.

30. OMB, *Circular A-4*, 19.

31. For an excellent discussion of these issues see Thomas O. McGarity and Ruth Ruttenberg, "Counting the Cost of Health, Safety, and Environmental Regulation," *Texas Law Review* 80 (2002): 1997. McGarity and Ruttenberg conclude that cost estimates are generally not based on empirical analysis.

32. Ibid., 2030–2033.

33. OMB, *Circular A-4*, 26–27.

34. Alan Krupnick et al., "Age, Health, and the Willingness to Pay for Mortality Risk Reductions: A Contingent Valuation Survey of Ontario Residents," *Journal of Risk and Uncertainty* 24, no. 2 (2000): 161–186. http://ideas.repec.org/a/kap/jrisku/v24y2002i2p161-86.html.

35. OMB, *Circular A-4*, 33–34.

36. Ibid., 31.

37. Ibid., 35–36.

38. Ibid.

39. Ibid., 36.

40. Ibid., 35.

41. For a general overview of the federal courts' jurisdiction and operations see U.S. Courts, *Understanding the Federal Courts*, http://www.uscourts.gov/understand02/index.html.

42. For an example of such a provision see *Clean Air Act*, § 7604.

43. In his annual report on the state of the federal courts, former Chief Justice William Rehnquist warned: "The Judiciary's funding for Fiscal Year 2004 included in the omnibus appropriations bill, however, is inadequate. The continuing uncertainties and delays in the funding process have necessitated substantial effort on the part of judges and judiciary managers and staff to modify budget systems, develop contingency plans, cancel activities, and attempt to cut costs. Many courts may face hiring freezes, furloughs, or reductions in force." William Rehnquist, *2003 Year-End Report on the Federal Judiciary*, U.S. Supreme Court, January 2004. http://www.supremecourtus.gov/publicinfo/year-end/2003year-endreport.html. Later Year-End Reports also reflect this crisis. See generally Supreme Court of the United States, Chief Justice's Year-End Reports of the Federal Judiciary, http://www.supremecourtus.gov/publicinfo/year-end/year-endreports.html.

44. For aggregate statistics concerning federal court caseload see U.S. Courts, *Federal Caseload Statistics 2004*, http://www.uscourts.gov/caseload2004/front/judbus03.pdf.

45. *Industrial Union Dept., AFL-CIO v. American Petroleum Institute*, 448 U.S. 607, 642 (1980).

46. *Ethyl* was decided by the D.C. Circuit Court of Appeals, the level of courts right below the Supreme Court. Although the opinion has never been overruled, it was the high-water mark of judicial support for ambitious EPA rulemaking.

47. *Industrial Union Dept., AFL-CIO v. American Petroleum Institute,* 653.

48. Ibid.

49. Ibid., 722–723.

50. These events are explained in Robert V. Percival et al., *Environmental Regulation, Law, Science, and Policy,* 4th ed. (New York: Aspen, 2003), 378.

51. The Supreme Court takes a fraction of the cases sent to it for review. Denial of a petition for certiorari leaves the decision by a Court of Appeals in effect.

52. *Corrosion Proof Fittings v. EPA,* 947 F.2d 1201 (5th Cir. 1991).

53. Thomas O. McGarity, "Some Thoughts on De-Ossifying the Rulemaking Process," *Duke Law Journal* 41, no. 6 (1992): 1385.

54. Examples of these provisions are *Clean Air Act, U.S. Code* 42 (1994), § 7410(a)(2); *Clean Water Act, U.S. Code* 33 (1994), § 1342 (b); *Safe Drinking Water Act, U.S. Code* 42 (1994 and Supp. 1997), § 300g-3(e); *Resource Conservation and Recovery Act, U.S. Code* 42 (1994), §§ 6929(b), 6991(g).

55. Environmental Council of the States, "Delegation by Environmental Act," Environmental Council of the States, http://ecos.org/section/states/enviro_actlist. The 75 percent figure is as of 2001.

56. For a superb description of this history and its implications for public policy today see David B. Walker, *The Rebirth of Federalism: Slouching Toward Washington* (Riverside: Chatham Press, 1995), 23–24, 67–91. The discussion here is based largely on his explanation of this history.

57. For a discussion of these events see Timothy J. Conlan, "Federalism and Competing Values in the Reagan Administration," *Publius: The Journal of Federalism* 16 (1986): 29–47.

58. Unfunded Mandates Reform Act of 1995, Public Law 104-4, *U.S. Statutes at Large* 109: 48, codified as amended in scattered sections of U.S. Code Service (USCS). During the floor debate, senators and representatives told anecdote after anecdote about ostensibly senseless mandates. The majority were about environmental rules.

59. To her credit, Carol Browner, President Clinton's EPA administrator, attempted to shift to a performance-based system that would reward good states, but these efforts fell by the wayside as George W. Bush took office.

### Chapter 4

1. Hardin, "Tragedy of the Commons."

2. Ibid., 1244.

3. Friedman, *Capitalism and Freedom,* 30.

4. Smith, *Wealth of Nations,* 423.

5. Terry L. Anderson and Donald R. Leal, *Free Market Environmentalism,* rev. ed. (New York: Palgrave, 2001), 3.

6. Ibid.

7. Angela Logomasini and David Riggs, "Chemical Risk." In *The Environmental Source* (Washington, DC: Competitive Enterprise Institute, 2004), 22–36. http://www.cei.org/gencon/026,01623.cfm.

8. Angela Logomasini, "Deploy DDT to Fight Malaria." Competitive Enterprise Institute, June 18, 2002. http://www.cei.org/gencon/019,03078.cfm.

9. "The air pollution scare industry is at it again—in a very timely manner to help the Environmental Protection Agency impose more dubious regulations on us," Steven J. Milloy exhorts in an editorial for FoxNews.com. Steven J. Milloy, "EPA Whips Up Air Pollution Scare," FoxNews.com, March 9, 2006. http://www.foxnews.com/story/0,2933,187390,00.html.

10. Gregg Easterbrook, *A Moment on Earth: The Coming of Age of Environmental Optimism* (New York: Viking, 1995). Bjorn Lomborg, *The Skeptical Environmentalist: Measuring the Real State of the World*, translated by Hugh Matthews (Cambridge, England: Viking, 2001). Both books were heavily criticized when they appeared. For examples of negative reviews of Easterbrook's book see Mark Jones, "On Gregg Easterbrook, Author," *World Overpopulation Awareness*, May 2000, http://www.overpopulation.org//Op_Eds/MarkJones_Easterbrook.html. Douglas A. Kysar, "Some Realism about Environmental Skepticism: The Implications of Bjorn Lomborg's *The Skeptical Environmentalist* for Environmental Law and Policy," *Ecology Law Quarterly* 30 (2003): 223–278.

11. All of the quotations in this paragraph appear at Easterbrook, *Moment on Earth*, xvi. The author has become more concerned about global warming since he wrote *A Moment on Earth*, announcing that "in roughly the last decade, the evidence of artificial global warning has gone from sketchy to overpowering." Gregg Easterbrook, "Case Closed: The Debate about Global Warming Is Over," Brookings Institution, *Issues in Governance Studies*, no. 3 (June 2006): 2. Nevertheless, he announces "optimistically," solutions will be "much more practical and affordable than currently assumed" (1) so long as we turn our backs on unduly burdensome approaches like the Kyoto Protocol and follow a "market-driven, innovative approach" (6).

12. Lomborg, *Skeptical Environmentalist*, 3.

13. Ibid., 34–42.

14. Ibid., 5.

15. Ibid., 119 (emphasis in original).

16. Ibid., 120.

17. Ibid., 42.

18. Joint Science Academies, "Joint Science Academies' Statement: Global Response to Climate Change," June 7, 2005. http://nationalacademies.org/onpi/06072005.pdf.

19. For details of the Chamber of Commerce study see Nancy Ognanovich, "Business Interests Urge Administration to Remove Burdensome Regulations," *Environment Reporter* (BNA) 35 (December 24, 2004): 2641–2643.

20. John D. Graham, Office of Information and Regulatory Affairs, Testimony Before the U.S. House of Representatives Small Business Committee. May 19, 2004. http://www.whitehouse.gov/omb/legislative/testimony/graham/04059_graham_reg_reform.html.

21. Steven Breyer, *Breaking the Vicious Circle: Toward Effective Risk Regulation*

(Boston: Harvard University Press, 1993). Justice Breyer was not on the Supreme Court bench when the book was originally published.

22. Frank Ackerman and Lisa Heinzerling, *Priceless: On Knowing the Price of Everything and the Value of Nothing* (New York: New Press, 2004), 47–52.

23. Ibid., 41–55.

24. Bill Cohen, quoted in E. J. Dionne, "When Government Is 'Good,'" *Washington Post*, September 2, 2005.

25. Philip K. Howard, *The Death Of Common Sense: How Law Is Suffocating America* (New York: Random House, 1994).

26. Ibid., 31–32.

27. Ibid., 32.

28. Ibid., 19–20, all quotations in this paragraph.

29. Mass. Regs. Code 105, §§ 460.110 (basic cleanup requirements), 460.160 (occupant removal) (2002). For the text of the regulations see Massachusetts, Trial Court Law Libraries, "Lead Paint Law: A Pathfinder." http://www.lawlib.state.ma.us/lead.html. For a general overview of the program see Massachusetts Department of Public Health, "Childhood Lead Poisoning Prevention Program."

30. In 1994 the chemical and oil industry trade associations refused to support an effort by the insurance industry to gut Superfund's liability scheme, instead joining with environmentalists in support of a proposal to revitalize the program. The proposal died in the 1994 Newt Gingrich Congress, never to be resurrected. For a description of these events see Rena I. Steinzor, "The Reauthorization of Superfund: Can the Deal of the Century Be Saved?" *Environmental Law Reporter* 15 (1985): 10016–10059, and Rena I. Steinzor, "The Reauthorization of Superfund: The Public Works Alternative," *Environmental Law Reporter* 25 (1995): 10078–10104. In 1996 pesticide manufacturers and environmentalists cut a deal that allowed passage of the Food Quality Protection Act. For a critical evaluation of the new law and its implementation see Thomas McGarity, "Politics by Other Means: Law, Science, and Policy in EPA's Implementation of the Food Quality Protection Act," *Administrative Law Review* 53, no. 1 (2001): 103.

31. Once again, this approach is still used today. See Natural Resources Defense Council (NRDC), "Unchecked Development and Pollution Threatens Water Quality and Recreation For Millions in New York and New Jersey," December 3, 2002. http://www.nrdc.org/media/pressReleases/021203.asp.

32. The term is still in use today. See Sierra Club, "Superfund 'Polluter Pays' Amendment Loses in Senate," March 11, 2004, http://www.sierraclub.org/pressroom/releases/pr2004-03-11a.asp, reporting on efforts by Senator Frank Lautenberg to reinstate the corporate taxes that support the Superfund program.

33. For example, from 1983 to 1987, I worked for Congressman James Florio (D-NJ), often referred to as the father of the original Superfund statute, in his and others' contentious campaign to reauthorize the statute; this effort was completed in 1986 with the passage of the Superfund Amendments and Reauthorization Act, which greatly enlarged the size of the program. At one point, the legislation called for imposition of a "waste end tax" on companies that generated regulated categories of hazardous waste in order to raise additional funds for cleanup of abandoned dump sites. Individual companies' output of such waste

varied considerably, and the ink on the proposal was not dry when each one ran an analysis of the amount of new taxes that might be imposed on it or its competitors. Large Fortune 100 New Jersey petrochemical manufacturers circulated these estimates to members of Florio's staff but continued their overall opposition to Florio's bill.

34. See, for example, Thomas P. Lyon and John W. Maxwell, *Corporate Environmentalism and Public Policy* (New York: Cambridge University Press, 2004); Hilary Stone and John Washington-Smith, *Profit and the Environment: Common Sense of Contradictions* (New York: Wiley, 2002); Hoffman, *From Heresy to Dogma;* Marc J. Epstein, *Measuring Corporate Environmental Performance: Best Practices for Costing and Managing an Effective Environmental Strategy* (Chicago: Irwin Professional Publishing, 1996).

35. Hoffman, *From Heresy to Dogma.* The volume won the 2001 Rachel Carson Prize from the Society of Social Studies of Science. The cover and front page of the revised edition feature endorsements from former EPA Administrator William Ruckelshaus (then chairman and chief executive officer of Browning Ferris Industries), Environmental Defense Fund Executive Director Fred Krupp, and Robert D. Kennedy, retired chairman and chief executive officer of Union Carbide Corporation, a company that was among the first to become converted to the idea of corporate environmentalism in the wake of the disastrous 1984 explosion at its plant in Bhopal, India, that killed thousands.

36. For a description see Barnaby J. Feder, "Chemistry Cleans Up a Factory," *New York Times,* July 18, 1999. See also the materials NRDC has posted on its Web site about the project; NRDC, "Preventing Industrial Pollution at Its Source," http://www.nrdc.org/water/pollution/ndow.asp. I spent my sabbatical year in 2001–2002 at NRDC's Washington, DC, office and became very familiar with its work.

37. For information on green accounting see Daryl Ditz, Janet Ranganathan, and R. Darryl Banks, editors, *Green Ledgers: Case Studies in Corporate Environmental Accounting* (Washington, DC: World Resources Institute, 1995).

38. For an explanation of environmental management systems and trends see Hoffman, *From Heresy to Dogma,* 219–221, and Epstein, *Measuring Corporate Environmental Performance,* 50–74.

## Chapter 5

The first chapter epigraph is from the NRC, *Toxicological Effects of Methyl Mercury* (Washington, DC: National Academy Press, 2000), 9, 11. http://books.nap.edu/openbook/0309071402/html/index.html. The second is from Bill Kovacs, vice president of Environment, Technology and Regulatory Affairs of U.S. Chamber of Commerce, "Mercury Emissions," radio actuality, December 3, 2003.

1. This chapter is based in part on a pair of articles I co-authored with my friend and colleague Professor Lisa Heinzerling of the Georgetown Law Center in 2004, soon after EPA proposed its power plant rule. Those citations are: Rena Steinzor and Lisa Heinzerling, "A Perfect Storm: Mercury and the Bush Administration," *Environmental Law Reporter* 34 (2004): 10297–10333; Rena Steinzor

and Lisa Heinzerling, "A Perfect Storm: Mercury and the Bush Administration, Part II," *Environmental Law Reporter* 34 (2004): 10485–10512.

2. NRC, *Toxicological Effects of Methyl Mercury*, 9, 11.

3. These numbers conflict because the independent doctors use different tests to determine levels of mercury in the body. Venous blood tests of mothers are on average 70 percent *lower* than tests of the blood in the umbilical cord that connects the baby to the mother in utero. For lower estimates see CDC, *Third National Report on Human Exposure to Environmental Chemicals*, July 2005, 45–51. http://www.cdc.gov/exposurereport/3rd/pdf/thirdreport.pdf. For the contrasting Harvard analysis see Leonardo Transande, Philip J. Landrigan, and Clyde Schechter, "Public Health and Economic Consequences of Methyl Mercury Toxicity to the Developing Brain," *Environmental Health Perspectives* 113 (2005): 590, 593, http://ehp.niehs.nih.gov/docs/2005/113-5/toc.html. Dr. Transande is affiliated with the Mount Sinai School of Medicine, Children's Hospital in Boston, the Harvard Medical School, and the Albert Einstein College of Medicine in New York. His co-authors, Philip Landrigan and Clyde Schechter, are affiliated with Mount Sinai School of Medicine and Albert Einstein College of Medicine, respectively.

4. EPA, "Mercury: Laws and Regulations." http://www.epa.gov/mercury/regs.htm.

5. EPA, *National Emission Standards for Hazardous Air Pollutants: Mercury Emissions from Mercury Cell Chlor-Alkali Plants, Federal Register* 68 (December 19, 2003): 70,904 (to be codified at 40 CFR pt. 63). http://www.epa.gov/ttn/atw/hg cellcl/fr19deo3.pdf.

6. EPA, *Standards for Performance for New and Existing Stationary Sources.* A fact sheet containing a plain-English summary of the rule appears at EPA, "Clean Air Mercury Rule." http://www.epa.gov/oar/mercuryrule/hg_factsheet1_29_04.htm. For an account of the states' lawsuit see BNA, "11 States File Lawsuit Over Mercury as EPA Published Emissions-Trading Rule," *Environment Reporter* 36 (May 20, 2005): 1021. Environmental groups have also sued, and the cases are likely to be consolidated. BNA, "Five Environmental Groups Sue to Halt Trading Rule for Mercury Emissions," *Environment Reporter* 36 (July 15, 2005): 1446.

7. Mark Clayton, "America's New Coal Rush," *Christian Science Monitor,* February 26, 2004. http://www.csmonitor.com/2004/0226/p01s04-sten.html.

8. For more information on these trends see P. F. Schuster et al., "Atmospheric Mercury Deposition During the Last 270 Years: A Glacial Ice Core Record of Natural and Anthropogenic Sources," *Environmental Science and Technology* 36, no. 11 (2002): 2303–2310. http://www.ngdc.noaa.gov/paleo/pubs/schuster2002/schuster2002.html.

9. EPA, "Mercury: The Global Context," http://www.epa.gov/mercury/control_emissions/global.htm. For a more comprehensive but somewhat outdated discussion see EPA, *Mercury Study: Report to Congress*, 1997: O-1 (EPA-452/R-97-003), http://www.epa.gov/mercury/report.htm.

10. NRC, *Toxicological Effects of Methyl Mercury.*

11. Ibid., 11.

12. Ibid., 4–10, 250–270.

13. Gary Myers speaking on July 23, 2003, to the Senate Committee on Envi-

ronment and Public Works, *Climate History and Mercury Emissions*, 108th Cong., 1st sess. http://epw.senate.gov/hearing_statements.cfm?id=212851.

14. Joint Institute for Food Safety and Applied Nutrition (JIFSAN), *Annual Report 1998–1999*, http://web.archive.org/web/20020818011614/www.jifsan.umd.edu/Rev99AnRep.htm. "JIFSAN played a crucial role in bringing together the resources to continue [the Seychelles Child Development Study] on the developmental effects of mercury. Funding for the project was provided by the FDA . . . , the Electric Power Research Institute (present funding $486,000), the National Tuna Foundation ($10,000), and the National Fisheries Institute ($5,000)."

15. EPA, *2004 National Listing of Fish Advisories*, September 2005, http://www.epa.gov/waterscience/fish/advisories/fs2004.pdf.

16. EPA, "Mercury: The Global Context."

17. EPA, *Regulatory Finding on Emissions of Hazardous Air Pollutants from Electric Utility Steam Generating Units, Federal Register* 65 (December 20, 2000): 79825, 79827, http://frwebgate.access.gpo.gov/cgi-bin/getdoc.cgi?dbname=2000_register&docid=00-32395-filed.pdf. In a relatively careful piece of technical writing that cited experts working for the industry-sponsored Electric Power Research Institute, Carola Hanisch explained the scientific uncertainties of mercury deposition without challenging these figures. Carola Hanisch, "Where Is Mercury Deposition Coming From?" *Environmental Science and Technology* 32, no. 7 (1998): 176–179, http://pubs.acs.org/hotartcl/est/98/apr/mer.html.

18. Florida Department of Environmental Protection, *Integrating Atmospheric Mercury Deposition with Aquatic Cycling in South Florida: An Approach for Conducting a Total Maximum Daily Load Analysis for an Atmospherically Derived Pollutant*, October 2002, revised November 2003, http://www.dep.state.fl.us/secretary/news/2003/nov/pdf/mercury_report.pdf.

19. Patrick J. Michaels, "EPA: Shoot First, Ask Later," *Cato Institute* (March 19, 2003), http://www.cato.org/dailys/03-19-03.html.

20. *U.S. Code* 42 (2000), §§ 7412(b), (c).

21. Ibid., § 7412(e).

22. For a good description of this industrial segment and the problems it causes see Jeff Johnson, "Where Goes the Missing Mercury?" *Chemical and Engineering News* 82, no. 11 (March 15, 2004): 31–32. For figures on storage, use, and purchase see Chlorine Institute, *Eighth Annual Report to EPA for the Year 2004*, May 13, 2005, http://www.epa.gov/region5/air/mercury/8thcl2report.pdf.

23. Those companies and their sales in 2004 are: Ashta Chemicals Inc. ($70.7 million); Occidental Chemical Corp. ($3.6 billion, and its parent, Occidental Petroleum Corp., had revenues of $11.3 billion); Olin Corp. ($1.9 billion); PPG Industries ($9.5 billion); Pioneer Americas LLC. ($407 million); Vulcan Materials Company ($2.2 billion). Source: Disclosure® online U.S. Public Company Profiles, Lexis-Nexis, and www.hoovers.com. The list in Table 5.1 was valid as of the date EPA issued its chlor-alkali regulations in December 2003. The Ninth Annual Report to EPA for the Year 2005, prepared by the Chlorine Institute Inc. and released on May 15, 2006, states that the Occidental Chemical Company Delaware plant closed in 2005. The report is available at http://www.chlorineinstitute.org/newsdetail.cfm?ItemNumber=2907.

24. EPA, *National Emission Standards*, 70920.

25. Ibid.

26. *U.S. Code* 42 (2000), § 7412(n)(1).

27. EPA, *Regulatory Finding on Emissions,* 79825–79831.

28. The agreement settled the case of *Natural Resources Defense Council v. EPA,* No. 92-1415 (D.C. Cir. 1998).

29. For an account of these events see Tom Hamburger and Alan C. Miller, "Mercury Emissions Rule Geared to Benefit Industry, Staffers Say," *Los Angeles Times,* March 16, 2004.

30. EPA, *Proposed National Emission Standards for Hazardous Air Pollutants; and, in the Alternative, Proposed Standards for Performance of New and Existing Sources: Electric Utility Steam-Generating Units, Federal Register* 69 (proposed January 30, 2004): 4652. The proposal came out in December, but it took several weeks to get it published in the *Federal Register.*

31. Hamburger and Miller, "Mercury Emissions Rule."

32. EPA, *Standards for Performance for New and Existing Stationary Sources;* EPA, *Revision of December 2000 Regulatory Finding on Emissions of Hazardous Air Pollutants from Electric Utility Steam Generating Units and the Removal of Coal- and Oil-Fired Electric Utility Steam Generating Units from the Section 112(c) List, Federal Register* 70 (March 29, 2005): 15994 (to be codified at 40 CFR pt. 63), http://a257.g.akamaitech.net/7/257/2422/01jan20051800/edocket.access.gpo .gov/2005/pdf/05-6037.pdf.

33. Information about the rule can be found at EPA, "Clean Air Interstate Rule, Regulatory Actions," http://epa.gov/cair/rule.html. For the text of the rule see EPA, *Rule to Reduce Interstate Transport of Fine Particulate Matter and Ozone (Clean Air Interstate Rule); Revisions to Acid Rain Program; Revisions to the NOx SIP Call, Federal Register* 70 (May 12, 2005): 25162 (to be codified at 40 CFR pts. 51, 72, et al.), http://a257.g.akamaitech.net/7/257/2422/01jan20051800/edocket .access.gpo.gov/2005/pdf/05-5723.pdf.

34. David Hawkins speaking on April 8, 2003, to the Senate Committee on Environment and Public Works, Subcommittee on Clean Air, Climate Change, and Nuclear Safety, *Clear Skies Act of 2003: Hearings on S. 485,* 108th Cong., 1st sess., http://epw.senate.gov/108th/Hawkins_040803.htm.

35. Michael Janofsky, "Groups Propose Alternative To E.P.A. Rules on Mercury," *New York Times,* November 14, 2005.

36. The State and Territorial Air Pollution Program Administrators and the Association of Local Air Pollution Control Officials (STAPPA/ALAPCO), the preeminent professional association for state regulators, announced release of a model state rule on mercury emissions on November 14, 2005. Janofsky, "Groups Propose Alternative." These are the figures that would result from two alternative proposals to impose strict technology-based standards on power plants that were under discussion by a multi-stakeholder advisory committee in 2001. *Clear Skies Act of 2003: Hearings on S. 485 Before the Senate Commission on Environment and Public Works, Subcommittee on Clean Air, Climate Change, and Nuclear Safety,* 108th Congress (April 8, 2003) (statement of David Hawkins, Director, NRDC Climate Center Natural Resources Defense Council), *available at* http://epw.senate.gov/108th/Hawkins_040803 .htm.

37. A chart showing the status of the states is available at STAPPA/ALAPCO,

"State Mercury Programs for Utilities," http://www.4cleanair.org/StatePrograms
.pdf.

38. For descriptions and analyses of these programs see Richard Toshiyuki
Drury et al., "Pollution Trading and Environmental Injustice: Los Angeles'
Failed Experiment in Air Quality Policy," *Duke Environmental Law and Policy
Journal* 9 (1999): 231; Rena Steinzor, "Toward Better Bubbles and Future Lives: A
Progressive Response to the Conservative Agenda for Reforming Environmental
Law," *Environmental Law Reporter* 32 (2002): 11421–11455.

39. O'Neill, "Mercury, Risk, and Justice," 11070–11071.

40. Executive Order 12291 (Reagan order, continued by President George
H. W. Bush); Executive Order 12866 (Clinton order, left in place by President
George W. Bush). Presidents have the option of continuing, withdrawing, or re-
writing executive orders issued by previous administrations and some of the basic
orders have remained in effect through several administrations. The Bush administration has been far more enthusiastic about the application of the executive
order's language than the Clinton Administration ever was, although the fact that
the document was written under Clinton offers conservatives substantial political
cover for this zeal.

41. For an analysis of these issues see McGarity and Ruttenberg, "Counting
the Cost," 1997.

42. U.S. Government Accountability Office (GAO), *Clean Air Act, Emerging Mercury Control Technologies Have Shown Promising Results, but Data on Long-
Term Performance Are Limited*, May 2005, 8 (GAO-05-216), http://www.gao
.gov/new.items/d05612.pdf.

43. EPA, *Regulatory Impact Analysis of Final Clean Air Mercury Rule*, March
2005, http://www.epa.gov/ttn/atw/utility/ria_final.pdf.

44. EPA, *Standards for Performance for New and Existing Stationary Sources.*

45. GAO, *Clean Air Act, Emerging Mercury Control Technologies.*

46. EPA, *Regulatory Impact Analysis of Final Clean Air Mercury Rule*, 10-5.

47. Ibid., 10-46.

48. Ibid., 10-47.

49. EPA, *Standards for Performance for New and Existing Stationary Sources*,
28606, 28642.

50. Transande, Landrigan, and Schechter, "Public Health and Economic
Consequences."

51. Glenn Rice and James Hammitt, "Economic Valuation of Human Health
Benefits of Controlling Mercury Emissions from U.S. Coal-Fired Plants," report, Northeast States Coordinated Air Use Management (NESCAUM), February 2005, xviii, http://bronze.nescaum.org/airtopics/mercury/rpt050315mercury
health.pdf.

52. William Becker, quoted in Margaret Kriz, "The Next Arsenic: Safeguarding the Food Chain," *National Journal*, February 14, 2004, 458.


## Chapter 6

The chapter epigraph is from a speech by David Ozonoff, on October 19, 1995,
to the Senate Committee on Environmental and Public Works, *Safe Drinking*

*Water Act Amendments of 1995: Hearing on S. 1316,* 104th Cong, 1st sess., 102–103. Dr. Ozonoff chaired the Department of Environmental Health at Boston University between 1983 and 2003; he now directs the Superfund Basic Research Program.

1. For excellent background on the invention, mismanagement, and environmental consequences of perchlorate see Peter Waldman, "Seeping Threat: A Fuel of Cold War Defenses Now Ignites Health Controversy," *Wall Street Journal,* December 16, 2002.

2. NRC, *Health Implications of Perchlorate Ingestion,* 57.

3. Joseph G. Hollowell et al., "Iodine Nutrition in the United States. Trends and Public Health Implications: Iodine Excretion Data from National Health and Nutrition Examination Surveys I and III (1971–1974 and 1988–1994)," *Journal of Clinical Endrocrinology and Metabolism* 83, no. 10 (1998): 3398–3400.

4. The Environmental Working Group study revealed that 18 percent of the samples contained perchlorate above detectable levels and that a single serving would expose the person who ate it to levels four times more than the then-prevailing EPA drinking water guidance. EWG, "Suspect Salads: Toxic Rocket Fuel Found in Samples of Winter Lettuce," 2003, http://www.ewg.org/reports/suspectsalads/es.php. The military's decision was reported in Waldman, "EPA Bans Staff from Discussing Issue."

5. For a detailed account of the study results see U.S. Food and Drug Administration (FDA), Center for Food Safety and Applied Nutrition, *Exploratory Data on Perchlorate in Food,* November 2004, http://www.cfsan.fda.gov/~dms/clo4data.html. The five states are Arizona, California, Florida, New Jersey, and Texas.

6. Ibid. The thirteen states are Arizona, California, Georgia, Kansas, Maryland, Missouri, Louisiana, New Jersey, Pennsylvania, South Carolina, Texas, Virginia, and Washington.

7. Andrea B. Kirk et al., "Perchlorate and Iodide in Dairy and Breast Milk," *Environmental Science and Technology* 39, no. 7 (2005): 2011–2017. The states were California, Connecticut, Florida, Georgia, Hawaii, Maine, Maryland, Michigan, Missouri, Nebraska, New Jersey, New Mexico, New York, North Carolina, Texas, Virginia, Washington, and West Virginia. Peter Waldman, "Perchlorate Level in Human Milk Exceeds Regulator's 'Safe Dose,'" *Wall Street Journal,* February 23, 2005.

8. For an excellent account of these events see Jennifer Sass, "U.S. Department of Defense and White House Working Together to Avoid Cleanup and Liability for Perchlorate Pollution," *International Journal of Occupational and Environmental Health* 10, no. 3 (2004): 330–334.

9. Waldman, "EPA Bans Staff from Discussing Issue."

10. NRC, *Health Implications of Perchlorate Ingestion.*

11. Ibid., 5–8, presents a succinct account of the research preceding perchlorate's use as a drug.

12. Michael Girard, chairman of the Perchlorate Study Group, letter to EPA Information Quality Guidelines staff, December 3, 2003, 1, 11. http://www.epa.gov/quality/informationguidelines/iqg-list.html. The Perchlorate Study Group does not have an immediately available Web site—that is, several searches

did not reveal its location, although users of the Internet know that, like life on other planets, one can never derive a definitive answer from such methodology. A subset of the group's member companies founded the Council on Water Quality, which does have a Web site, at http://www.councilonwaterquality.org.

13. GAO, *Perchlorate: A System to Track Sampling and Cleanup Results Is Needed*, May 2005 (GAO-05-462), 45, http://www.gao.gov/new.items/d05462.pdf. Studies co-sponsored by EPA and DOD were counted as DOD-sponsored studies.

14. This document is no longer available on EPA's Web site. A copy is on file with the author.

15. EPA, Office of Research and Development, National Center for Environmental Assessment, *Perchlorate Contamination: Toxicological Review and Risk Characterization*, 2002 External Review Draft (NCEA-1-0503, 2002), http://oaspub.epa.gov/eims/eimsapi.dispdetail?deid=24002.

16. Paul Gilman, science advisor to EPA, letter to Bruce M. Alberts, president of National Academy of Sciences, March 19, 2003, http://oaspub.epa.gov/eims/eimscomm.getfile?p_download_id=442275.

17. *U.S. Code* 5 (2000), § 552. The act requires the government to turn over records in its custody to the public upon request, unless the material falls within narrow exemptions, including the need to protect the confidentiality of certain internal agency deliberations. EPA withheld the actual text of many documents but did furnish phone logs that show the participants in these conversations. For a complete account of this effort and links to the documents themselves see NRDC, *White House and Pentagon Bias National Academy Perchlorate Report*, January 10, 2005, http://www.nrdc.org/media/pressreleases/050110.asp.

18. Jennifer Sass (Natural Resources Defense Council), Richard Wiles (Environmental Working Group), and Michael Jacobson (Center for Science in the Public Interest), letter to Dr. Bruce Alberts, president of National Academy of Sciences, October 9, 2003 (copy on file with author).

19. *U.S. Code* 5 (2000), app. § 15 (b)(1)(A).

20. Colonel Daniel Rogers, U.S. Air Force, presentation to the National Academy of Sciences Committee to Assess the Health Implications of Perchlorate Ingestion, October 27, 2003, 2–3 (copy on file with author) (emphasis added).

21. Monte A. Greer et al., "Health Effects Assessment for Environmental Perchlorate Contamination: The Dose Response for Inhibition of Thyroidal Radioiodine Uptake in Humans," *Environmental Health Perspectives* 110, no. 9 (2002): 927–937.

22. One of the panel's own members was troubled by this limitation and dissented when his colleagues did not adopt additional safety factors to compensate for it, although he signed onto the rest of the report. He was not identified in the report. NRC, *Health Implications of Perchlorate Ingestion*, 16. A more comprehensive critique of the NAS report is provided in Gary Ginsberg and Deborah Rice, "The NAS Perchlorate Review: Questions Remain about the Perchlorate RfD," *Environmental Health Perspectives* 113 (2005): 1117.

23. NRC, *Health Implications of Perchlorate Ingestion*, 7.

24. Felicity Barringer, "Science Panel Issues Report on Exposure to Pollutant," *New York Times*, January 11, 2005; Rob Stein, "Dangers of Rocket Fuel Chemical Downplayed," *Washington Post*, Jan. 11, 2005; Marla Cone and Lisa

Getter, "Study Disagrees with EPA on Perchlorate," *Los Angeles Times*, January 11, 2005.

25. The provisions of the act that govern such standard setting appear at *U.S. Code* 42 (2000), § 300g-1 (2000).

26. Susan Parker Bodine (assistant administrator, EPA Office of Solid Waste and Emergency Response), Memorandum on Assessment Guidance for Perchlorate, January 26, 2006, http://clu-in.org/download/contaminantfocus/perchlorate/jan06perchguidassess.pdf.

27. Superfund was created by the Comprehensive Environmental Response, Compensation and Liability Act (CERCLA), *U.S. Code* 42 (2000), §§ 9601-9675. To consult the National Priorities List see EPA, "NPL Site Totals by Status and Milestone as of April 25, 2006," http://www.epa.gov/superfund/sites/query/queryhtm/npltotal.htm.

28. Melanie A. Marty (chair of Children's Health Protection Advisory Committee), letter to Stephen L. Johnson (administrator of the EPA), March 8, 2006, http://yosemite.epa.gov/ochp/ochpwebnsf/content/30806_3.htm/$file/30806_3.pdf.

29. Susan Parker Bodine (assistant administrator of Office of Solid Waste and Emergency Response, EPA), letter to Melanie A. Marty (chair of Children's Health Protection Advisory Committee), May 11, 2006, 1, http://yosemite.epa.gov/ochp/ochpweb.nsf/content/5112006.htm/$file/5112006.pdf.

30. Those are: Arizona (14 ppb), Maryland (1 ppb), Nevada (18 ppb), New Mexico (1 ppb), New York (5 ppb for drinking water and 18 ppb for public notification regarding contamination), and Texas (17 ppb for the cleanup of residential sites and 51 ppb for cleanups of industrial sites). EPA, "State Perchlorate Advisory Levels as of 4/20/05," http://www.epa.gov/fedfac/pdf/stateadvisorylevels.pdf.

31. Carolyn Whetzel, "Drinking Water: Stronger Standard for Perchlorate Urged to Better Protect Pregnant Women, Infants," *Environment Report* (BNA) 36 (April 15, 2005): 766.

32. CDC, "Study of Perchlorate Exposure and Thyroid Function in the U.S. Population." Perchlorate Fact Sheet, October 5, 2006, http://www.cdc.gov/nceh/publications/factsheets/perchlorate.htm.

33. GAO, *Perchlorate: A System to Track Sampling*.

34. For an excellent discussion of perchlorate contamination in drinking water see Mary Tiemann, *Perchlorate Contamination of Drinking Water: Regulatory Issues and Legislative Actions*, Congressional Research Service (Washington, DC: Library of Congress, June 15, 2005), http://www.ncseonline.org/nle/crsreports/05feb/RS21961.pdf.

35. GAO, *Perchlorate: A System to Track Sampling*.

36. *U.S. Code* 42 (2000), §§ 6902-6992k.

37. *U.S. Code* 42 (2000), §§ 9601-9675.

38. *U.S. Code* 33 (2000), §§ 1251-1387.

39. *U.S. Code* 42 (2000), §§ 300f-300j-26.

40. Nevada required Kerr-McGee to treat contaminated groundwater until perchlorate was present in amounts no higher than 18 ppb. GAO, *Perchlorate: A System to Track Sampling*, 18.

41. Ibid., 16. Texas has required the Navy to limit perchlorate levels in waste-water discharges at the McGregor Weapons Industrial Reserve Plant to 4 ppb.

42. Ibid, 19.

43. It is only fair to the reader to disclose that I have a professional and personal interest in the Aberdeen situation because I was legal counsel to the citizens' group that was an active participant in the events described here. The following account is based on those observations, supplemented by a series of documents that EPA turned over to NRDC under the Freedom of Information Act and available at NRDC, *White House and Pentagon Bias National Academy Perchlorate Report*, January 10, 2005, http://www.nrdc.org/media/pressreleases/050110.asp.

44. Lane Harvey Brown, "Town Closes 1 of 11 Wells," *Baltimore Sun*, June 14, 2002.

45. Peter Waldman, "The Economy: Bush Seeks Liability Shield on Water Pollutant," *Wall Street Journal*, March 14, 2003.

46. Felicity Barringer, "Pentagon Is Pressing to Bypass Environmental Laws for War Games and Arms Testing," *New York Times*, December 28, 2004.

47. Paul Wolfowitz, "Consideration of Requests for Use of Existing Exemptions Under Federal Environmental Law," Memorandum to Secretaries of the Army, Navy, and Air Force, March 7, 2003, 3.

48. GAO, *DOD Operational Ranges: More Reliable Cleanup Cost Estimates and a Proactive Approach to Identifying Contamination Are Needed*, May 2004 (GAO-04-601), http://www.gao.gov/new.items/d04601.pdf.

## Chapter 7

The chapter epigraph is from *U.S. Code* 42 (2000), § 7409(b).

1. EPA, *Air Quality Classifications for the 8-Hour Ozone National Ambient Air Quality Standards, Federal Register* 69 (September 22, 2004): 56697 (to be codified at 40 C.F.R. pt. 81). Ground-level ozone should not be confused with "atmospheric" or "stratospheric" ozone, which occurs much further from the earth's surface and provides an essential, protective barrier to the sun's rays.

2. For more information on these health effects see EPA, *Smog—Who Does It Hurt? What You Need to Know About Ozone and Your Health*, 1999 (EPA-452K-99-001), http://www.epa.gov/airnow/health.

3. CDC, *Summary Health Statistics for U.S. Children: National Health Interview Survey, 2003*, 2005 (Series 10, No. 223), 4, http://www.cdc.gov/nchs/data/series/sr_10/sr10_223.pdf.

4. For a good general background on the act see Percival et al., *Environmental Regulation*, 491–568.

5. EPA, *Latest Findings on National Air Quality: 2002 Status and Trends*, 2003 (EPA 454/K-03-001), http://www.abuse.com/environment/airtrends/2002_air trends_final.pdf.

6. EPA, *EPA and States Not Making Sufficient Progress in Reducing Ozone Precursor Emissions in Some Major Metropolitan Areas*, 2004 (Report No. 2004-P-00033), http://www.epa.gov/oig/reports/2004/20040929-2004-P-00033.pdf.

7. For a comprehensive discussion of air quality and its implications for pub-

lic health see American Lung Association, *State of the Air 2005*, 2005, http://www.lungusa2.org/embargo/sota05/SOTA05_final.pdf. For a critique of the report see Roy Cordato, "Caution Needed on 'State of the Air': JLF Analysts offer Response to American Lung Association Report," John Locke Foundation, April 28, 2005, http://www.johnlocke.org/press_releases/display_story .html?id=81. Dr. Cordato is an economist.

8. EPA, *Air Trends: Ozone*, http://www.epa.gov/airtrends/ozone.html; EPA, *Green Book: 8-Hour Ozone Area Summary*, http://www.epa.gov/oar/oaqps/greenbk/gnsum.html.

9. *Whitman v. American Trucking Associations*, 531 U.S. 457 (2001).

10. EPA, *Clear Skies*, http://www.epa.gov/ebtpages/airairpoclearskies.html. For a critical analysis of the Clear Skies proposal and what would happen under the existing statute see Larry Parker and James E. McCarthy, "Clear Skies and the Clean Air Act: What's the Difference?" Congressional Research Service, February 25, 2005, http://www.ncseonline.org/NLE/CRSreports/05Feb/RL32782.pdf.

11. *U.S. Code* 42 (2000), § 7409(d).

12. Sheila Jasanoff, *The Fifth Branch: Science Advisers as Policymakers* (Cambridge, MA: Harvard University Press, 1990); Professor Jasanoff's book has a compelling account of EPA's relationship with CASAC that is the basis for this description of the process at 101-122. Also see Wendy Wagner, "The Science Charade in Toxic Risk Regulation," *Columbia Law Review* 95, no. 7 (1995): 1613-1723.

13. The standard is that levels measured at an ambient air quality monitoring site are in compliance if you take the three-year average of the fourth-highest eight-hour period for each year, average them, and come up with a number at or less than the 0.08 ppm limit. EPA, *National Ambient Air Quality Standards, Federal Register* 62 (July 18, 1997): 38856 (to be codified at 40 C.F.R. pt. 50). As noted in the introduction, the CAA is not a subject for those who have difficulty attending to precise, counter-intuitive technical details.

14. "More Research Needed on Health Effects of Ozone, PM Proposals, Senate Panel Told," *Environment Reporter* (BNA) 27 (February 7, 1997): 2022-2024.

15. Ibid.

16. Readers wishing to pursue these arguments should see Gary Koop and Lisa Tole, "Measuring the Health Effects of Air Pollution: To What Extent Can We Really Say That People Are Dying from Bad Air?" *Journal of Environmental Economics and Management* 47 (2004): 30-54; Cary Coglianese and Gary E. Marchant, "The EPA's Risky Reasoning," *Regulation* (Summer 2004): 16-22; C. Boyden Gray, "The Clean Air Act Under Regulatory Reform," *Tulane Environmental Law Journal* 11 (1998): 235-260; Margaret Kriz, "Heavy Breathing," *National Journal*, January 4, 1997, 8; Angela Antonelli, "Can No One Stop the EPA?" Heritage Foundation, July 8, 1997, http://www.heritage.org/Research/PoliticalPhilosophy/BG1129.cfm; Kenneth Green, "Rethinking EPA's Proposed Ozone and Particulate Standards," Reason Public Policy Institute, June 1997, http://www .rppi.org/environment/ps224.html; "Industry, Environmental Groups Disagree On Need For Tighter Standards," *Environment Reporter* (BNA) 27 (January 24, 1997): 1947-1955.

17. EPA, *Draft Air Quality Criteria for Ozone and Related Photochemical Oxi-

*dants*, E-Docket No. ORD-2004-0015, *Federal Register* 70 (August 31, 2005): 5180.

18. NRC, *Interim Report of the Committee on Changes in New Source Review Programs for Stationary Sources of Air Pollutants* (Washington, DC: National Academy Press, 2005), 57.

19. *American Trucking Associations v. EPA*, 175 F.3d 1027 (D.C. Cir. 1999).

20. *U.S. Code* 42 (2000), § 7409.

21. Ibid., § 7410. The provisions instructing EPA to provide designations and review SIPs for non-attainment areas appear at § 7502.

22. Provisions authorizing EPA to issue pollution control requirements appear at *U.S. Code* 42 (2000), §§ 7411 (standards of performance for new stationary sources) and 7412 (hazardous air pollutants).

23. Two excellent critiques are Thomas O. McGarity, "Missing Milestones: A Critical Look at the Clean Air Act's VOC Emissions Reduction Program in Non-attainment Areas," *Virginia Environmental Law Journal* 18, no. 1 (1999): 41, and Howard Latin, "Regulatory Failure, Administrative Incentives, and the New Clean Air Act," *Environmental Law* 21, no. 4 (1991): 1647.

24. GAO, *Air Pollution: Emission Sources Regulated by Multiple Clean Air Act Provisions*, 2000 (GAO/RCED-00-155), 1.

25. GAO routinely testifies before Congress about its reports. The $140 million estimate appeared in the statement of GAO Associate Director David G. Wood testifying on May 17, 2000, before the U.S. Senate Subcommittee on Clean Air, Wetlands, Private Property, and Nuclear Safety, Committee on Environment and Public Works, "Air Pollution: Implementation of the Clean Air Act Amendments of 1990," 7, http://www.gao.gov/archive/2000/rc00183t.pdf. The expert is described as the director of an organization that represents state and local governments but is not identified by name.

26. NRC, *Air Quality Management in the United States* (Washington, DC: National Academy Press, 2004), 128. This single volume is a terrific source of both background on the Clean Air Act and ideas for reforming it.

27. *U.S. Code* 42 (2000), §§ 7509, 7511(d). EPA also has enforcement authority under *U.S. Code* 42 (2000), § 7413.

28. EPA's authority to write Federal Implementation Plans appears at *U.S. Code* 42 (2000), § 7410(c).

29. *U.S. Code* 42 (2000), §§ 7501–7515.

30. Any private citizen can bring such a lawsuit and recover attorney's fees under *U.S. Code* 42 (2000), §7604.

31. Howard Latin, "Regulatory Failure," 1692 (emphasis in original).

32. OMB, *Circular A-4*.

33. Executive Order 12866.

34. EPA, *The Benefits and Costs of the Clean Air Act, 1970 to 1990*, 1997 (EPA 410-R-97-002), http://www.epa.gov/oar/sect812. Cost figures appear at page ES-2; benefit numbers are set forth at ES-8; and value of health effects numbers are on ES-6.

35. EPA, *Benefits and Costs of the Clean Air Act 1990 to 2010*, 1999 (EPA 410-R-99-001), http://www.epa.gov/oar/sect812. Monetized direct cost and benefit figures are at page iii; monetized adverse health effects are at 70.

36. Ralph L. Keeney and Kenneth Green, "Estimating Fatalities Induced by Economic Impacts of EPA's Ozone and Particulate Standards," Reason Public Policy Institute (1997) (Reason Public Policy Institute Policy Study No. 225), http://www.reason.org/ps225.PDF. For an opposing view see Ackerman and Heinzerling, *Priceless*, 41–60.

### Chapter 8

1. Christopher Schroeder and Rena Steinzor, editors, *A New Progressive Agenda for Public Health and the Environment* (Durham, NC: Carolina Academic Press, 2004). The Center for Progressive Reform (CPR) is a think tank composed of working academics in the disciplines of law, economics, philosophy, and science. Our scholarly work focuses on environmental law and policy; the protection of public health from pollution, bad drugs, and bad food; natural resources preservation; occupational health and safety; and energy policy. Our funding is provided by the Deer Creek Foundation, the Beldon Fund, and the Baumann Foundation. For more information see Center for Progressive Reform, http://www.progressivereform.org.

2. Luntz Research Companies, "Environment" (emphasis omitted).

3. Ibid.

4. Pew Research Center, *Trends 2005* (Washington, DC: Pew Research Center, 2005), 17, http://pewresearch.org/trends.

5. Polling Report, "ABC News/Time/Stanford University Poll, March 9–14, 2006," http://pollingreport.com/enviro.htm.

6. Linda Lyons, "Daily Concerns Overshadow Environment Worries, Two-Thirds of Americans Distressed About Environment," Gallup Organization, April 19, 2005.

7. Pew Research Center, *Trends 2005*, 19.

8. Duke University, Nicolas Institute for Environmental Policy Solutions, *Public Opinion Strategies and Hart Research Present a Report of Key Findings and Analysis from Research Conducted on Behalf of the Nicholas Institute*, 2005, http://www.nicholas.duke.edu/institute/surveywhitepaper.pdf.

9. Ibid., 15.

10. Ibid., 16.

11. Ibid., 17.

12. Ibid., 18.

13. Ibid., 19.

14. Ibid., 20.

15. Ibid.

16. Michael Janofsky, "When Cleaner Air Is a Biblical Obligation: Evangelical Groups Join Call for Tougher Environmental Laws," *New York Times*, November 7, 2005.

17. Polling Report, "Gallup Poll, March 13–16, 2006," http://pollingreport.com/enviro.htm.

18. Ibid.

19. Fairbank, Maslin, Maullin, and Associates (Democratic) and Public Opinion Strategies (Republican), 2004 Polling on the Environment, polling for the Nature Conservancy and Trust for Public Land (April 3–12, 2004), available to subscribers at http://nationaljournal.com/members/polltrack/2004/todays/04/0421fmmapos.htm. Between 7 and 10 percent of each group were "undecided," and the remainder were described as "unwilling."

20. U.S. Census Bureau, "Nation's Population One-Third Minority," press release, May 10, 2006, http://www.census.gov/Press-Release/www/releases/archives/population/006808.html.

21. Eban Goodstein, *The Trade-Off Myth: Fact and Fiction About Jobs and the Environment* (Washington, DC: Island Press 1999), 8.

22. Claudia Dean, "Trust in Government Declines: Post-9/11 Jump in Americans' Confidence in Washington Is Fading," *Washington Post*, May 31, 2002.

23. Sam Roberts, "In Government We Trust (as Far as We Can Throw It)," *New York Times*, January 4, 2004.

24. Ibid.

25. Pew Research Center, *Trends 2005*, 21.

26. Christopher Lee, "Image Problem Looms for U.S. Civil Service: Poll Suggests Need for Better Recruiting," *Washington Post*, August 18, 2004.

27. Polling Report, "Environment: CBS/New York Times Poll, Nov. 20–24, 2002," http://pollingreport.com/enviro.htm.

28. Pew Research Center, *Trends 2005*, 17.

29. Polling Report, "Environment: The Harris Poll, Aug. 9–16, 2005," http://pollingreport.com/enviro.htm. Some 53 percent said the president was not doing his share, and 57 percent similarly criticized Congress.

30. Paul Farhi, "When the Blue Chips Are Down, in Government We Trust," *Washington Post*, April 30, 2002.

31. "Inequality and the American Dream," *Economist*, June 17–23, 2006, 13. If the phrase "work hard and play by the rules" sounds familiar, it is because the phrase was repeatedly intoned by President Bill Clinton in his own efforts to explain why he was governing in a way consistent with American traditional values. See, e.g., William Jefferson Clinton, President's Radio Address, December 10, 1994, http://www.presidency.ucsb.edu/ws/index.php?pid=49577. ("And I'm talking about hard-working Americans who play by the rules; they're tired of watching their earnings benefit people who don't.")

32. Phil Ochs authored the lyrics of this well-known song from the 1960s and also put out an album with the title for Elektra Records. Wikipedia, "There but for Fortune," http://en.wikipedia.org/wiki/There_but_for_Fortune.

33. U.S. Census Bureau, *Income, Poverty, and Health Insurance Coverage in the United States: 2004*, August 2005, http://www.census.gov/prod/2005pubs/p60-229.pdf; David Wood, "Effect of Child and Family Poverty on Child Health in the United States," *Pediatrics* 112, no. 3 (September 2003): 707–711, http://pediatrics.aappublications.org/cgi/content/full/112/3/S1/707; National Center for Children in Poverty, "Basic Facts about Low-Income Children: Birth to Age 18" (2006), http://www.nccp.org/pub_lico6.html; North Carolina State University, Department of Sociology and Anthropology, "The Causes and Consequences of

Child Poverty," *Quality of Life in North Carolina* 3, no. 1 (undated), http://www
.ces.ncsu.edu/depts/sociology/pub/qol/the_causes_and_consequenses_of_
children_poverty.pdf.

34. Wood, "Effect of Child and Family Poverty," 707.

35. Department of Health and Human Services, Office of the Secretary, *Annual Update of the HHS Poverty Guidelines*, notice, *Federal Register* 71 (January 24, 2006): 3848–3849.

36. Wood, "Effect of Child and Family Poverty," 708.

37. Janean E. Dilworth-Bart and Colleen F. Moore, "Mercy Mercy Me: Social Injustice and the Prevention of Environmental Pollutant Exposures Among Ethnic Minority and Poor Children," *Child Development* 77, no. 2 (March 2006): 247–265.

38. Paul Krugman, "Losing Our Country," *New York Times*, June 10, 2005.

39. Ibid.

40. Ibid.

41. Ibid.

42. Thomas R. Malthus, *An Essay on Population as It Affects the Future Improvement of Society*, 1st ed. (London: J. Johnson, 1798).

43. Ibid., chapter 2, page 1.

44. David R. Francis, "How to Slow the Population Clock," *Christian Science Monitor* (July 3, 2006): 15; http://www.csmonitor.com/2006/0703/p15s01-cogn
.html.

45. Al Gore, *An Inconvenient Truth* (Emmaus: Rodale Books, 2006); Jim Hansen, "The Threat to the Planet," *New York Review of Books*, July 13, 2006, http://www.nybooks.com/articles/19131.

46. Millennium Ecosystem Assessment Board, *Living Beyond Our Means: Natural Assets and Human Well-being*, statement prepared for Kofi Annan (Secretary-General of the United Nations), March 2005, http://www.maweb
.org//en/Products.BoardStatement.aspx.

## Chapter 9

The chapter epigraph is from Adam Clymer, "Barry Goldwater, Conservative and Individualist, Dies at 89," *New York Times*, May 29, 1998.

1. Many of the ideas presented here were first developed in a book written by scholars at the Center for Progressive Reform, including me; Schroeder and Steinzor, *New Progressive Agenda*. For more information about the Center for Progressive Reform see www.progressivereform.org.

2. Andrews, *Managing the Environment*, 109–135.

3. Ibid., 120.

4. The cases were *Gibbons v. Ogden*, 22 U.S. 1 (1824), and *Lochner v. New York*, 198 U.S. 45 (1905).

5. Upton Sinclair, *The Jungle* (originally published 1906; New York: Bantam Books, 1981).

6. Dwight D. Eisenhower, *Public Papers of the Presidents of the United States:*

*Dwight D. Eisenhower, 1953–61*, vol. 1 (Washington, DC: Government Printing Office, 1983), 207, 714.

7. Wendy E. Parmet, "From Slaughter-House to Lochner: The Rise and Fall of the Constitutionalization of Public Health," *American Journal of Legal History* 40, no. 1 (1996): 476–505.

8. Ibid., 477, 503–505.

9. *Nebraska ex rel. Stenberg v. U.S.*, 238 F.3d 946 (8th Cir. 2001), *cert. denied*, 533 U.S. 929 (2001). Ultimately, the case was thrown out on jurisdictional grounds that it had filed its complaint in the wrong court.

10. As any professional manager will tell you, there are real limits to the amount of money that any institution can feasibly absorb and use effectively in the short term.

11. The Agency last convened a panel of outside experts to review its mandates and programs and give it a sense of what its priorities should be in 1987; that report remains a classic in the field but is long overdue for updating. EPA, *Unfinished Business: A Comparative Assessment of Environmental Protection*, 1987.

12. For an excellent description of the theories and practice that underlie this approach see Clifford Rechtschaffen and David Markell, *Reinventing Environmental Enforcement and the State/Federal Relationship* (Washington, DC: Environmental Law Institute, 2003).

13. Mary Jane K. Selgrade et al., "Induction of Asthma and the Environment: What We Know and Need to Know," *Environmental Health Perspectives* 114 (April 2006): 615, 616.

14. Ibid., 616.

15. For more information see Rena Steinzor and Margaret Clune, *The Toll of Superfund Neglect: Toxic Waste Dumps and Communities at Risk*, June 15, 2006. http://www.progressivereform.org/articles/Superfund_061506.pdf.

16. Chris Mooney, *The Republican War on Science* (New York: Basic Books, 2005), 102–120; Wendy Wagner and Rena Steinzor, editors, *Rescuing Science from Politics: Regulation and the Distortion of Scientific Research* (New York: Cambridge University Press, 2006).

17. Wagner and Steinzor, introduction to *Rescuing Science*, 8–9.

18. John Applegate, "The Government Role in Scientific Research, Who Should Bridge the Data Gap in Chemical Regulation," in *Rescuing Science*, edited by Wagner and Steinzor, 268–275.

19. David Kriebel et al., "The Precautionary Principle in Environmental Science," *Environmental Health Perspectives* 109 (September 2001): 871–876. Apart from the authors' enthusiasm for European approaches, the article contains a well-reasoned analysis of why precaution is so important in the formulation of environmental policy.

# Bibliography

Ackerman, Frank, and Lisa Heinzerling. *Priceless: On Knowing the Price of Everything and the Value of Nothing.* New York: New Press, 2004.

American Lung Association. *State of the Air 2005.* 2005. http://www.lungusa2.org/embargo/sota05/SOTA05_final.pdf.

American Lung Association, Epidemiology and Statistics Unit, Research and Program Services. *Trends in Asthma Morbidity and Mortality.* May 2005. http://www.lungusa.org/atf/cf/{7A8D42C2-FCCA-4604-8ADE-7F5D5E762256}/ASTHMA1.PDF.

*American Trucking Associations v. EPA.* 175 F.3d 1027 (D.C. Cir. 1999).

Anderson, Terry L., and Donald R. Leal. *Free Market Environmentalism.* Rev. ed. New York: Palgrave, 2001.

Andrews, Richard N. L. *Managing the Environment, Managing Ourselves: A History of American Environmental Policy.* New Haven: Yale University Press, 1999.

Antonelli, Angela. "Can No One Stop the EPA?" Heritage Foundation. July 8, 1997. http://www.heritage.org/Research/PoliticalPhilosophy/BG1129.cfm.

Applegate, John. "The Government Role in Scientific Research, Who Should Bridge the Data Gap in Chemical Regulation." In *Rescuing Science from Politics: Regulation and the Distortion of Scientific Research*, edited by Wendy Wagner and Rena Steinzor, 255–278. New York: Cambridge University Press, 2006.

Barringer, Felicity. "Pentagon Is Pressing to Bypass Environmental Laws for War Games and Arms Testing." *New York Times*, December 28, 2004.

Barringer, Felicity. "Science Panel Issues Report on Exposure to Pollutant." *New York Times*, January 11, 2005.

Bodine, Susan Parker. Letter to Melanie A. Marty, May 11, 2006. http://yosemite.epa.gov/ochp/ochpweb.nsf/content/5112006.htm/$file/5112006.pdf.

———. Memorandum on Assessment Guidance for Perchlorate. January 26, 2006. http://clu-in.org/download/contaminantfocus/perchlorate/jan06perchguidassess.pdf.

Breyer, Steven. *Breaking the Vicious Circle: Toward Effective Risk Regulation.* Boston: Harvard University Press, 1993.

Brown, Lane Harvey. "Town Closes 1 of 11 Wells." *Baltimore Sun*, June 14, 2002.

Bureau of National Affairs Inc. (BNA). "CMA More Optimistic than EDF On

Lack of Data for 100 Chemicals." *Daily Environment Report* 230 (December 1, 1997): A-4.

———. "Eleven States File Lawsuit Over Mercury as EPA Published Emissions-Trading Rule." *Environment Reporter* 36 (May 20, 2005): 1021.

———. "Five Environmental Groups Sue to Halt Trading Rule for Mercury Emissions." *Environment Reporter* 36 (July 15, 2005): 1446.

———. "Industry, Environmental Groups Disagree On Need For Tighter Standards." *Environment Reporter* 27 (January 24, 1997): 1947.

———. "More Research Needed on Health Effects of Ozone, PM Proposals, Senate Panel Told." *Environment Reporter* 27 (February 7, 1997): 2022.

Burkhard, Bruce. "Year in Review, Congress vs. Environment: Environmental Laws Suffer Under GOP-Controlled Congress." Cable News Network. December 29, 1995.

Carson, Rachel. *Silent Spring.* 40th anniv. ed. Boston: Mariner Books, 2002.

Centers for Disease Control and Prevention (CDC). *Third National Report on Human Exposure to Environmental Chemicals.* July 2005. http://www.cdc.gov/exposurereport/3rd/pdf/thirdreport.pdf.

———. National Center for Environmental Health. *Preventing Lead Poisoning in Young Children.* October 1991. http://www.cdc.gov/nceh/lead/publications/books/plpyc/contents.htm.

———. "Study of Perchlorate Exposure and Thyroid Function in the U.S. Population." Perchlorate Fact Sheet. October 5, 2006. http://www.cdc.gov/nceh/publications/factsheets/perchlorate.htm.

———. *Summary Health Statistics for U.S. Children: National Health Interview Survey, 2003.* 2005. Series 10, no. 223. http://www.cdc.gov/nchs/data/series/sr10/sr10223.pdf.

Chlorine Institute. *Eighth Annual Report to EPA for the Year 2004.* May 13, 2005. http://www.epa.gov/region5/air/mercury/8thcl2report.pdf.

Clayton, Mark. "America's New Coal Rush." *Christian Science Monitor,* February 26, 2004. http://www.csmonitor.com/2004/0226/p01s04-sten.html.

*Clean Air Act. U.S. Code* 42 (2000), §§ 7401–7671q.

*Clean Air Act Amendments of 1990.* Public Law 101-549. *U.S. Statutes at Large* 104 (1990): 2399.

Clinton, William Jefferson. *State of the Union Address as Delivered,* January 23, 1996. http://clinton4.nara.gov/WH/New/other/sotu.html.

———. President's Radio Address, December 10, 1994. http://www.presidency.ucsb.edu/ws/index.php?pid=49577.

Clymer, Adam. "Barry Goldwater, Conservative and Individualist, Dies at 89." *New York Times,* May 29, 1998.

Coglianese, Cary, and Gary E. Marchant. "The EPA's Risky Reasoning." *Regulation* (Summer 2004): 16–22.

Colborn, Theo, Dianne Dumanoski, and John Peterson Myers. *Our Stolen Future.* New York: Plume, 1997.

*Comprehensive Environmental Response, Compensation and Liability Act* (CERCLA). *U.S. Code* 42 (2000), §§ 9601–9675.

Cone, Marla, and Lisa Getter. "Study Disagrees with EPA on Perchlorate." *Los Angeles Times,* January 11, 2005.

Conlan, Timothy J. "Federalism and Competing Values in the Reagan Administration." *Publius: The Journal of Federalism* 16 (1986): 29–47.

Cordato, Roy. "Caution Needed on 'State of the Air': JLF Analysts offer Response to American Lung Association Report." John Locke Foundation, April 28, 2005. http://www.johnlocke.org/press_releases/display_story.html?id=81.

*Corrosion Proof Fittings v. EPA.* 947 F.2d 1201 (5th Cir. 1991).

Covello, Vincent T., and Miley W. Merkhofer. *Risk Assessment Methods.* New York: Plenum Press, 1993.

Crane, Edward H. "The Republican Congress in Historical Context." In *The Republican Revolution 10 Years Later: Smaller Government or Business as Usual?*, edited by Chris Edwards and John Samples, 17–22. Washington, DC: Cato Institute, 2005.

Davies, J. Clarence, and Jan Mazurek. *Pollution Control in the United States: Evaluating the System.* Washington, DC: Resources for the Future, 1998.

Dean, Claudia. "Trust in Government Declines." *Washington Post*, May 31, 2002.

Dilworth-Bart, Janean E., and Colleen F. Moore. "Mercy Mercy Me: Social Injustice and the Prevention of Environmental Pollutant Exposures Among Ethnic Minority and Poor Children." *Child Development* 77, no. 2 (March 2006): 247.

Dionne, E. J. "When Government Is 'Good.'" *Washington Post*, September 2, 2005.

Ditz, Daryl, Janet Ranganathan, and R. Darryl Banks, editors. *Green Ledgers: Case Studies in Corporate Environmental Accounting.* Washington, DC: World Resources Institute, 1995.

Drury, Richard Toshiyuki, Michael E. Belliveau, J. Scott Kuhn, and Shipra Bansal. "Pollution Trading and Environmental Injustice: Los Angeles' Failed Experiment in Air Quality Policy." *Duke Environmental Law and Policy Forum* 9 (1999): 231–290.

Duke University, Nicolas Institute for Environmental Policy Solutions. *Public Opinion Strategies and Hart Research Present a Report of Key Findings and Analysis from Research Conducted on Behalf of the Nicholas Institute.* 2005. http://www.nicholas.duke.edu/institute/surveywhitepaper.pdf.

Easterbrook, Gregg. "Case Closed: The Debate About Global Warming Is Over." Brookings Institution, *Issues in Governance Studies*, no. 3 (June 2006).

——. *A Moment on Earth: The Coming of Age of Environmental Optimism.* New York: Viking, 1995.

*Economist.* "The Conservative Movement, A Hammer Blow." October 1, 2005, 27–29.

——. "The Fiscal Mess, or Is It an Opportunity?" October 1, 2005, 29–32.

——. "Inequality and the American Dream." June 17, 2006, 13.

Edwards, Chris, and John Samples, editors. *The Republican Revolution 10 Years Later: Smaller Government or Business as Usual?* Washington, DC: Cato Institute, 2005.

Eisenhower, Dwight D. *Public Papers of the Presidents of the United States: Dwight D. Eisenhower, 1953–61*, vol. 1. Washington, DC: Government Printing Office, 1983.

Environmental Council of the States. "Delegation by Environmental Act." 2001. http://ecos.org/section/states/enviro_actlist.

Environmental Defense Fund. *Toxic Ignorance: The Continuing Absence of Basic Health Testing for Top-Selling Chemicals in the United States.* New York: Environmental Defense Fund, 1997.

Environmental Working Group (EWG). "Suspect Salads: Toxic Rocket Fuel Found in Samples of Winter Lettuce." 2003. http://www.ewg.org/reports/suspectsalads/es.php.

Epstein, Marc J. *Measuring Corporate Environmental Performance: Best Practices for Costing and Managing an Effective Environmental Strategy.* Chicago: Irwin Professional Publishing, 1996.

*Ethyl Corporation v. EPA.* 541 F.2d 1, 6 (D.C. Cir. 1976).

Executive Order 12291. February 17, 1981. *Federal Register* 46 FR 13193, 3 CFR, 1981 Comp., p. 127. http://www.archives.gov/federal-register/codification/executive-order/12291.html.

Executive Order 12866. Regulatory Planning and Review. September 30, 1993. *Federal Register* 58, no. 190 (October 4, 1993): 51735–51744. http://www.whitehouse.gov/omb/inforeg/eo12866.pdf.

Farhi, Paul. "When the Blue Chips Are Down, in Government We Trust." *Washington Post,* April 30, 2002.

Feder, Barnaby J. "Chemistry Cleans Up a Factory." *New York Times,* July 18, 1999.

*Federal Insecticide, Fungicide, and Rodenticide Act Amendments of 1988.* Public Law 100-532, § 102. *U.S. Statutes at Large* 102 (1988): 2654.

*Federal Water Pollution Control Act. U.S. Code* 33 (2000), § 1251(a)(1).

Florida Department of Environmental Protection. *Integrating Atmospheric Mercury Deposition with Aquatic Cycling in South Florida: An Approach for Conducting a Total Maximum Daily Load Analysis for an Atmospherically Derived Pollutant.* October 2002, revised November 2003. http://www.dep.state.fl.us/secretary/news/2003/nov/pdf/mercury_report.pdf.

*Food Quality Protection Act.* Public Law 104-170. *U.S. Statutes at Large* 110 (1996): 1489 et seq.

Francis, David R. "How to Slow the Population Clock." *Christian Science Monitor,* July 3, 2006. http://www.csmonitor.com/2006/0703/p15s01-cogn.html.

Friedman, Milton. *Capitalism and Freedom.* 40th anniv. ed. Chicago: University of Chicago Press, 2002.

*Gibbons v. Ogden.* 22 U.S. 1 (1824).

Gillespie, Ed, and Bob Schellhas, editors. *Contract with America: The Bold Plan by Rep. Newt Gingrich, Rep. Dick Armey, and the House Republicans to Change the Nation.* Washington, DC: Republican National Committee, 1994.

Gilman, Paul, science advisor to EPA. Letter to Bruce M. Alberts, president of National Academy of Sciences, March 19, 2003. http://oaspub.epa.gov/eims/eimscomm.getfile?p_download_id=442275.

Girard, Michael. Letter to U.S. Environmental Protection Agency Information Quality Guidelines staff, December 3, 2003. http://www.epa.gov/quality/informationguidelines/iqg-list.html.

Goodstein, Eban. *The Trade-Off Myth: Fact and Fiction About Jobs and the Environment.* Washington, DC: Island Press 1999.

Gore, Al. *An Inconvenient Truth.* Emmaus: Rodale Books, 2006.

Graham, John D. Office of Information and Regulatory Affairs. Testimony Before the U.S. House of Representatives Small Business Committee, May 19, 2004. http://www.whitehouse.gov/omb/legislative/testimony/graham/040519_graham_reg_reform.html.

Gray, C. Boyden. "The Clean Air Act Under Regulatory Reform." *Tulane Environmental Law Journal* 11 (1998): 235–260.

Green, Kenneth. "Rethinking EPA's Proposed Ozone and Particulate Standards." Reason Public Policy Institute, June 1997. http://www.rppi.org/environment/ps224.html.

Greer, Monte A., Gay Goodman, Richard C. Pleus, and Susan E. Greer. "Health Effects Assessment for Environmental Perchlorate Contamination: The Dose Response for Inhibition of Thyroidal Radioiodine Uptake in Humans." *Environmental Health Perspectives* 110, no. 9 (2002): 927–937.

Hamburger, Tom, and Alan C. Miller. "Mercury Emissions Rule Geared to Benefit Industry, Staffers Say." *Los Angeles Times,* March 16, 2004.

Hamilton, Alexander, James Madison, and John Jay. *The Federalist Papers,* edited by Clinton Rossiter. New York: New American Library, 1961. First published 1788.

Hanisch, Carola. "Where Is Mercury Deposition Coming From?" *Environmental Science and Technology* 32, no. 7 (1998): 176–179. http://pubs.acs.org/hotartcl/est/98/apr/mer.html.

Hansen, Jim. "The Threat to the Planet." *New York Review of Books,* July 13, 2006. http://www.nybooks.com/articles/19131.

Hardin, Garrett. "The Tragedy of the Commons." *Science* 162, no. 3859 (1968): 1243–1248.

Hayek, F. A. *The Road to Serfdom.* 50th anniv. ed. Chicago: University of Chicago Press, 1994.

*Hazardous and Solid Waste Amendments of 1984.* Public Law 98-616. *U.S. Statutes at Large* 98 (1984): 3221.

Hoffman, Andrew J. *From Heresy to Dogma: An Institutional History of Corporate Environmentalism.* Stanford, CA: Stanford University Press, 2001.

Hollowell, Joseph G., N. W. Staehling, W. H. Hannon, D. W. Flanders, E. W. Gunter, G. F. Maberly, L. E. Braverman, S. Pino, D. T. Miller, P. L. Garbe, D. M. DeLozier, and R. J. Jackson. "Iodine Nutrition in the United States. Trends and Public Health Implications: Iodine Excretion Data from National Health and Nutrition Examination Surveys I and III (1971–1974 and 1988–1994)." *Journal of Clinical Endocrinology and Metabolism* 83, no. 10 (1998): 3398–3400.

Howard, Philip K. *The Death Of Common Sense: How Law Is Suffocating America.* New York: Random House, 1994.

*Industrial Union Dept., AFL-CIO v. American Petroleum Institute.* 448 U.S. 607 (1980).

Janofsky, Michael. "Groups Propose Alternative To E.P.A. Rules on Mercury." *New York Times,* November 14, 2005.

———. "When Cleaner Air Is a Biblical Obligation." *New York Times,* November 7, 2005.

Jasanoff, Sheila. *The Fifth Branch: Science Advisers as Policymakers.* Cambridge, MA: Harvard University Press, 1990.

Johnson, Jeff. "Where Goes the Missing Mercury?" *Chemical and Engineering News* 82, no. 11 (March 15, 2004): 31–32.

Joint Institute for Food Safety and Applied Nutrition (JIFSAN). *Annual Report 1998–1999.* http://web.archive.org/web/20020818011614/www.jifsan.umd.edu/Rev99AnRep.htm.

Joint Science Academies. "Joint Science Academies' Statement: Global Response to Climate Change." June 4, 2005. http://nationalacademies.org/onpi/0607 2005.pdf.

Jones, Mark. "On Gregg Easterbrook, Author." *World Overpopulation Awareness.* May 2000. http://www.overpopulation.org//Op_Eds/MarkJones_Easter brook.html.

Keeney, Ralph L., and Kenneth Green. "Estimating Fatalities Induced by Economic Impacts of EPA's Ozone and Particulate Standards." Reason Public Policy Institute Policy Study No. 225. 1997. http://www.reason.org/ps225 .PDF.

Kirk, Andrea B., P. Kalyani Martinelango, Kang Tian, Aniruddha Dutta, Ernest E. Smith, and Purnendu K. Dasgupta. "Perchlorate and Iodide in Dairy and Breast Milk." *Environmental Science and Technology* 39, no. 7 (2005): 2011–2017.

Koop, Gary, and Lisa Tole. "Measuring the Health Effects of Air Pollution: To What Extent Can We Really Say That People Are Dying From Bad Air?" *Journal of Environmental Economics and Management* 47 (2004): 30–54.

Kovacs, Bill. "Mercury Emissions." U.S. Chamber of Commerce Radio Actuality. December 3, 2003. http://www.uschamber.com/NR/rdonlyres/eykqfj3b vnibjgahe5rbv55m2qmzl6pwlaq4u4ynlahvvl5502qsumt3xbkgkm6zkk44 abojuydm4tu50pfzfrpwyze/mercurykovacs120303.txt.

Kozinski, Alex, and Steven A. Engel. "Recapturing Madison's Constitution: Federalism Without the Blank Check." In *James Madison and the Future of Limited Government,* edited by John Samples. Washington, DC: Cato Institute, 2002.

Kriebel, David, Joel Tickner, Paul Epstein, John Lemons, Richard Levins, Edward L. Loechler, Margaret Quinn, Ruthann Rudel, Ted Schettler, and Michael Stoto. "The Precautionary Principle in Environmental Science." *Environmental Health Perspectives* 109 (September 2001): 871–876.

Kriz, Margaret. "Heavy Breathing." *National Journal,* January 4, 1997.

———. "The Next Arsenic: Safeguarding the Food Chain." *National Journal,* February 14, 2004.

Krugman, Paul. "Losing Our Country." *New York Times,* June 10, 2005.

Krupnick, Alan, Anna Alberini, Maureen Cropper, Nathalie Simon, Bernie O'Brien, Ron Goeree, and Martin Heintzelman. "Age, Health, and the Willingness to Pay for Mortality Risk Reductions: A Contingent Valuation Survey of Ontario Residents." *Journal of Risk and Uncertainty* 24, no. 2 (2000): 161–186. http://ideas.repec.org/a/kap/jrisku/v24y2002i2p161-86.html.

Kysar, Douglas A. "Some Realism About Environmental Skepticism: The Implications of Bjorn Lomborg's *The Skeptical Environmentalist* for Environmental Law and Policy." *Ecology Law Quarterly* 30 (2003): 223–278.

Latin, Howard. "Regulatory Failure, Administrative Incentives, and the New Clean Air Act." *Environmental Law* 21, no. 4 (1991): 1647-1720.

Lavelle, Marianne. "Environmental Vise: Law, Compliance." *National Law Journal* (August 30, 1993): S1.

Lazarus, Richard J. "The Tragedy of Distrust in the Implementation of Federal Environmental Law." *Law and Contemporary Problems* 54 (1991): 311-374.

Lee, Christopher. "Image Problem Looms for U.S. Civil Service." *Washington Post*, August 18, 2004.

Liasson, Mara. "Conservative Advocate." *Morning Edition*, National Public Radio, May 25, 2001. http://www.npr.org/templates/story/story.php?storyId =1123439.

*Lochner v. New York.* 198 U.S. 45 (1905).

Logomasini, Angela. "Deploy DDT to Fight Malaria." Competitive Enterprise Institute. June 18, 2002. http://www.cei.org/gencon/019,03078.cfm.

Logomasini, Angela, and David Riggs. "Chemical Risk." In *Environmental Source*. Washington, DC: Competitive Enterprise Institute, 2004. http://www.cei .org/gencon/026,01623.cfm.

Lomborg, Bjorn. *The Skeptical Environmentalist: Measuring the Real State of the World.* Translated by Hugh Matthews. Cambridge, England: Viking, 2001.

Luntz Research Companies. "The Environment: A Cleaner, Safer, Healthier America." National Environmental Trust. 2004. http://www.luntzspeak.com/ graphics/LuntzResearch.Memo.pdf.

Lyon, Thomas P., and John W. Maxwell. *Corporate Environmentalism and Public Policy.* New York: Cambridge University Press, 2004.

Lyons, Linda. "Daily Concerns Overshadow Environment Worries, Two-Thirds of Americans Distressed About Environment." Gallup Organization. April 19, 2005.

Malthus, Thomas R. *An Essay on Population as It Affects the Future Improvement of Society.* London: J. Johnson, 1798.

Marty, Melanie A. Letter to Stephen L. Johnson, March 8, 2006, http://yosemite .epa.gov/ochp/ochpweb.nsf/content/30806_3.htm/$file/30806_3.pdf.

Massachusetts, Commonwealth of. "Lead Paint Law: A Pathfinder." Trial Court Law Libraries. http://www.lawlib.state.ma.us/lead.html.

———, Department of Public Health. "Childhood Lead Poisoning Prevention Program." http://www.mass.gov?pageID=eohhs2terminal&L=5&L0=Home&L1=Government&L2=Departments+and+Divisions&L3=Department+of+Public+Health&L4=Programs+and+Services+A+-+J&sid=Eeohhs2&b=terminalcontent&f=dph_environmental_lead_g_clppp_about&csid=Eeohhs2.

McGarity, Thomas O. "The Courts and Ossification of Rulemaking: A Response to Professor Seidenfeld." *Texas Law Review* 75 (1997): 525-558.

———. "Missing Milestones: A Critical Look at the Clean Air Act's VOC Emissions Reduction Program in Nonattainment Areas." *Virginia Environmental Law Journal* 18, no. 1 (1999): 41-102.

———. "Politics by Other Means: Law, Science, and Policy in EPA's Implementation of the Food Quality Protection Act." *Administrative Law Review* 53, no. 1 (2001): 103-222.

———. "Some Thoughts on De-Ossifying the Rulemaking Process." *Duke Law Journal* 41, no. 6 (1992): 1385–1462.

McGarity, Thomas O., and Ruth Ruttenberg. "Counting the Cost of Health, Safety, and Environmental Regulation." *Texas Law Review* 80 (2002): 1997–2058.

Michaels, Patrick J. "EPA: Shoot First, Ask Later." Cato Institute. March 19, 2003. http://www.cato.org/dailys/03-19-03.html.

Millennium Ecosystem Assessment Board. *Living Beyond Our Means: Natural Assets and Human Well-Being.* March 2005. http://www.maweb.org/en/Products. BoardStatement.aspx.

Milloy, Steven J. "EPA Whips Up Air Pollution Scare." FoxNews.com, March 9, 2006. http://www.foxnews.com/story/0,2933,187390,00.html.

Mooney, Chris. *The Republican War on Science.* New York: Basic Books, 2005.

Moore, Colleen F. *Silent Scourge: Children, Pollution and Why Scientists Disagree.* New York: Oxford University Press, 2003.

National Center for Children in Poverty. "Basic Facts About Low-Income Children: Birth to Age 18." 2006. http://www.nccp.org/pub_lico6.html.

National Research Council (NRC). *Air Quality Management in the United States.* Washington, DC: National Academy Press, 2004.

———. *Health Implications of Perchlorate Ingestion.* Washington, DC: National Academy Press, 2005.

———. *Interim Report of the Committee on Changes in New Source Review Programs for Stationary Sources of Air Pollutants.* Washington, DC: National Academy Press, 2005.

———. *Toxicological Effects of Methyl Mercury.* Washington, DC: National Academy Press, 2000. http://books.nap.edu/openbook/0309071402/html/ index.html.

Natural Resources Defense Council (NRDC). "Preventing Industrial Pollution at Its Source." Report. 1999. http://www.nrdc.org/water/pollution/msri/ msriinx.asp.

———. "Unchecked Development and Pollution Threatens Water Quality and Recreation For Millions in New York and New Jersey." Press release. December 3, 2002. http://www.nrdc.org/media/pressReleases/021203.asp.

———. "White House and Pentagon Bias National Academy Perchlorate Report." Press release. January 10, 2005. http://www.nrdc.org/media/press releases/050110.asp.

*Natural Resources Defense Council v. EPA*, No. 92-1415 (D.C. Cir. 1998).

*Natural Resources Defense Council v. U.S. EPA.* 422 F. Supp. 2d 105 (D.D.C. 2006).

*Nebraska ex rel. Stenberg v. U.S.* 238 F.3d 946 (8th Cir. 2001), *cert. denied*, 533 U.S. 929 (2001).

North Carolina State University, Department of Sociology and Anthropology. "The Causes and Consequences of Child Poverty." *Quality of Life in North Carolina* 3, no. 1. http://www.ces.ncsu.edu/depts/sociology/pub/qol/the_ causes_and_consequenses_of_children_poverty.pdf.

O'Neill, Catherine A. "Mercury, Risk, and Justice." *Environmental Law Reporter* 34 (2004): 11070–11071.

O'Rourke, P. J. *All the Trouble in the World: The Lighter Side of Overpopulation, Famine, Ecological Disaster, Ethnic Hatred, Plague, and Poverty.* Boston: Atlantic Monthly Press, 1994.

Ognanovich, Nancy. "Business Interests Urge Administration to Remove Burdensome Regulations." *Environment Reporter* (BNA) 35 (December 24, 2004): 2641–2643.

Parker, Larry, and James E. McCarthy. "Clear Skies and the Clean Air Act: What's the Difference?" Congressional Research Service. February 25, 2005. http://www.ncseonline.org/NLE/CRSreports/05Feb/RL32782.pdf.

Parmet, Wendy E. "From Slaughter-House to Lochner: The Rise and Fall of the Constitutionalization of Public Health." *American Journal of Legal History* 40, no. 1 (1996): 476–505.

Percival, Robert V., Christopher H. Schroeder, Alan S. Miller, and James P. Leape. *Environmental Regulation, Law, Science, and Policy.* 4th ed. New York: Aspen, 2003.

Pew Research Center. *Trends 2005.* Washington, DC: Pew Research Center, 2005. http://pewresearch.org/trends.

Pierce, Richard J. Jr., Sydney A. Shapiro, and Paul R. Verkuil. *Administrative Law and Process.* 2d ed. Westbury, NY: Foundation Press, 1992.

Polling Report. "ABC News/Time/Stanford University Poll, March 9–14, 2006." http://pollingreport.com/enviro.htm.

———. "Environment: CBS/New York Times Poll, Nov. 20–24, 2002." http://pollingreport.com/enviro.htm.

———. "Environment: The Harris Poll, Aug. 9–16, 2005." http://pollingreport.com/enviro.htm.

———. "Gallup Poll, March 13–16, 2006." http://pollingreport.com/enviro.htm.

Read, Stephen J., and Lynn Carol Miller. "Dissonance and Balance in Belief Systems: The Promise of Parallel Constraint Satisfaction Processes and Connectionist Modeling Approaches." In *Beliefs, Reasoning, and Decision Making: Psycho-Logic in Honor of Bob Abelson*, edited by Roger C. Schank and Ellen Langer. Hillsdale, New Jersey: Lawrence Erlbaum Associates, 1994.

Reagan, Ronald. Acceptance of the Republican Nomination for President, July 17, 1980. http://www.4president.org/speeches/reagan1980convention.htm.

———. "A New Republican Party." Address to the Fourth Annual Conservative Political Action Conference (CPAC) Convention, February 6, 1977. http://www.presidentreagan.info/speeches/new_republican_party.cfm.

———. "To Restore America." Speech. March 31, 1976. http://www.reaganlegacy.org/speeches/reagan.torestore.3.31.76.htm.

Rechtschaffen, Clifford, and David Markell. *Reinventing Environmental Enforcement and the State/Federal Relationship.* Washington, DC: Environmental Law Institute, 2003.

Rehnquist, William. *2003 Year-End Report on the Federal Judiciary.* U.S. Supreme Court. January 2004. http://www.supremecourtus.gov/publicinfo/year-end/2003year-endreport.html.

Rice, Glenn, and James Hammitt. "Economic Valuation of Human Health Benefits of Controlling Mercury Emissions from U.S. Coal-Fired Plants." Report.

Northeast States Coordinated Air Use Management (NESCAUM). February 2005. http://bronze.nescaum.org/airtopics/mercury/rpto50315mercuryhealth.pdf.

Roberts, Sam. "In Government We Trust (As Far as We Can Throw It)." *New York Times*, January 4, 2004.

Rodricks, Joseph V. *Calculated Risks*. New York: Cambridge University Press, 1992.

Rogers, Daniel. U.S. Air Force, presentation to the National Academy of Sciences Committee to Assess the Health Implications of Perchlorate Ingestion. October 27, 2003. Copy on file with author.

Ruckelshaus, William D. "Stopping the Pendulum." *Environmental Forum* 12, no. 6 (November/December 1995): 25–29.

*Safe Drinking Water Act Amendments of 1985*. Public Law 99-339. *U.S. Statutes at Large* 100 (1985): 642.

*Safe Drinking Water Act Amendments of 1996*. Public Law 104-182. *U.S. Statutes at Large* 110 (1996): 1613.

Sass, Jennifer. "U.S. Department of Defense and White House Working Together to Avoid Cleanup and Liability for Perchlorate Pollution." *International Journal of Occupational and Environmental Health* 10, no. 3 (2004): 330–334.

Sass, Jennifer, Richard Wiles, and Michael Jacobson. Letter to Dr. Bruce Alberts, October 9, 2003. Copy on file with author.

Schroeder, Christopher, and Rena Steinzor, editors. *A New Progressive Agenda for Public Health and the Environment*. Durham: Carolina Academic Press, 2004.

Schudson, Michael. *The Good Citizen: A History of American Civic Life*. Cambridge, MA: Harvard University Press, 1998.

Schuster, P. F., David P. Krabbenhoft, David L. Naftz, L. Dewayne Cecil, Mark L. Olson, John F. Dewild, David D. Susong, Jaromy R. Green, and Michael L. Abbott. "Atmospheric Mercury Deposition During the Last 270 Years: A Glacial Ice Core Record of Natural and Anthropogenic Sources." *Environmental Science and Technology* 36, no. 11 (2002): 2303–2310. http://www.ngdc.noaa.gov/paleo/pubs/schuster2002/schuster2002.html.

*Section-by-Section Analysis of Water Quality Act of 1987*. 133 *Congressional Record* H1131 (1987). Reprint, 1987 USCCAN 5.

Selgrade, Mary Jane K., Robert F. Lemanske Jr., M. Ian Gilmour, Lucas M. Neas, Marsha D. W. Ward, Paul K. Henneberger, David N. Weissman, Jane A. Hoppin, Rodney R. Dietert, Peter D. Sly, Andrew M. Geller, Paul L. Enright, Gillian S. Backus, Philip A. Bromberg, Dori R. Germolec, and Karin B. Yeatts. "Induction of Asthma and the Environment: What We Know and Need to Know." *Environmental Health Perspectives* 114 (April 2006): 615–619.

Sierra Club. "Superfund 'Polluter Pays' Amendment Loses in Senate." Press release. March 11, 2004. http://www.sierraclub.org/pressroom/releases/pr2004-03-11a.asp.

Simmons, John G. *Doctors and Discoveries: Lives That Created Today's Medicine*. Boston: Houghton Mifflin, 2002.

Sinclair, Upton. *The Jungle*. 1906. Reprint, New York: Bantam Books, 1981.

Smith, Adam. *The Wealth of Nations*. New York: Modern Library, 1937.

State and Territorial Air Pollution Program Administrators and the Association of Local Air Pollution Control Officials (STAPPA/ALAPCO). "State Mercury Programs for Utilities." Report. STAPPA/ALAPCO, 2006. http://www.4cleanair.org/StatePrograms.pdf.

Stein, Rob. "Dangers of Rocket Fuel Chemical Downplayed." *Washington Post*, January 11, 2005.

Steingraber, Sandra. *Having Faith: An Ecologist's Journey to Motherhood*. New York: Berkley Books, 2001.

Steinzor, Rena. "The Reauthorization of Superfund: Can the Deal of the Century Be Saved?" *Environmental Law Reporter* 15 (1985): 10016–10059.

———. "The Reauthorization of Superfund: The Public Works Alternative." *Environmental Law Reporter* 25 (1995): 10078–10104.

———. "Toward Better Bubbles and Future Lives: A Progressive Response to the Conservative Agenda for Reforming Environmental Law." *Environmental Law Reporter* 32 (2002): 11421–11455.

Steinzor, Rena, and Margaret Clune. *The Toll of Superfund Neglect: Toxic Waste Dumps and Communities at Risk*. Center for American Progress and Center for Progressive Reform, June 15, 2006. http://www.progressiveregulation.org/articles/Superfund_061506.pdf.

Steinzor, Rena, and Lisa Heinzerling. "A Perfect Storm: Mercury and the Bush Administration." *Environmental Law Reporter* 34 (2004): 10297–10333.

———. "A Perfect Storm: Mercury and the Bush Administration, Part II." *Environmental Law Reporter* 34 (2004): 10485–10512.

Stone, Hilary, and John Washington-Smith. *Profit and the Environment: Common Sense of Contradictions*. New York: Wiley, 2002.

Tiemann, Mary. *Perchlorate Contamination of Drinking Water: Regulatory Issues and Legislative Actions*. Congressional Research Service. Washington, DC: Library of Congress, June 15, 2005. http://www.ncseonline.org/nle/crsreports/05feb/RS21961.pdf.

Tolchin, Susan J., and Martin Tolchin. *Dismantling America: The Rush to Deregulate*. Boston: Houghton Mifflin, 1983.

Transande, Leonardo, Philip J. Landrigan, and Clyde Schechter. "Public Health and Economic Consequences of Methyl Mercury Toxicity to the Developing Brain." *Environmental Health Perspectives* 113, no. 5 (May 2005): 590–596. http://ehp.niehs.nih.gov/docs/2005/113-5/toc.html.

*Unfunded Mandates Reform Act of 1995*. Public Law 104-4. *U.S. Statutes at Large* 109: 48.

United Press International (UPI). "Environmentalists: Reagan Is Soiling the Nest." March 11, 1983.

U.S. Census Bureau. *Income, Poverty, and Health Insurance Coverage in the United States: 2004*. August 2005. http://www.census.gov/prod/2005pubs/p60-229.pdf.

———. "Nation's Population One-Third Minority." Press release, May 10, 2006. http://www.census.gov/Press-Release/www/releases/archives/population/006808.html.

*U.S. Code* 5 (2000). app. § 15 (b)(1)(A); § 552.

*U.S. Code* 33 (2000). §§ 1251–1387.

*U.S. Code* 42 (2000). § 300; §§ 6902–6992; § 7409–7413; §§ 7501–7515; § 7604; §§ 9601–9675.

U.S. Congress, House of Representatives. *H.R. Conf. Rep. on Clean Air Act Amendments of 1990.* H.R. Conf. Rep. No. 101-952. Reprint, 1990 USCCAN 3385.

———. *H.R. Conf. Rep. on Hazardous and Solid Waste Amendments of 1984.* H.R. Conf. Rep. No. 98-1113. Reprint. 1984 USCCAN 5576.

———. *H.R. Conf. Rep. on Safe Drinking Water Act Amendments of 1986.* H.R. Rep. No. 99-575. Reprint, 1986 USCCAN 1566.

———. *H.R. Conf. Rep. on Safe Drinking Water Act Amendments of 1996.* H.R. Conf. Rep. No. 104-741 (1996).

U.S. Congress, Senate. *Climate History and Mercury Emissions.* 108th Cong., 1st sess. http://epw.senate.gov/hearing_statements.cfm?id=212851.

———. *Hearings on Clear Skies Act of 2003.* S. 485. 108th Cong., 1st sess. http://epw.senate.gov/108th/Hawkins_040803.htm.

———, Committee on Environment and Public Works, Subcommittee on Clean Air, Wetlands, Private Property, and Nuclear Safety. "Air Pollution: Implementation of the Clean Air Act Amendments of 1990." Statement of David G. Wood, GAO associate director, Environmental Protection Issues, May 17, 2000. http://www.gao.gov/archive/2000/rc00183t.pdf.

U.S. Courts. *Federal Caseload Statistics 2004.* http://www.uscourts.gov/caseload 2004/front/judbus03.pdf.

———. *Understanding the Federal Courts.* http://www.uscourts.gov/understand02/ index.html.

U.S. Department of Health and Human Services (HHS), Office of the Secretary. Annual Update of the HHS Poverty Guidelines, notice. *Federal Register* 71 (January 24, 2006): 3848.

U.S. Department of Labor, Bureau of Labor Statistics. *Consumer Price Index.* ftp://ftp.bls.gov/pub/special.requests/cpi/cpiai.txt.

U.S. Environmental Protection Agency (EPA). *2004 National Listing of Fish Advisories.* September 2005, http://www.epa.gov/waterscience/fish/advisories/ fs2004.pdf.

———. *Air Quality Classifications for the 8-Hour Ozone National Ambient Air Quality Standards. Federal Register* 69 (September 22,2004): 56697.

———. *Air Trends: Ozone.* http://www.epa.gov/airtrends/ozone.html.

———. *The Benefits and Costs of the Clean Air Act, 1970 to 1990.* 1997. EPA 410-R-97-002. http://www.epa.gov/oar/sect812.

———. *Benefits and Costs of the Clean Air Act 1990 to 2010.* 1999. EPA 410-R-99-001. http://www.epa.gov/oar/sect812.

———. *Budget in Brief.* http://www.epa.gov/adminweb/budget-goals.htm.

———. "Clean Air Interstate Rule, Regulatory Actions." http://epa.gov/cair/ rule.html.

———. "Clean Air Mercury Rule." http://www.epa.gov/oar/mercuryrule/hg_ factsheet1_29_04.htm.

———. *Clear Skies.* http://www.epa.gov/ebtpages/airairpoclearskies.html.

———. *Draft Air Quality Criteria for Ozone and Related Photochemical Oxidants.* E-Docket No. ORD-2004-0015. *Federal Register* 70 (August 31, 2005): 5180.

———. *EPA and States Not Making Sufficient Progress in Reducing Ozone Precursor Emissions in Some Major Metropolitan Areas*, 2004. Report no. 2004-P-00033. http://www.epa.gov/oig/reports/2004/20040929-2004-P-00033.pdf.

———. *Green Book: 8-Hour Ozone Area Summary.* http://www.epa.gov/oar/oaqps/greenbk/gnsum.html.

———. *Latest Findings on National Air Quality: 2002 Status and Trends*, 2003. (EPA 454/K-03-001). http://www.abuse.com/environment/airtrends/2002_airtrends_final.pdf.

———. "Mercury: Laws and Regulations." http://www.epa.gov/mercury/regs.htm.

———. *Mercury Study: Report to Congress*. 1997: O-1 (EPA-452/R-97-003). http://www.epa.gov/mercury/report.htm.

———. "Mercury: The Global Context." http://www.epa.gov/mercury/control_emissions/global.htm.

———. *National Ambient Air Quality Standards. Federal Register* 62 (July 18, 1997): 38856.

———. *National Emission Standards for Hazardous Air Pollutants: Mercury Emissions from Mercury Cell Chlor-Alkali Plants. Federal Register* 68, no. 244 (December 19, 2003) (to be codified at 40 CFR pt. 63). http://www.epa.gov/ttn/atw/hgcellcl/fr19deo3.pdf.

———. "NPL Site Totals by Status and Milestone as of April 25, 2006." http://www.epa.gov/superfund/sites/query/queryhtm/npltotal.htm.

———. *Proposed National Emission Standards for Hazardous Air Pollutants; and, in the Alternative, Proposed Standards for Performance of New and Existing Sources: Electric Utility Steam-Generating Units. Federal Register* 69 (proposed January 30, 2004): 4652.

———. *Regulatory Finding on Emissions of Hazardous Air Pollutants from Electric Utility Steam Generating Units. Federal Register* 65 (December 20, 2000): 79825. http://frwebgate.access.gpo.gov/cgi-bin/getdoc.cgi?dbname=2000_register&docid=00-32395-filed.pdf.

———. *Regulatory Impact Analysis of Final Clean Air Mercury Rule.* U.S. Environmental Protection Agency, March 2005. http://www.epa.gov/ttn/atw/utility/ria_final.pdf.

———. *Revision of December 2000 Regulatory Finding on Emissions of Hazardous Air Pollutants from Electric Utility Steam Generating Units and the Removal of Coal- and Oil-Fired Electric Utility Steam Generating Units from the Section 112(c) List, Federal Register* 70 (March 29, 2005) (to be codified at 40 CFR pt. 63). http://a257.g.akamaitech.net/7/257/2422/01jan20051800/edocket.access.gpo.gov/2005/pdf/05-6037.pdf

———. *Rule to Reduce Interstate Transport of Fine Particulate Matter and Ozone (Clean Air Interstate Rule); Revisions to Acid Rain Program; Revisions to the NOx SIP Call. Federal Register* 70 (May 12, 2005): 25162. http://a257.g.akamaitech.net/7/257/2422/01jan20051800/edocket.access.gpo.gov/2005/pdf/05-5723.pdf.

———. *Smog—Who Does It Hurt? What You Need to Know About Ozone and Your Health.* 1999. EPA-452K-99-001. http://www.epa.gov/airnow/health.

———. *Standards for Performance for New and Existing Stationary Sources: Electric Utility Steam Generating Units. Federal Register* 70, no. 95 (May 18, 2005):

28606–28700 (to be codified at 40 CFR pts. 60, 72, and 75). http://a257
.g.akamaitech.net/7/257/2422/01jan20051800/edocket.access.gpo.gov/2005/
pdf/05-8447.pdf.

———. "State Perchlorate Advisory Levels As of 4/20/05." http://www.epa.gov/
fedfac/pdf/stateadvisorylevels.pdf.

———. *Unfinished Business: A Comparative Assessment of Environmental Protection*,
1987.

U.S. Environmental Protection Agency, Office of Pollution Prevention and Toxics. "What Do We Really Know About the Safety of High Production Volume
Chemicals?" *Chemical Regulation Reporter* (BNA) 22 (May 1, 1998): 261.

U.S. Environmental Protection Agency, Office of Research and Development, National Center for Environmental Assessment. *Perchlorate Contamination: Toxicological Review and Risk Characterization*. 2002 External Review Draft (NCEA-
1-0503, 2002). http://oaspub.epa.gov/eims/eimsapi.dispdetail?deid=24002.

U.S. Food and Drug Administration (FDA), Center for Food Safety and Applied
Nutrition. *Exploratory Data on Perchlorate in Food*. November 2004. http://
www.cfsan.fda.gov/~dms/clo4data.html.

U.S. General Accounting Office/Government Accountability Office (GAO). *Air
Pollution: Emission Sources Regulated by Multiple Clean Air Act Provisions*. 2000.
GAO/RCED-00-155.

———. "Air Pollution: Implementation of the Clean Air Act Amendments of
1990." Testimony Before the Committee on Environment and Public Works,
Subcommittee on Clean Air, Wetlands, Private Property, and Nuclear Safety.
Statement of David G. Wood, GAO associate director, Environmental Protection Issues, May 17, 2000. http://www.gao.gov/archive/2000/rc00183t.pdf.

———. *Clean Air Act, Emerging Mercury Control Technologies Have Shown Promising Results, but Data on Long-Term Performance Are Limited*. May 2005. http://
www.gao.gov/new.items/do5612.pdf.

———. *DOD Operational Ranges: More Reliable Cleanup Cost Estimates and a Proactive Approach to Identifying Contamination Are Needed*. GAO-04-601. May
2004. http://www.gao.gov/new.items/do4601.pdf.

———. *Perchlorate: A System to Track Sampling and Cleanup Results Is Needed*.
GAO-05-462. May 2005. http://www.gao.gov/new.items/do5462.pdf.

U.S. Office of Management and Budget (OMB), Executive Office of the President. *Budget of the United States Government, Fiscal Year 2005*. http://www.white
house.gov/omb/budget/fy2005/sheets/outlays.xls.

———. *Circular A-4*. September 17, 2003. http://www.whitehouse.gov/omb/
circulars/a004/a-4.pdf.

Wagner, Wendy E. "Commons Ignorance: The Failure of Environmental Law
to Produce Needed Information on Health and the Environment." *Duke Law
Journal* 53, no. 6 (1997): 1619–1746.

———. "The Science Charade in Toxic Risk Regulation." *Columbia Law Review*
95, no. 7 (1995): 1613–1723.

Wagner, Wendy, and Rena Steinzor, editors. *Rescuing Science from Politics: Regulation and the Distortion of Scientific Research*. New York: Cambridge University
Press, 2006.

Waldman, Peter. "The Economy: Bush Seeks Liability Shield on Water Pollutant." *Wall Street Journal*, March 14, 2003.

———. "EPA Bans Staff from Discussing Issue of Perchlorate Pollution." *Wall Street Journal*, April 28, 2003.

———. "Perchlorate Level in Human Milk Exceeds Regulator's 'Safe Dose.'" *Wall Street Journal*, February 23, 2005.

———. "Seeping Threat: A Fuel of Cold War Defenses Now Ignites Health Controversy—Perchlorate Runoff Makes Way to Water Supply of Millions." *Wall Street Journal*, December 16, 2002.

Walker, David B. *The Rebirth of Federalism: Slouching Toward Washington*. Riverside, CT: Chatham Press, 1995.

Wargo, John. *Our Children's Toxic Legacy*. New Haven, CT: Yale University Press, 1996.

*Water Quality Act of 1987*. Public Law 100-4. *U.S. Statutes at Large* 101 (1987).

Whetzal Carolyn. "Drinking Water: Stronger Standard for Perchlorate Urged to Better Protect Pregnant Women, Infants." *Environment Reporter* (BNA) 36 (April 15, 2005): 766.

*Whitman v. American Trucking Associations*. 531 U.S. 457 (2001).

Wigle, Donald T. *Child Health and the Environment*. New York: Oxford University Press, 2003.

Wolfowitz, Paul. "Consideration of Requests for Use of Existing Exemptions Under Federal Environmental Law." Memorandum to Secretaries of the Army, Navy, and Air Force. March 7, 2003.

Wood, David. "Effect of Child and Family Poverty on Child Health in the United States." *Pediatrics* 112, no. 3 (September 2003): 707-711. http://pediatrics.aappublications.org/cgi/content/full/112/3/S1/707.

# Index

Aberdeen, Maryland, perchlorate incident, 146–147, 233n43
Ackerman, Frank, 83
Aerojet company, 126, 128, 131
African Americans, 168, 191
agency capture, 220n18
Agent Orange, 91
air pollution: and Clean Air Interstate Rule (AIR), 116; Code Red days for, 13, 118, 169, 197; and electoral politics, 153; EPA achievements on lowering, 49, 151–152; and mercury emissions, 104, 111–118; and National Ambient Air Quality Standards (NAAQS), 52, 151–158, 161–165, 168, 170, 206, 234n13. *See also* asthma; Clean Air Act (CAA); ozone
Air Pollution Control (or Clean Air) Act (1955), 219n10. *See also* Clean Air Act (CAA)
Alabama, 113
ALAPCO. *See* Association of Local Air Pollution Control Officials (ALAPCO)
*Alice in Wonderland*, 103
Allen, Bruce, 81
American Lung Association, 151–152
American Pacific Corporation, 131
*American Prospect*, 99
ammonium perchlorate, 128. *See also* perchlorate

Anderson, Terry, 77–78
Andrews, Richard, 40, 48, 49, 202, 218–219n3
Annan, Kofi, 193
appellate courts, 68–69, 71–72, 158–160. *See also* federal courts
Arizona, 230nn5–6, 232n30
Arkansas, 143
asbestos, 71–72, 212–213
Ashta Chemicals Inc., 113, 227n23
Association of Local Air Pollution Control Officials (ALAPCO), 124, 228–229nn36–37
asthma: cost for treatment of, 206; monetary cost assigned to, 167; and ozone, 10, 13, 101, 150–151, 157, 167, 206; statistics on adults with, 216n6; statistics on childhood asthma, 13, 50, 150–151, 206
atrazine, 56
automobile industry, 46, 70, 85, 124

*Baltimore Sun*, 146
battled-agency syndrome, 49–50. *See also* Environmental Protection Agency (EPA)
Bauman Foundation, 236n1
Becker, William, 124
Beldon Fund, 236n1
Bentham, Jeremy, 202
benzene, 70–71
Bhopal, India, explosion (1984), 225n35

big business. *See* corporations

Bodine, Susan, 139

Brazil, 81

*Breaking the Vicious Circle* (Breyer), 83, 223–224n21

Brent, Gregory, 135

Breyer, Stephen, 83, 223–224n21

Browner, Carol, 42–43, 156, 160, 167, 208, 222n59

Browning Ferris Industries, 225n35

budget deficits in federal government, 36–37, 43, 73

Bull, Richard, 135

Bureau of National Affairs, 99

bureaucracy: advantages of, 198; legal infrastructures of, 44; regulation and stupid bureaucrats, 84–85; and workforce competency and morale, 200–202. *See also* Environmental Protection Agency (EPA); hollow government; *and other government agencies*

Burford, Ann Gorsuch, 39, 49

Bush, George H. W.: and Clean Air Act amendments (1990), 152; conservatism of, 40–41; and cost-benefit analysis, 119, 229n40; as vice president, 38

Bush, George W.: and Clear Skies proposal, 153; conservatism of, 43–44; and cost-benefit analysis, 62, 77, 119, 165–166, 229n40; and Iraq war, 1, 28, 43; and perchlorate exposure, 12

business. *See* corporations

CAA. *See* Clean Air Act (CAA)

California: and mercury, 117–118; and ozone, 158; and perchlorate, 12, 126, 128, 129, 140–141, 143, 148, 230nn5–7

California Institute of Technology, 127

Canada, 64–65, 81

cancer, 20–21

*Capitalism and Freedom* (Friedman), 33–35, 216n1

carbon monoxide, 152

Carroll, Lewis, 103

Carson, Rachel, 47

CASAC. *See* Clean Air Scientific Advisory Committee (CASAC)

Cato Institute, 32, 36–37, 110, 217n22

CDC. *See* Centers for Disease Control (CDC)

Census Bureau, 189–190

Center for Progressive Reform (CPR), 175, 236n1, 238n1

Center for Science in the Public Interest, 135

Centers for Disease Control (CDC), 46, 104, 141

CERCLA. *See* Comprehensive Environmental Response, Compensation and Liability ("Superfund") (1980)

Chamber of Commerce, U.S., 80, 82, 103

checks and balances, 68–69

chemical industry: and chlor-alkali plants, 104, 112–114, 125, 227n23; and Dow's corporate environmentalism, 90–91; and EPA beginnings, 48; and harmfulness versus importance of chemicals, 79–82; mercury pollution from, 11; perchlorate from, 11; safety information on chemicals, 59; and Superfund legislation, 224n30, 225n33. *See also* mercury; perchlorate; toxic waste

Chemical Manufacturers Association, 59

Chevron, 207

childhood asthma. *See* asthma

children: adverse effects of toxic chemicals on generally, 9; and lead poisoning, 21, 46, 85; maximum safe blood lead levels for, 46; poverty of, 189–193; statistics on, 3. *See also* asthma; mercury; ozone; perchlorate; water pollution

China, 81, 110

chlor-alkali plants, 104, 112–114, 125, 227n23

chlorine, 112–114, 227n23

Christian right, 22, 28, 180

*Christian Science Monitor*, 105

Clean Air Act (CAA): appropriations
for, 163; cost-benefit analysis of, 63,
165–170; deadlines in, 13, 163–166;
and EPA "market-based" trading,
11, 114–118, 120, 124, 125; and federal implementation plans (FIPs),
163; funding for, 51; goals of, 18;
harmful impact of, 168; health-
based approach of, 153; and maximum achievable control technology
(MACT), 111–112, 114–116, 119–
121; and mercury emissions, 104,
111–118; on National Ambient Air
Quality Standards (NAAQS), 151–
158, 161–165, 168, 170, 206, 234n13;
1970 amendments to, 13, 163; 1977
amendments to, 154, 163–164;
1990 amendments to, 41, 51, 52–53,
111–112, 114–118, 119–120, 152–153,
219n11; and "non-attainment areas,"
13, 150, 162; and ozone, 151–165,
168–170; passage of, 151, 219n10

Clean Air Interstate Rule (AIR), 116

Clean Air Scientific Advisory Committee (CASAC), 154–156

Clean Water Act (CWA), 52, 145,
219n10

climate change, 81–82, 110, 180, 193–
194, 223n11

Clinton, Bill: and cost-benefit analysis, 62, 119, 165, 229n40; economic
policies of, 73; and EPA, 42–43,
114, 222n59; presidency of, 29, 41–
43; on working hard and playing
by the rules, 237n31

Code Red days for air pollution, 13,
118, 169, 197

cognitive and political dissonance,
14–15, 184

Cohen, Bill, 84

Commerce Clause, 196–197, 204–205

companies. *See* corporations

Competitive Enterprise Institute
(CEI), 79, 80

complexification, 15–21, 198–199

compliance costs, 119–121. *See also*
cost-benefit analysis

Comprehensive Environmental Response, Compensation and Liability ("Superfund") (1980), 88,
91, 139, 145, 207, 218n30, 219n10,
224n30, 224–225n33

Congress: and Clean Air Act amendments (1977), 154; and Clean Air
Act amendments (1990), 152–153;
and Clear Skies proposal, 153;
conservatives' criticism of, 23; and
environmental issues generally,
97, 99–100; and environmental
statutes (1940s–1980), 49, 219n10;
and environmental statutes (1980s–
1990s), 39–40, 52–53, 218n30; EPA's
difficulties in interpretation of
statutes of, 17–18, 21, 52–54, 70;
EPA's relationship with, 17–18, 21,
48–50; Republican Revolution in,
41, 88; and riders on appropriations bills, 55–56, 99–100

*Congressional Quarterly*, 99

Connecticut, 158, 230n7

Conoco Phillips, 207

conservatism: of George H. W. Bush,
40–41; of George W. Bush, 43–44;
and case against regulation, 78–86,
156–158; and Christian right, 22,
28; and Clinton, 29, 41–43; and
Contract with America, 41–42,
177; and devolution of government intervention to state and
local levels, 23–24, 29; different
approaches to, 22, 27–28; of Friedman, 33–35; modern conservative
ideology, 33–36; neoconservatives,
22, 28; overview of, 26–27; of Reagan, 22, 36–40; and sound science
campaign, 16–17, 107, 155; and special interests, 29; and trading systems, 115–116; traditional vision of,
for limited government, 22, 27; and
U.S. Constitution's compromise
of federalist republic with divided
responsibilities between federal
and state governments, 30–33; and
vision of future, 187–188

Constitution, U.S.: checks and balances in, 68–69; Commerce Clause of, 196–197, 204–205; compromise in, on responsibilities of federal and state governments, 30–33; and conservatism, 30–33; and EPA's power, 159–160; judiciary in, 68–69; strict construction interpretation of, 160

Contract with America, 41–42, 177

corporate environmentalism: Hoffman on, 89, 91–92; incentives and disincentives for, 89–91; rhetoric and reality of, 86–89

corporations: and case against regulation, 78–86, 156–158; compliance with environmental laws and corporate counsel, 18; and corporate environmentalism, 86–92; and devolution, 29; diversity of regulated industries and firms, 87, 98–99; and EPA's 1997 decisions on ozone NAAQS, 158–159; and free market environmentalism, 76–78; and global warming, 194; goal of, 76; and green accounting, 91; and Hardin's tragedy of the commons, 76–78; incentives and disincentives for voluntary environmental programs by, 89–91; multinational corporations, 29; opposition to environmental regulation of, 18–19, 86–89, 98–99; taxation of, for Superfund cleanups, 207; and trading systems for pollution control, 11, 24, 114–118, 120, 124, 125. *See also* regulation

*Corrosion Proof Fittings v. EPA*, 71–72, 212–213

cost-benefit analysis: and benefits analysis, 20–21, 63–65, 121–123, 211–212; and G. H. W. Bush presidency, 119, 229n40; and G. W. Bush presidency, 62, 77, 119, 165–166, 229n40; of Clean Air Act (CAA), 63, 165–170; and Clinton presidency, 62, 119, 165, 229n40; and compliance costs, 119–121; and cost analysis, 20, 62–63, 119–121,

212; and discounting, 65–67; and environmental issues generally, 19–21, 24, 60–62; and EPA, 54, 59–68, 74; and human health benefits, 20–21, 63–65, 121–123, 167; and maximum achievable control technology (MACT), 119–121; on mercury, 118–123, 125; and monetary value of human life, 20–21, 63, 167, 211–212; and monetary value of IQ points, 21, 121–122, 167; and number crunching in the face of uncertainty, 59–62, 119; OMB's requirements for, 62, 66–67; on ozone, 165–170; problems with, 119, 170; and Reagan presidency, 38–39, 62, 118, 229n40; reform of, by monetization of costs, not benefits, 197, 211–212; steps of, 62–68; and willingness to accept (WTA), 63–65; and willingness to pay (WTP), 63–65, 170

Council on Water Quality, 231n12

court cases. *See* federal courts; Supreme Court, U.S.

CPR. *See* Center for Progressive Reform (CPR)

Crane, Edward, 36–37, 217n22

CWA. *See* Clean Water Act (CWA)

Davies, Terry, 56–57

DDT, 79

deadline performance of EPA, 13, 21, 39–40, 52, 163–166

*Death of Common Sense, The* (Howard), 84–85

Deer Creek Foundation, 236n1

Defense Department (DOD), 12, 129, 132–138, 140, 144–148, 154, 207

Delaware, 113

Delay, Tom, 45

Democratic Party, 47–48, 178. *See also* progressivism; *and specific presidents*

deregulation, 38–39, 200. *See also* regulation

devolution of government intervention, 23–24, 29

Dichlorvos, 56

Dilworth-Bart, Janean, 191
discounting, 65–67
*Dismantling America* (Tolchin and Tolchin), 38
district courts, 68, 69
distrust, 21–23
DOD. *See* Defense Department (DOD)
DOE. *See* Energy Department (DOE)
DOI. *See* Interior Department (DOI)
Dow Chemical Company, 25, 90–91
drinking water: and Aberdeen, Maryland, perchlorate incident, 146–147, 233n43; legislation on, 51, 53, 139, 145, 146, 219nn10–11; perchlorate in, 10, 11–12, 126–130, 140–144, 146–147. *See also* perchlorate; water pollution
Duke University, 178–180, 181
Dursban, 90

Earth Day, 18, 48
Easterbrook, Gregg, 80–82, 223n11
*Economist, The*, 43, 185
Eisenhower, Dwight, 203
Electric Power Research Institute, 108–109, 227n14, 227n17
electric utility. *See* utility industry
employment. *See* jobs
EMS. *See* environmental management systems (EMS)
Energy Department (DOE), 96, 105, 121, 133, 134
Enlightenment movement, 202
Enron, 182
*Environment Reporter*, 99
Environmental Council of the States, 72
Environmental Defense Fund, 59, 225n35
*Environmental Forum*, 99
environmental issues: and childhood poverty, 191–192; complexification of, 15–19; corporate environmentalism, 86–92; and cost-benefit analysis, 19–21, 24; devolution of, to state and local governments,

23–24; free market environmentalism, 24, 76–78; global perspective on, 193–194; and Hardin's tragedy of the commons, 75–78, 193; hollow government and "tragedy of distrust" syndrome, 21–23; Luntz on, 177; media coverage of, 19, 99; O'Rourke on environmental protection as luxury good, 24; policy making on, 19–21; polls on environmental protection, 177–180; polls on jobs versus environment, 180–182; public debate on generally, 175–177; and public relations war against regulation, 18–19; and religious beliefs, 180; and sound science campaign, 16–17, 107, 155; and values, 175–177, 184–187. *See also* air pollution; Environmental Protection Agency (EPA); mercury; ozone; perchlorate; reform measures; water pollution; *and specific laws*
Environmental Law Institute, 99
*Environmental Law Reporter*, 99
environmental laws: and Hardin's tragedy of the commons, 75–78; lists of, 39–40, 49, 52–53, 218n30, 219n10, 219n11; on mercury, 104, 111–118; on ozone, 151, 152–154, 158–165; on perchlorate, 144–148; and state governments, 72–74. *See also specific laws*
environmental management systems (EMS), 91
environmental policy making. *See* policy making
Environmental Protection Agency (EPA): achievements of, 46, 49–50; and asbestos, 71–72, 212–213; and battled-agency syndrome, 49–50; budget of, 21, 41, 49, 50–54, 74, 164, 206; and G. H. W. Bush presidency, 41; and Clean Air Act goals, 18; and Clinton presidency, 41–43, 114; constitutionality of power of, 158–160; and cost-benefit analysis, 54, 59–68, 74; deadline

performance and work delays of, 13, 21, 39–40, 52, 163–166; and defensive governing, 17–18; difficulties of, in interpretation of statutes, 17–18, 21, 52–54, 70; and dockets for federal courts, 97; and environmental statutes (1940s–1980), 49, 219n10; and environmental statutes (1980s–1990s), 39–40, 52–53, 218n30, 219n11; establishment and beginnings of, 22, 46–48, 209–210, 218–219n3; federal court cases involving, 68–72, 97–98, 158–160; and federal implementation plans (FIPs), 163; guidance documents from, 100; independent priority setting by, 197, 205–206; institutional autonomy for, 197–200; judicial deference to decisions by, 197, 198, 212–213; lawsuits against, 56, 115, 125; and lead in gasoline, 46, 70, 85, 124; management problems of, 54–57; and mercury, 11, 104–105, 113–125, 154; and ozone, 150–156, 158–165; and paralysis by analysis, 57–68; and perchlorate exposure, 12, 128, 129, 133–134, 138–141, 144, 146–149, 154; and pesticides, 56; progressives' suspicions of, 39–40; and Reagan presidency, 38–39, 49; reform measures for, 197–202; regional offices of, 73–74; relationship between Congress and, 17–18, 21, 48–49, 50; review of mandates and programs of, by outside experts, 239n11; and risk assessment, 54, 57–59, 74; and special interests, 54; stakeholders of generally, 54; and state governments, 72–74; and Stockholm Syndrome, 54–56; stovepipe organizational structure of, 56–57; and technology-based controls, 210–211; and trading systems for pollution control, 11, 24, 114–118, 120, 124, 125; weakness of, in enforcement of regulations,

23–24; workforce competence and morale in, 200–202. *See also* regulation; *and specific laws*
Environmental Working Group (EWG), 128, 135, 230n4
EPA. *See* Environmental Protection Agency (EPA)
epidemiological studies: definition of, 107; of mercury, 107–109, 227n14
*Ethyl* case, 45, 46, 69, 222n46
EWG. *See* Environmental Working Group (EWG)
Exxon Mobil, 207

factories. *See* industrial pollution
Farhi, Paul, 183–184
Faroe Islands, 108
Fatz, Raymond, 147
FDA. *See* Food and Drug Administration (FDA)
federal courts: appellate courts, 68–69, 71–72, 158–160; appointment of judges to, 68; cases of, involving EPA, 68–72, 97–98; and constitutionality of EPA's power, 158–160; and deference to EPA's decisions, 197, 198, 212–213; district courts, 68, 69; and EPA's ozone decision, 158–160; lawsuits against EPA's mercury trading system, 115, 125; levels of, 68; number of cases heard by, 69; number of judges in, 69; and Supreme Court's denial of petition for certiorari, 222n51. *See also* Supreme Court, U.S.
federal implementation plans (FIPs), 163
Federal Insecticide, Fungicide, and Rodenticide Act (1947), 219n10
Federal Insecticide, Fungicide, and Rodenticide Act Amendments (1988, 1996), 51, 53, 219n11
Federal Reserve System, 217n13
*Federalist Papers, The*, 30–33, 216n6
FIFRA. *See* Federal Insecticide, Fungicide, and Rodenticide Act (1947)

FIPs. *See* federal implementation plans (FIPs)

fish contaminated with mercury, 10, 100, 103, 104, 105, 109, 111, 118, 121

Fisher, Linda, 147

Florida, 109, 203n5, 203n7

Florio, James, 39, 218n30, 224–225n33

Food and Drug Administration (FDA), 108, 128, 133, 227n14

Food Quality Protection Act (1996), 50, 51, 219n11, 224n30

France, 81

free market environmentalism, 24, 76–78

*Free Market Environmentalism* (Anderson and Leal), 77–78

Freedom of Information Act, 134, 231n17

Friedman, Milton, 4, 33–35, 76, 216n1, 217n13, 217n20

*From Heresy to Dogma* (Hoffman), 89, 91–92, 225n35

fungicides. *See* pesticides

future: conservative vision of, 187–188; progressive vision of, 188–189

Gallup Organization, 178, 180

GAO. *See* Government Accountability Office (GAO)

gasoline, lead in, 46, 70, 85, 124

General Motors, 156

Georgia, 113, 230nn6–7

Germany, 81

*Gibbons v. Ogen*, 238n4

Gingrich, Newt, 41, 224n30

Ginsburg, Douglas, 159

global mercury cycle, 106

global warming, 81–82, 110, 180, 193–194, 223n11

Goldwater, Barry, 195, 196

Goodstein, Eban, 181

government. *See* Congress; Environmental Protection Agency (EPA); hollow government; reform measures; *specific presidents; and specific government agencies*

Government Accountability Office

(GAO), 120–121, 142–144, 148, 162–163, 235n25

Graham, John, 82

Great Depression, 22, 34

Great Lakes, 118

Great Society, 34, 183, 203

green accounting, 91

greenhouse gas emissions, 81. *See also* global warming

Greenpeace, 80

Greer, Monte, 137, 138

guidance documents, 100

Hamilton, Alexander, 30–31

Hanisch, Carola, 227n17

Hardin, Garrett, 35, 75–78, 193

Harris Poll, 183

Hart (Peter D.) Research Associates, 178–180

Harvard Center for Risk Analysis, 123

Hawaii, 230n7

Hayek, F. A., 4, 35, 76, 217n20

Hazardous and Solid Waste Amendments (1984), 51, 219n11

Health and Human Services Department (HHS), 108

health of children. *See* children

Heinzerling, Lisa, 83

herbicides. *See* pesticides

Heritage Foundation, 25

HHS. *See* Health and Human Services Department (HHS)

Hispanics, 191

Hoffman, Andrew J., 89, 91–92, 225n35

hollow government: and legal infrastructures of bureaucracy, 44; polls on, 182–184; and "tragedy of distrust" syndrome, 21–23. *See also* reform measures

Holmstead, Jeffrey, 114–115, 118, 120

Howard, Philip, 84–85

Hurricane Katrina, 105, 148, 182

ideology, definition of, 27

India, 81, 225n35

industrial pollution: and mercury pollution, 11, 104–106; and ozone

"precursors," 13; trading systems for pollution control, 11, 24, 114–118, 120, 124, 125. *See also* chemical industry; oil industry
infants. *See* mercury; perchlorate
insecticides. *See* pesticides
*Inside EPA*, 99
Institute of Environmental Medicine, New York University, 156
Institute of Medicine, 98
Integrated Risk Information System (IRIS), 139
intelligence. *See* IQ
Interagency Perchlorate Steering Committee (IPSC), 12, 129, 133–134
Interior Department (DOI), 38–39, 49
iodide deficiency, 127
IPSC. *See* Interagency Perchlorate Steering Committee (IPSC)
IQ: and lead poisoning, 21; and mercury poisoning, 100, 119, 121–123; monetary value of IQ points, 21, 121–122, 167
Iraq war, 1, 28, 43, 105, 148, 182
IRIS. *See* Integrated Risk Information System (IRIS)
Italy, 81

Japan, 81
Jarabek, Annie, 133
Jasanoff, Sheila, 155, 234n12
Jay, John, 30–31
JIFSAN. *See* Joint Institute for Food Safety and Applied Nutrition (JIFSAN)
jobs: creation of, for environmental cleanup, 181; environment versus, 180–182; public opinion on public service jobs, 183; statistics on working-age adults, 180
Johnson, Lyndon, 196
Joint Institute for Food Safety and Applied Nutrition (JIFSAN), 227n14
judicial branch. *See* federal courts
*Jungle, The* (Sinclair), 203
Justice Department, 97

Kansas, 230n6
Kennedy, Robert D., 225n35
Kerr-McGee Chemical, 11, 128, 131, 141–142, 232n40
Kovacs, Bill, 103
Krugman, Paul, 192–193
Krupp, Fred, 225n35
Kyoto Protocol, 223n11

Lake Erie, 49
Lamb, James, 135
Latham and Watkins law firm, 115
Latin, Howard, 165
laws. *See* environmental laws; *and specific laws*
lead: as air pollutant, 152; consequences of lead poisoning for children, 21, 46; EPA's lead-in-gasoline decision, 46, 70, 85, 124; regulation of lead paint in Massachusetts, 85; safe exposure level of, for children, 46; statistics on lead poisoning in children, 85
Leal, Donald, 77–78
left wing. *See* progressivism
liberalism. *See* progressivism
Lippmann, Morton, 156
*Lochner v. New York*, 238n4
Locke, John, 202
Lockheed-Martin, 131
Logomasini, Angela, 79
Lomborg, Bjorn, 80–82
*Los Angeles Times*, 115
Louisiana, 113, 230n6
Luntz, Frank, 42, 177

MACT. *See* maximum achievable control technology (MACT)
Madison, James, 30–31, 35
Maine, 158, 230n7
malaria, 79
Malthus, Thomas, 75, 193
Marathon Oil, 207
Marshall, Thurgood, 71
Maryland, 146–147, 158, 230nn6–7, 232n30
Massachusetts, 85, 129, 140, 142, 158
maximum achievable control tech-

nology (MACT), 111–112, 114–116, 119–121
Mayer, Kevin, 141
Mazurek, Jan, 56–57
McClain, R. Michael, 135
McGarity, Thomas, 72
McGee Corporation, 126
media and environmental issues, 19, 99
Mercer, George, 146
mercury: amount of, from U.S. sources, 109–110; case study on, 103–125; and chlor-alkali plants, 104, 112–114, 125, 227n23; and Clean Air Act (CAA), 104, 111–118; and compliance costs, 119–121; conclusion on, 124; cost-benefit analysis on, 118–123, 125; EPA regulation of, 11, 104–105, 113–125, 154; epidemiological studies of, 107–109, 227n14; in fish, 10, 100, 103, 104, 105, 109, 111, 118, 121; global mercury cycle, 106; human health benefits for regulation of, 121–123; and IQ, 100, 119, 121–123; lessons from case study on, 124–125; and maximum achievable control technology (MACT), 111–112, 114–116, 119–121; model state rule on mercury emissions, 116, 124, 228n36; National Research Council (NRC) report on, 103, 104, 106–108, 154; overview on, 103–105; and precautionary principle, 210; prenatal exposure to, 10, 100–101; public health implications of, 105–109, 121–123; reference dose (RfD) for methylmercury, 106; scientific research on, 105–111, 154, 207; sources of mercury air emissions, 104; state requirements for mercury control, 116–117, 124; statistics on infants with blood mercury levels above maximum recommended level, 104, 109, 123, 226n3; as threat to children's neurological development, 9–11, 100–101, 104, 121–122; TPY limit on mercury emissions,

116–117, 123; and trading systems, 114–118, 120, 124, 125; and utility industry, 11, 104–111; and water pollution, 9–11; women's blood mercury levels, 10, 100, 104, 109, 123; worldwide emissions total per year (TPY), 106, 109
methylmercury, 10, 105–111. *See also* mercury
Michaels, Patrick, 110
Michigan, 90–91, 118, 158, 230n7
military. *See* Defense Department (DOD)
military uses of and cleanup programs for perchlorate, 11, 126, 128, 129, 137, 143–149
Millennium Ecosystem Assessment Board, 193–194
Milloy, Steven J., 223n9
Minnesota, 118
Mississippi, 230n6
Missouri, 230n7
*Moment on Earth, A* (Easterbrook), 80–82, 223n11
Mooney, Chris, 208
Moore, Colleen, 191
Morrall, John, 82–83
*Mother Jones*, 99
motor vehicles: and EPA's lead-in-gasoline decision, 46, 70, 85, 124; and ozone "precursors," 13
multinational corporations. *See* corporations
Muskie, Edmund, 39
Myers, Gary, 108–109, 207

NAAQS. *See* National Ambient Air Quality Standards (NAAQS)
napalm, 91
NAS. *See* National Academy of Sciences (NAS)
NASA, 96, 133, 134
*Nation, The*, 99
National Academies, 12, 98, 104, 107, 127, 134–135
National Academy of Engineering, 98
National Academy of Sciences (NAS), 81, 98, 106, 134–139, 199

National Aeronautics and Space Administration (NASA), 96, 133, 134
National Ambient Air Quality Standards (NAAQS), 52, 151–158, 161–165, 168, 170, 206, 234n13
National Association of Manufacturers, 80
National Environmental Policy Act (1970), 219n10
National Fisheries Institute, 227n14
National Health and Nutrition Examination Surveys (NHANES), 127
National Institutes of Health (NIH), 108
*National Journal*, 99
National Pollutant Discharge Elimination System (NPDES), 145
National Research Council (NRC): and complexification, 199; on mercury, 103, 104, 106–108, 154, 207; in National Academies, 98, 104; on ozone, 158, 163; on perchlorate, 12, 141, 210
National Tuna Foundation, 227n14
Native Americans, 10, 118
Natural Resources Defense Council (NRDC): and Dow Chemical's pollution prevention program, 90–91; lawsuit against EPA by, 56; and mercury, 114, 115, 128; and perchlorate, 128, 134–135, 231n22
Nature Conservancy, 90, 180, 237n19
Nebraska, 204, 230n7
*Nebraska ex rel. Stenberg v. U.S.*, 204, 239n9
neighborhood effects theory, 34–35
neoconservatives, 22, 28
Nevada, 11–12, 126, 128, 142, 143, 232n30, 232n40
New Deal, 22, 34, 183, 203–204
New Hampshire, 158
New Jersey, 158, 230nn5–7
New Mexico, 230n7, 232n30
*New Progressive Agenda for Public Health and the Environment, A* (Schroeder and Steinzor), 175

New York state, 158, 230n7, 232n30
*New York Times*, 182
New York University, 156
New Zealand, 108
news media. *See* media and environmental issues
Nicholas Institute for Environmental Policy Solutions, Duke University, 178–180, 181
NIH. *See* National Institutes of Health (NIH)
nitrogen oxides ($NO_x$), 116, 117, 151, 152, 161
Nixon, Richard, 47–48, 209, 218–219n3
Norquist, Grover, 26
North Carolina, 230n7
NPDES. *See* National Pollutant Discharge Elimination System (NPDES)
NRC. *See* National Research Council (NRC)
NRDC. *See* Natural Resources Defense Council (NRDC)
nuclear weapons, 1

Occidental Chemical, 113, 227n23
Occupational Safety and Health Administration (OSHA), 70–71, 72, 82–83
Ochs, Phil, 237n32
Office of Information and Regulatory Affairs (OIRA), 82
Office of Management and Budget (OMB), 62, 66–67, 82, 96, 134–135, 164
Ohio, 113, 158
oil industry, 46, 48, 224n30, 225n33
OIRA. *See* Office of Information and Regulatory Affairs (OIRA)
Olin Corp., 113, 126, 227n23
OMB. *See* Office of Management and Budget (OMB)
Omenn, Gilbert, 135
O'Neill, Catherine, 118
O'Rourke, P. J., 24–25
OSHA. *See* Occupational Safety and Health Administration (OSHA)

ozone: and asthma in children, 10, 13, 101, 150–151, 157, 167, 206; case study on, 150–170; and Clean Air Act, 151–165, 168–170; and Clean Air Scientific Advisory Committee (CASAC), 154–156; and Code Red days, 13, 118, 169, 197; conclusion on, 168–169; conservative case against regulation of, 156–158; cost-benefit analysis on, 165–170; cost of regulation of, 84; eight-hour standard for, 156, 160, 164, 169, 170; and EPA, 150–156, 158–165; formation of, 151; GAO report on, 162–163; ground-level ozone versus atmospheric or stratospheric ozone, 233n1; lessons from case study on, 169–170; and NAAQS for ground-level ozone, 151–158, 161–165, 168, 170, 206, 234n13; and "non-attainment areas," 13, 150, 162; one-hour standard for, 155–156, 164; overview on, 150–154; and pulmonary disease generally, 156–158, 167; questions on, 15; scientific research on, 154–158, 208; sources of, 13; and state governments, 73; state implementation plans (SIPs) for, 161–163, 165; trends in levels of, 151–152
Ozonoff, David, 126

Paracelsus, 57
Parmet, Wendy, 203–204
Partnership for Public Service, 182–183
Pennsylvania, 158, 230n6
perchlorate: and Aberdeen, Maryland incident, 146–147, 233n43; activities causing perchlorate contamination, 143–144; case study on, 126–149; characteristics of, as environmental contaminant, 127–128; cleanup costs for, 12, 129; conclusion on, 148; cost of research on, 128, 129, 149; in drinking water, 10, 11–12, 126–130, 140–144; economics of cleanup of, 148, 149; and EPA, 12, 128, 129, 133–134, 139–141, 146–149, 154; GAO report on, 142–144; health effects of, on babies, 10, 11–12, 101, 127, 139, 140; industry-dominated research on, 131–133; Interagency Perchlorate Steering Committee (IPSC) on, 12, 129, 133–134; laws on, 144–148; lessons from case study on, 149; map of maximum perchlorate concentrations in U.S., 142; maximum safe exposure level for, 12; as medication, 130; military uses of and cleanup by, 11, 126, 128, 129, 137, 143–149; National Academy of Sciences (NAS) peer review on, 134–139, 231n22; overview on, 126–130; and precautionary principle, 210; reference dose (RfD) for, 138–141, 210; scientific research on, 12, 127, 128–141, 207, 230n4; state regulations on, 129, 140–141, 144, 230n6; statistics on contamination by, 128–129, 140; and Superfund cleanup program, 139; and thyroid hormones, 10, 11–12, 101, 127, 130–131, 133, 141
Perchlorate Study Group (PSG), 131–133, 135, 138, 230–231n12
pesticides, 51, 53, 56, 79, 90, 219n10, 224n30
Pew Research Center, 177, 182
Pioneer Americas LLC, 113, 227n23
police power for protection of public health, 196–197, 202–205
policy making: and complexification, 19–21, 198–199; and Congress, 99–100; and cost-benefit analysis, 19–21, 24, 38–39, 54, 59–68; devolution of, to state and local governments, 23–24, 29; and executive branch, 96; and judicial branch, 97–98; and legislative branch, 97; and media, 99; and National Academies, 98; process of, 99–101; and public-interest organizations, 99;

and regulated industries, 98–99; and rulemaking, 100; science versus, 155–156. *See also* Environmental Protection Agency (EPA); *and specific U.S. presidents*

political dissonance, 14–15

polls: conservatives' critique of, 14–15; on environmental protection, 177–180; on government, 182–184; on jobs versus environment, 180–182

pollution. *See* air pollution; children; mercury; ozone; perchlorate; water pollution

*Pollution Control in the United States* (Davies and Mazurek), 56–57

Pollution Prevention Act (1990), 219n10

poverty, 189–193

power plants. *See* utility industry

PPG Industries, 113, 227n23

precautionary principle, 197, 209–210

pregnancy. *See* women

*Priceless* (Heinzerling and Ackerman), 83

progressivism: ideology of, 28–29; and precautionary principle, 210; and Reagan presidency, 39–40; and special interests, 29; and "tragedy of distrust," 22–23; and vision of future, 188–189

PSG. *See* Perchlorate Study Group (PSG)

public health: federal police power for protection of, 196–197, 202–205; and New Deal, 203–204; and sanitation movement (1850s), 202; underlying ideas on, 3. *See also* asthma; mercury; ozone; perchlorate; water pollution

public-interest organizations, 99. *See also specific organizations*

public opinion. *See* polls

Public Opinion Strategies, 178–180

public policy. *See* policy making

Pure Food and Drug Act (1906), 203

RCRA. *See* Resource Conservation and Recovery Act (1976)

Reagan, Ronald: and bully pulpit on big government, 37–38, 72, 183; as California governor, 37–38; conservatism of, 22, 36–40; and cost-benefit analysis, 38–39, 62, 118, 229n40; and deregulation, 38–39; on environmentalism, 217n28; and EPA, 38–39, 49; Friedman on, 34, 217n14; and limited government and runaway deficits, 36–37; and new federalism, 72–73; and progressive backlash, 39–40

reference dose (RfD): definition of, 106; for methylmercury, 106; for perchlorate, 138–141, 210

reform measures: best available solutions, 197, 210–211; clean science, 197, 207–209; conclusion on, 213; EPA institutional autonomy, 197–200; EPA workforce competence and morale, 200–202; federal police power to protect public health, 196–197, 202–205; funding for environmental programs, 197, 206–207; independent priority setting by EPA, 197, 205–206; judicial deference, 197, 198, 212–213; list of, 196–197; monetization of costs, not benefits, 186, 211–212; overview of, 195–197; precautionary principle, 209–210

regulation: conservative case against, 78–86, 156–158; and corporate environmentalism, 86–92; cost of, 82–84; diversity of regulated industries and firms, 87, 98–99; harm caused by, 82–85; and harmfulness versus importance of chemicals, 79–82; and lost opportunity costs, 86; opposition to environmental regulation, 86–89, 98–99; and stupid bureaucrats, 84–85. *See also* deregulation; Environmental Protection Agency (EPA); mercury; ozone; perchlorate; *and other federal agencies*

Rehnquist, William, 221n43

Reilly, William, 41

religious beliefs and environmental issues, 22, 28, 180

Republican Party: and Contract with America, 41–42, 177; and different approaches to conservatism, 22, 28; and environmental issues, 47–48, 178; and Reagan presidency, 36. *See also* conservatism; *and specific presidents*

*Republican War on Science, The* (Mooney), 208

*Rescuing Science from Politics* (Wagner and Steinzor), 208

research. *See* scientific research

Resource Conservation and Recovery Act (1976), 53, 144–145, 219n10

Resources for the Future, 65

RfD. *See* reference dose (RfD)

Rhode Island, 158

riders on appropriations bills, 55–56, 99–100

right wing. *See* conservatism

risk assessment, and EPA, 54, 57–59, 74, 197, 209–210

*Road to Serfdom, The* (Hayek), 35, 217n20

Rogers, Dan, 12, 133, 136–137, 147

Roosevelt, Teddy, 47

Ruckelshaus, William, 45, 47, 49, 58, 225n35

Russia, 81

Safe Drinking Water Act (1974), 139, 145, 146, 204, 219n10

Safe Drinking Water Act Amendments (1985, 1996), 51, 53, 219n11

sanitation movement (1850s), 202

SCAQMD. *See* South Coast Air Quality Management District (SCAQMD)

Schudson, Michael, 19

*Science*, 75

scientific research: and animal studies, 107, 137–138; and conservatives' sound science campaign, 16–17, 107, 155; epidemiological studies, 107–109, 227n14; funding for basic research, 208–209; industry-dominated research on perchlorate, 131–133; on mercury, 105–111, 154, 207; on ozone, 154–158, 208; and peer review, 134–139; on perchlorate, 12, 127, 128–141, 207; policy versus, 155–156; politics versus, 136–137; reform on, for clean science, 197, 207–209; and weight of the available scientific evidence, 107, 137–138

SDWA. *See* Safe Drinking Water Act (1974)

September 11 terrorist attack, 1, 28, 43

Seychelle Islands, 108, 227n14

Sierra Club, 80

*Silent Spring* (Carson), 47

Sinclair, Upton, 203

SIPs. *See* state implementation plans (SIPs) for ozone

*Skeptical Environmentalist, The* (Lomborg), 80–82

slavery, 211–212

Smith, Adam, 60, 77, 202

smog. *See* ozone

Society of Social Studies of Science, 225n35

sodium perchlorate, 128. *See also* perchlorate

sound science campaign, 16–17, 107, 155

South Carolina, 230n6

South Coast Air Quality Management District (SCAQMD), 117–118

Soviet Union, collapse of, 217n14

special interests, 27, 29, 54, 55–56

Stafford, Robert, 39

stakeholders, 54

Stanford University, 177–178

STAPPA. *See* State and Territorial Air Pollution Program Administrators (STAPPA)

State and Territorial Air Pollution Program Administrators (STAPPA), 124, 228–229nn36–37

state governments: and environmental laws, 72–74; and mercury control, 116–117, 124; and ozone, 73, 161–163; and perchlorate, 129,

140–141, 144, 230n6; and public
health in nineteenth century, 203;
and Reagan presidency, 72–73; and
Unfunded Mandates Reform Act
(1995), 73, 222n58; in U.S. Constitution, 30–33
state implementation plans (SIPs) for
ozone, 161–163, 165
Stockholm Syndrome, 54–56
sulfur dioxide (SO$_2$), 116, 117, 152
Sunoco, 207
Superfund Amendments and Reauthorization Act (1986),
224–225n33
Superfund sites and cleanups, 88, 91,
139, 207, 218n30, 219n10, 224n30,
224–225n33
Supreme Court, U.S.: choice of cases
heard by, 69, 222n51; on Clean Air
Act amendments (1990), 153; and
denial of petition for certiorari,
222n51; and EPA's ozone decision,
160; and OSHA, 70–71, 72; on
states' role in public health, 203

Tatel, David, 159
technology. *See* maximum achievable
control technology (MACT)
Tennessee, 113
TERA. *See* Toxicology Excellence in
Risk Assessment (TERA)
terrorism, 1, 28, 43
Texas, 143, 230nn5–7, 232n30, 233n41
Texas Tech University, 128–129
Thomas, Lee, 41
thyroid gland, 130–131, 132
thyroid hormones and perchlorate, 10,
11–12, 101, 127, 130–131, 133, 141
thyroxine, 130
*Time*, 177–178
Tolchin, Susan and Martin, 38
Toxic Substances Control Act (1976),
213, 219n10
toxic waste: cost of burying, 83;
and electoral politics, 153; EPA
achievements on lowering, 49–
50; EPA regulations and reports

on, 53; Superfund law on, 88, 91,
139, 207, 218n30, 219n10, 224n30,
224–225n33
Toxicology Excellence in Risk Assessment (TERA), 132, 135
*Trade-Off Myth, The: Fact and Fiction
About Jobs and the Environment*
(Goodstein), 181
trading systems for pollution control,
11, 24, 114–118, 120, 124, 125
"tragedy of distrust" syndrome, 21–23
tragedy of the commons, 75–78, 193
triiodothyronine, 130
Trust for Public Land, 180, 237n19

*Unfinished Business: A Comparative
Assessment of Environmental Protection*, 239n11
Unfunded Mandates Reform Act
(1995), 73, 222n58
Union Carbide Corporation, 225n35
unitary executive theory, 144
United Kingdom, 81
United Nations, 193
University of Michigan, 89
Utah, 143
utility industry: coal-fired power
plants, 104, 105, 114–118; and
maximum achievable control technology (MACT), 114–116, 119–121;
and mercury, 11, 104–111, 114–118;
and ozone "precursors," 13; and
trading system for regulating coal-
fired plants, 114–118, 120, 124, 125

Valero Energy, 207
values and environmental issues, 175–
177, 184–187
Vermont, 158
Vietnam War, 91, 182
Virginia, 230n6–7
VOCs. *See* volatile organic com-
pounds (VOCs)
volatile organic compounds (VOCs),
117–118, 151, 161
Voltaggio, Thomas, 146–147
Voltaire, 202

Von Karman, Theodore, 126
Vulcan Materials Co., 113, 227n23

Wagner, Wendy, 155, 208
Waldman, Peter, 129
*Wall Street Journal*, 12, 129, 147
*Washington Monthly*, 99
*Washington Post*, 183–184
Washington state, 230nn6–7
water pollution: EPA achievements
    on lowering, 49; fish contaminated
    with mercury, 10, 100, 103, 104,
    105, 109, 111, 118, 121; and mercury,
    9–11, 105–106; and perchlorate, 10,
    11–12, 126–130. *See also* Clean Water
    Act (CWA); Safe Drinking Water
    Act (1974), Safe Drinking Water
    Act Amendments (1985, 1996);
    Water Pollution Control (or Clean
    Water) Act (1948)
Water Pollution Control (or Clean
    Water) Act (1948), 219n10
Water Quality Act (1987), 51, 219n11
Watson, Robert, 193

Watt, James G., 39, 49
Waxman, Henry, 39
*Wealth of Nations, The* (Smith), 77
West Virginia, 113, 158, 230n7
Williams, Stephen, 159
willingness to accept (WTA), 63–65
willingness to pay (WTP), 63–65, 170
Wisconsin, 113, 118
Wolff, George, 156
Wolfowitz, Paul, 147
women: blood mercury levels of, 10,
    100, 104, 109, 123; iodide deficiency
    in, 127; perchlorate exposure of, 12,
    101, 129, 140, 141; pregnant women
    and fish contaminated with mer-
    cury, 10, 100, 103, 104, 105, 109, 118,
    121; thyroid hormones of, 11–12
Wood, David G., 189–190, 235n25
World Bank, 193
Wright, Skelly, 45, 46
WTA. *See* willingness to accept
    (WTA)
WTP. *See* willingness to pay (WTP)